THE GOLDEN STAR

By the same author

'Occult Enigmas'

A BOOK FOR INITIATES

THE GOLDEN STAR

A MYSTIC CRESCENDO IN TWELVE VISIONS

by

JEAN MICHAUD, Ph. D.

All rights reserved. No part of this publication may be reproduced, distributed, or transmitted in any form or by any means, including photocopying, recording, or other electronic or mechanical methods, without the prior written permission of the publisher, except in the case of brief quotations embodied in critical reviews and certain other noncommercial uses permitted by copyright law.

Printed in the United States of America

ISBN 978-1-941489-60-4

www.AudioEnlightenmentPress.com

DEDICATION

*This Book is Dedicated in deepest gratitude by
Ma-u and Ma-uti to Neteru-Hem — the Divine Messenger*

Commenced January 30th, 1939
Finished September 23rd, 1939

CONTENTS

Dedication v

Note ix

Vision 1: The Domains of Night 3

Vision 2: Demons and Devas 33

Vision 3: Elements and Elementals 67

Vision 4: Witchcraft 95

Vision 5: Spiritualism 131

Vision 6: The Astral Fire 171

Vision 7: The Symbol of the Cross 195

Vision 8: The Kosmos 221

Vision 9: Cosmic Consciousness 263

Vision 10: The Great Light 293

Vision 11: The Dwellers in the Celestial Spheres 317

Vision 12: God 341

NOTE

All the facts and data, as related by the Divine Messenger in this Book, are in accordance with the most advanced Occult Teachings, from the remotest times of antiquity until to-day. They are not figments of the Author's imagination, but rest on the solid basis of the Ancient Wisdom, gathered together over periods of untold thousands of years, which the profound learning of all the greatest Teachers, aided by Divine Inspiration, has been able to record for our minds to dwell on; so that our hearts and Souls shall bow in adoration to the Incomprehensible Highest All-Father-All-Mother, and the Holy Angels, Princes of Light, and their Sacred Ministers of the Celestial Spheres.

Several of the sayings of Neteru-Hem are based on parts of the 'Secret Doctrine', that great collection of ancient words of wisdom, so patiently assembled by Madame Blavatsky, to whom the world of Western Occultism owes a debt so great that it can never be repaid — except with deepest respect and gratitude for the wonderful Service she has rendered to Mankind.

The Author has essayed the almost impossible task of giving the name of every Sage whose words have been quoted; but to supply a complete list would turn this book into a catalogue! He therefore craves your indulgence in this and all the rest.

It will be noted that the style of writing varies considerably throughout the book. There is a definite Occult reason for this, which will be understood by the discerning reader.

* * *

The names of the three principal characters in this story should be pronounced as follows:—

Neteru-Hem — Net'roo Hém; the accent on the last syllable.
Ma-u — — Mah-oo.
Ma-uti — — Mah-oo-tee.

JET

Obsidian blackness of the sombre Night
Where dwell the shades of dark illusion;
And sullen Wings of evil flap about
In leaden, drooping Flight.

VISION 1
THE DOMAINS OF NIGHT

When Ma-u and Ma-uti watched the glorious sunset that evening, neither he nor she had any conception of the thrilling and unbelievable adventures to which it was the prelude. They could not think of aught but the superb beauties in the sky; a seeming fairyland upon which they appeared to be gazing *down*: a coast of rocky cliffs, coves and inlets, green and gold and orange-red, with blue seas bestrewed with crimson rocks.

At one unforgettable moment the sun sent out five purple rays from between the massed clouds, which like a hand of benediction overspread the pair; whilst a path of molten gold stretched from Ra to them, as if inviting them to stride along that road to glory under His protecting hand. An invitation and initiation into the Mysteries.

Thus they watched the radiant, resplendent spectacle in the heavens; lost in wonder; soaring on the wings of Vision. And they heard a soft rustling in the air, as if a Presence floated above on feathery pinions. Somewhat startled they looked around and there, under a great oak, stood a majestic but benign-looking figure dressed in white, smiling benevolently at the two, who stared at him in amazement.

Who was that marvellous Being, and how did he suddenly come to appear at that spot?

As if he could read their thoughts he raised a hand in greeting and said: "I am Neteru-Hem, a Messenger from the Divine, and I have come to conduct you to strange regions, along paths that few have trod. If you will, I can show you the mysteries that will give you understanding of that which is inexplicable to most, and I will light within you a lamp that can cast its rays in all that is yet dark, and bring a gleam of Truth and comfort unto the gloomy of heart. I will unite within your Souls the memory and splendour that you both had in the long lost ages, before this world was made. I can make your dreams come true; for both of you are true dreamers whose earthly shell is wearing thin, so that the light within and the light without are ready for a holy fusion that will send a stream of brilliance across the dark domains of night, redeeming those who are now awaiting that Holy Call which once again shall bring the children to the breast of God the Father and the Mother, to be received in Love Supreme. Follow me, then, across the golden path that lies before you, and have no fear when through the worlds of outer and inner illusion I lead you up the golden stairway, ending at God's Throne.

Saying this, he stepped upon the path of molten gold that stretched from Ra, and hand in hand Ma-u and Ma-uti followed him, speechless, trustingly, for there came from him a magnetism that cast out all doubt and fear.

Slowly they proceeded to those cliffs and coves that shone and glittered in the sky and a soft breeze, warm and caressing, enfolded them; and as onward they trod, so the magic beauty increased and all was glory unspeakable when they arrived at the celestial scenes they had first seen from below.

It was a rocky coast with mighty cliffs, at the foot of which the blue sea threw up its spume and rainbow-mists of shattered waves. There were stretches of silver sand bestrewed with glitt'ring precious stones. There were fantastic moss-agates with fairy trees and plants inside them; and jasper and jade, chrysoprase and chrysolite, crystal and jet, opals and topaz, turquoise and amethyst and too many more to mention; all of exceeding beauty. Mosses, ferns and alpine plants clung to the rifts of the rocks, and sea-birds mewed and moaned and sailed in mighty sweeps through space. Following the Divine Messenger, the two walked along a slowly rising and falling path over the cliffs, through dreadful chasms, with monstrous cyclopean rocks embedded in the yellow sands; and yawning caves spread wide their gaping jaws, as if in giant pangs of hunger they longed to devour the three. So, passing on they came at last to a stupendous tumbling of puissant rocks, vast, vehement, huge in their proportions; as if the very dome of heaven had cracked and fallen in impetuous avalanche, incredibly menacing.

A narrow track led through this scene of devastation and gradually the splendour of the sun began to fade away, and gloomily the overhanging cliffs shut out the light, until they reached the mightiest of all the caves yet seen.

Into this darkening region they followed Neteru-Hem and now beheld they a scene of further wonder; of stalactites and stalagmites, descending from above in heavy drops, or rising up in twisting pillared shapes; falling like velvet draperies of folding curtains, or in the form of huge cathedrals, complete with pulpits, altars, organs; to praise the Majesty of God.

But ever further did they penetrate into the caves and slowly the ebon shadows of the dark drew closer and enfolded them. Night cast its far-flung battlements of blackness and mystery, and the slow trickle of drops and tiny streams that built the mighty stalactites was no more heard; and stillness deep and sombre brooded over all.

And still the three proceeded on their way, in utter silence and deepest gloom, towards the regions where dwell the powers of the night, with the white raiment of the Messenger faintly visible in the murky shade, surrounded from all sides by a kabalistic, incomprehensible and enigmatical darkness; deep, impenetrable.

Now was felt a sigh of cold wind and heard a subdued whistling, like blowing of the breeze through a ship's cordage. Momentarily this wind became stronger and colder and the cavern seemed to widen out and become more spacious in all directions, until at last they stepped outside and found themselves under a starry vault, in which the constellations blazed like fervid, flaming jewels.

"Where are we?" asked Ma-uti.

"We are in the dread domains of forces of the Night and Darkness," replied the Messenger.

"What are those lights yonder?" asked Ma-u.

"Those are the Night Fires, which with their heat dry out the turbid dark waters; with their heat they quench them," quoth Neteru-Hem. "In these Regions the Self-Born, the CHHÂYÂS, dwell; they are the Shadows from the Bodies of the Sons of Twilight. What seems to you Darkness is in reality the Abstract and Absolute Light."

"But how can the Light be Darkness?" asked Ma-uti.

The Messenger replied: "Because it cannot be perceived with the physical senses, my child. It is the Dark Creation, the Evil Dragon, which can be conquered only by the Sun-God, who is one of the first Ministers of our Father-Mother, the sublime, great and only Creator of all that Is, including all the Minor Gods, His Elder Children; as you are his younger.

"When the Hidden Logos had first concentrated His Mind into Himself, the quality of Darkness pervaded His assumed Body, and when He finally abandoned this Body it was transformed into Night."

"And how long will this Night last, dear Messenger?" asked Ma-u. "It will last for one-hundred years of Brahmâ; or, according to mortal reckoning, 311,040 trillions of years; which figure represents one-hundred years of Days and Nights of Brahmâ. Perhaps this may seem a long time to your limited senses, but in terms of Eternity these Days and Nights are like a series of flashes from a light-house, which soon will cease when day returns.

"Born in the Body of Night are the Asuras, who form the first three classes of Pitris, and they—together with the other four classes of Pitris, who are called the Sons of Twilight—are amongst those Holy Rulers who endowed mankind with Mind. And they have made man in the form of a reflection of themselves, a sevenfold mystery of a sevenfold mystery. As the hearts of the Pitris have four lower cavities and three higher divisions, so is the heart of man constructed. As the bodies of the Pitris radiate seven Rays, so find we in man seven nervous plexuses, which radiate similar rays. And so it is with the seven layers of the skin in Pitris and man. Thus men became the shadows of the Shadows of the Gods, each a shadow of his own colour and kind, inferior to his Father; because the Creator is the substance of which man is the shadow, born in the darkness of the material, or in man the animal. In a similar manner, Earth is the Dark Night when compared with the glorious Day of the Heavenly Light. As the wise Pymander, one of the Ancient Sages, has said: 'I am thy Thought, thy God, more ancient than the moist Principle, the Light that radiates within Darkness, and the shining Word of God is the Son of Deity.' "

"Therefore," continued Neteru-Hem, "men are the Spirits of the Earth, clothed in shadow and linked with the higher regions by their Astral Selves, and warmed by the Solar Lhas, or Spirits; and the Earth, called Kliphoth, is the residence of the Prince of Darkness, whose name is Samaël, the Angel of Death.

"The first men were negative forms, ethereal astral shadows of their creative Progenitors, having neither astral nor physical bodies. These gradually melted away and became absorbed into the bodies of their own Sweat-Born progeny, which were of a more solid substance. And so, the shadow retiring and becoming covered with flesh, man's physical body was formed. And these bodies were vivified when the Sons of Wisdom, the Sons of Night, came down, ready for incarnation. The Lords said: 'We can choose, for we have Wisdom.' So they all chose those human vehicles that appealed most to their Wisdom. Some entered the Chhâyâs, some projected a dim burning spark; some entered the bodies of one race, others the bodies of another. One race was ready, the rest were not; and in this lies the secret of the subsequent inequalities of intellectual capacity, of birth, of social position.

"The angels that fell into generation became known as the Serpents and Dragons of Wisdom, born and created out of the secrecy and mystery of the Night.

"It was the Christian Saviour who came, like Krishna, to save mankind from eternal death and who conquered the Kingdom of Darkness, or Hell, as every Initiate does when he has developed within himself the Logos, or Christos, the Spiritual Ego, or Higher Self."

"But" — said, Ma-u — "you spoke just now about the Days and Nights of Brahmâ; what exactly is meant by that, Messenger?"

"The Days and Nights of Brahmâ", responded Nete-ru-Hem, "are those cycles of activity and rest, which, according to the ancient Teachings represented certain periods of 4,320,000,000 mortal years in which activity prevails on earth, making one Day of Brahmâ; and this is followed by a period of rest and darkness of equal duration, when all activity ceases, and this is called a Night of Brahmâ, to be followed by another Day, and so on. It is further taught that the Sons of Dark Wisdom — which in the Christian Theology are identical with the Archangels, the so-called Fallen Angels — that these Great Lords axe as Divine and as pure, if not purer, than all the Michaels and Gabriels so glorified in the Churches."

"How, then, came it to pass that the Churches have fallen into this error?" asked Ma-uti.

"One of the reasons is," replied the Messenger, "that the memories of Atlantis and the fall of its peoples, have continued up to the period of the birth of the Christian Church; and one of these memories is the story of *how* the Atlanteans were endowed with divine powers, just as all mankind is today — though many are not aware of it — and, feeling within themselves the inner God, Logos, or Christos, each felt that he was a Man-God in his nature, though physically an animal. From the day they realized this a struggle between the God-principle and the animal self began; a struggle for life between the spiritual and the physical. Those Atlanteans who conquered the lower, physical body, joined what they termed the Sons of Light. The others became slaves to matter and were termed the

Sons of Darkness. In other words, the first slaked off the shackles of the material, so that their minds became purified and ready to rejoin the Heavenly Hosts through union with the Soul; whilst the latter failed to do so and had to continue to be brought into incarnation after incarnation, until they too fought the good fight and conquered; and so won freedom. Therefore, we have the Kabalistic and symbolical teaching that God is Light — mirrored inversely in Nature and Matter — which is Darkness. This emblematical cosmogony was represented from time immemorial in the Temples of Egypt, where we find the two figures in black and white, the two Kabiri, personifying the opposite poles, north and south; or the commemoration of the passing of the original north pole of the earth to the south pole of heaven; or the inversion of the poles, when the great inclination of the earth's axis resulted in the displacement of the oceans, the submersion of the polar lands, and the consequent upheaval of new continents in the equatorial regions, and *vice versa*. The two figures also portray Set, the slayer of Osiris, as the Dark Night, and Osiris as the Light of Day and the Sun. And I want you to realize that Light, Life, Love, Goodness and Beauty, are as much the adversaries of darkness, death, hatred, evil and ugliness, as what the Christians call Satan, or the Devil is *their* great Enemy; the adversary of mankind and all that is good.

"So we find Light and Darkness engaged in an unending battle, each the reverse side of the other and representing the same principle in different ways."

"Will the struggle between Light and Darkness then be an eternal one, dear Messenger?" asked Ma-uti.

"No," he replied, "there is a prophecy which tells of the coming of the glorified spiritual Christos, who will deliver suffering mankind, or Chrestos. Only after He, who is called Sosiosh, or Kalki Avatâra appears, will the dark sides — the reverse of their natures — of Brahmâ, Ahura Mazda, Zeus, Jehovah, and all their kindred vanish and disappear in thin air. All those Gods of the Hindû, the

Zoroastrian, the Greco-Olympian, or the Israelite—cruel, tribal, jealous—will be no more, but melt away like the empty phantoms they are; once born in the mind of the zealot, the fanatic, the dreamer, taking form and *overshadowing* human ideals, instead of bringing the Light which will call home the wanderer on the ocean of illusion within a thousandfold illusion, which mortals call life—or death. Only then will all these dreams fade away into the limbo of things better forgotten.

"Then the egotism of the revengeful God 'I-AM' will be no more, and the higher realization of the one-ness of the children of the God of Light will be the heritage of all. The Jewish teachings of the Old Testamant—which surely is the basis of all the fiendish persecution mankind has suffered from for the last few thousands of years—will be replaced by the Super Gospel of Light and Love; and every dark and evil passion will be subdued."

So saying, the Messenger went forward, and Ma-u and Ma-uti followed him further into the dark domains.

Their way lay across a narrow path, just visible in the starlight, for there was no moon; and this path was like a razor-back in the Alps, astride a deep abyss. Beside the path the winds roared, howling with menace. To left and right reared mighty mountains, lifting up their giant masses to the black sky, which was bedecked with fiery gems. Restless shadows flitted here and there, more guessed at than beholden, and Ma-u and Ma-uti drew up a little closer to that white-clad figure, that fearlessly strode on.

"What are those shadows, dear Messenger?" asked Ma-uti.

"They are the Sons of the Lords of the Black Countenance, the gigantic Magicians of Ruta and Daitya, whose evil practices destroyed Atlantis, as surely they will destroy the present Race of Man, unless he turns to the Light. They dwell in cunningly devised subterranean caves, in twisting passages that lead to the nether worlds, where all the Lords of Darkness gather and bide their time. Deep in the murky depths they wait, shadows in the shadows, fearsome, deadly, merciless.

Skilful are they in the ancient Mysteries, divining their time for spinning their webs and weaving their snares in which to trap the unwary; preparing for the great catastrophe which, they hope, will end the Light for ever, so that ignorance and barbarism will prevail again. There they hide, until in the far distant future—the Krita Age as it is called by the Sages, in contradistinction to the present Kali Age—the 'Everlasting King' appears with his inspired teachers, who will awaken the minds of the peoples until they become pellucid as crystal. And already the heavens are full of signs and omens, and the dark ones gnash their teeth in rage, but impotent to prevent. Until that time, even the highest Angel will soil his immaculate wings when once he touches this dense and soiled atmosphere of darkling earth. Yet, darkness serves a holy purpose, as it was taught in all the ancient cosmogonies, and in Egypt it was said that Darkness was the principle of all things, and that Light comes from Darkness. Job said that Behemoth, the principle of Darkness, is the chief of the ways of God. Out of deep Darkness, or Chaos, with which the face of the earth was covered, came forth the creatures God created, when the Lord of the Sun sent forth his holy streams of Light and Life. This has happened many times when one of Brahmâ's Nights turned into Day. The Chhâyâs also perish and appear later on once more as Dhyânîs, who always remain, to watch and guide Man."

"How can we know them, Messenger?" asked Ma-u.

"Not by mortal sight, my son, but by the streams of Holy Light sent forth by them, enlightening the mind within with Wisdom; that which men call exaltation, genius, inspiration from on high."

Advancing farther still into the dreaded regions, flagitious, foul, they beheld monstrous shapes a-crawl the cavernous deeps, or chained to mighty rocks.

"Here are the shadows of the Giant Races that once abode upon the earth, stupendous beginnings out of Chaos; earthbound prodigies, vast and vile they linger on, until the final Age of Earth shall bring them, too. Salvation—if so they will.

"There are also those creatures here who were made by iniquitous sorcerers of Atlantis, from which the origin of the Prince of Tyrus can be traced."

"Is this the place then where Satan holds his Court?" asked Ma-u.

"No," said Neteru-Hem, "Satan is only a name; it is the name of Jehovah turned upside down. He is not a black God, but the negation of the White Deity. As God is the Light, so Satan is Darkness, and this Darkness is necessary for mortals, to set off the Light, or else to them the pure Light of the Sun would be invisible and incomprehensible."

Onwards went the Messenger with his two companions, and ever more increased the darkness, until it became visible and half showed and veiled the darker shades that flitted everywhere as on the silent wings of sable Gods, in rayless majesty, of Night's abode. A heavy, leaden movement became perceptible, as if ponderous tentacula stretched from unseen, hidden spiders; hairy, moribund with greed. A darkness pressing on the eyelids and searing in the brain with heavy throbs of sullen, persistent hammer-beats. All the candles of God's illumination dead, and the daggers of death, whose sudden visitation awes the stricken soul, a-point and ready to destroy. The sluggard shades of sleep, whose vapours rise and bind the lids with melancholy langour striking apathy, adrift like surging mists within the gloom.

No mystic Avilion is this, where Arthur's Soul was wafted by the maidens, when slain he was by Mordred, to rest in everlasting bliss. No gleam of light, no ray of hope, but endless grim despair, that chokes the pulsing throat with bitterness.

"Is not this darkness dreadful," sighed Ma-uti.

"Yes, my child," replied Neteru-Hem, "and yet, it is but the shadow of the Divine Light. The Spirits that dwell here and whom you both sense so unpleasantly, are but the Astral Shells of men, who themselves have determined their present condition. Some are incredibly old, and if you could see their shapes as once they were when in the flesh you would be truly terrified. They are the shades of the unknown Races who dwelt on earth many millions of years ago. Some are of the Chhiyis, or Shadows, others of the subsequent races such as the Androgynous, or third race, or of the fourth, symbolized by the Lion, and the fifth, or Aryan."

"Are these shades then entirely forsaken by God?" asked Ma-u.

"Nay, my son," was the reply, "remember that one of our wise men, named Pascal, once said that God is a circle, the centre of which is everywhere and the circumference nowhere. But that was ancient Wisdom, and God was also called the Cosmic Circle by wiser men of long ago, to whom both the terms God *and* Circle had the same meaning. The Nights and Days, or cycles of rest and activity, were also known as the Eternal Perpetual Motion, the Ever-Becoming, as well as the Ever Present and Ever-Existing: — making Absolute Unity in its perpetual and never ceasing evolution, circling back in incessant progress into its original status."

"Is darkness then caused by a turning away from the Sun-God?" asked Ma-uti.

"Yes," said the Messenger, "the quality of Darkness is — to an extent, though not always — the product of anger and wilful ignorance. In the body of the Sage, to whom realization has come by initiation along the way of error and temptation, there is no Darkness, but instead a Holy Light. The Cycles of the Nights and Days are the wheels of evolution and in them the Nights are periods of rest. It is taught that the Night of Brahmâ comes when the Sun passes away behind the 13th degree of Makara — the Tenth sign of the Zodiac — and does reach no more the Sign of Mina, or Pisces. This Sign Makara — the Crocodile, Dragon, or Leviathan, is connected with the birth of the spiritual Microcosm and the death of the physical Universe, and the Dhyân Chohans, called also the Kumâras, are connected with both.

"Mâra is the God of Darkness and Death, but also the unconscious quickener of the birth of the Spiritual. The Egyptians had a beautiful symbology for the Night of Brahmâ, as when Osiris, the defunct Sun, is buried and enters Amenti, and the Sacred Crocodiles plunge into thfe abyss of primordial Waters—the Great Green One. When the Sun of Life rises (or the Night ends), they re-emerge out of that Sacred River."

"And what happens during these, long Nights?" asked Ma-u.

"Nothing happens at all. The whole of Nature remains in a state of rest and slumber. There is neither construction nor destruction and all forms, as well as tneir Astral Types, remain as they were when Night commenced and they fell asleep. In those periods reigns the mystery of Non-Being; unconscious, yet absolutely conscious; unrealizable, yet the one Self-existing Reality; truly 'a chaos to the sense, a Kosmos to the reason,' as that great and wise woman, Blavatsky, the recorder of the secrets once said. When a Night commences there occurs a concentration of the Divine Essence, which during the Day was active by the expansion of this Essence from within outwardly, and inwardly from the without; an interchange of Cosmic Forces set in motion by immutable Laws. The 'breathing out' of these forces produces a world, the inhalation of the same causes this world to become static; a cyclic law that has existed from all eternity and will last for all eternity."

"I suppose that this cyclic law is the same as that which produces the ordinary day and night such as we know them in everyday life?" asked Ma-u.

"Yes," was the reply," and not only are there these cycles of the Nights and Days of Brahmâ, but there are cycles within these cycles. For instance, there are the Indian computations which take into consideration the reigns of the Manus, Gods, or Creators; the reign of one Manu lasting for 306,720,000 mortal years. The intervals between the reigns of each Manu are equal to 25,920,000 years; such intervals being termed Sandhis. During a Day of Brahmâ, fourteen such reigns and intervals constitute a Kalpa. You know already that one Night of Brahmâ lasts 4,320 millions of mortal years; so that a Day and a Night last twice as long. 360 of such Days and Nights make one Year of Brahmâ, equal to 3,110, 400 millions of years, and 100 such years constitute the whole period of Brahmâ's Age, or Mahâ Kalpa, namely 311,040 trillions of years.

"There are many different ways of arriving at such immense figures, and these Sacred Astronomical Cycles are of unbelievable antiquity. They are the calculations of Nârada and Asuramaya, the latter having the reputation of a Giant and a Sorcerer. But he was a white sorcerer, or White Magician, of Atlantis. Nârada, the Divine Rishi, was called Pesh-Hun, or Angelos. It is taught that He is the mysterious Power which sets in motion, and regulates, the cycles. Some call him the Eloquent Messenger of the Gods, who is for ever wandering about the earth giving good counsel; others regard Him as one of the Twelve Messiahs. He sometimes visits those nether regions which are called Pâtâla. He rules all worldly affairs and uses as his tools those who make wars and imagine that their own puny selves control the world. He is the indescribable, the greatest Sovereign of all times; unseen, unheard, yet everywhere. He is in the Effulgence of Light—the Ray of the Ever-Darkness—and in the OI-HA-HOU, which is Darkness, or the No-Number, according to the scripts of Dzyan.

An old Eastern Proverb says that 'Darkness is the Father-Mother: Light their Son.' Or, it is said that Darkness is the Eternal Matrix in which the Sources of Light appear and disappear. Or, that to the spiritual eye of the Initiate it is absolute Light."

As Neteru-Hem spoke it seemed as if a divine glow issued forth from him, lighting up the grim mansions of the dismal shapes and beings that flitted everywhere about, or crawled on loathsome bellies on the rocks and stones and floor. And they beheld a silent throng of monstrous dragons, mythical of mien, who, with unwinking, staring, glowing eyes, mirroring that mystic radiant glow, sat in a drooling ring about them, listening with slavering jaws agape; intense, as if with-flickering hope they too longed for salvation—as deep within ferocious souls they did. Dronish, drooped their sluggish trunks, prostrate with weary waiting for release and absolution; worn out with banishment, exile; the sport of witches, inexorable in their relentless grip, sealed down with mighty curses in the nether gloom. So they stared at that white shape and his companions.

"Oh, Messenger!" gasped Ma-uti.

"These are the thoughts of angry men and spiteful women," he replied.

"The thoughts of war, of lust, of hatred; jealousy and envy taking shape in bodies that would kill with fear the minds that thoughtlessly created them in brutish ignorance, or, in merciless mighty knowledge of the great Arcanum of Death. Here they abide; the work for which their masters formed them done; until by love and service their creators shall unloose the shackles that fetter, *both* to darkness and despair. For both are close connected, and in the eyes of men and women and behind the living masks of faces that shield the awful truth from all but the Initiate, abides the picture of each monster made in ages past or now, so dreadful to behold. Each deed of anger, giving pain, must be undone before these forms are free; and with their freedom comes exemption, disentluralment for their makers, who, until that time, will bear the mark of Cain upon their brows; and suffering is their lot."

"Are these thought-forms very old?" asked Ma-u.

"Yes; there are now in the nether heavens, such as you see here, some forms that were macle many millions of years ago. Thousands of incarnations have passed and still their makers have refused the Light. Instead of redeeming the creatures of their thoughts, they have made new ones to add and throngs of evil beings beset their path and lurk in unexpected comers, full of hatred for their masters, who with fresh hate respond and live and die in endless woe.

"Time, to God, does not exist in the same way as it does to mortals. A million years is but as one beat of the wings of a dragon-fly, when he trills his gauzy pennons on a day of sun. So He can wait, if man so wills with unrepenting mind."

As the Messenger and his companion stepped forward again the silent throng dissolved, as if his mere presence could melt these sad wraiths; and descending further into the twisting, tortuous galleries they came anon to a huge cavern, like unto a vast amphitheatre from which arose a soughing current of sobs and sighs. And in the radiance cast by his glowing form appeared a dim procession of ghostly men; all crowned with thorns, and heavy crosses athwart their drooping figures. In heavy agonizing drops the sweat and blood dripped from their foreheads; with droning sounds of murmured prayers they proceeded on an endless tour around that dim arena, on scabrous, un-hewn stones and flints with which bestrewed was everywhere the jaggéd ground. Harsh and austere their looks; shaggy hirsute faces, eyes fanatic, redly glowing in the dark. A grisly, horrid cavalcade of spectral spirits, heedless of the three who watched their agony.

"Behold the moulds in which the ancient persecutors of the faithful once were cast: the torturers, who with racks and gallows, fires and agonizing pains took toll of helpless victims in the name of Christ the King. There will be no release for them till all their prey in full realization descend into these regions, and with a holy kiss of pity forgive their trespasses, and take them by the hand to lead them to the Light—a merging, as ft were, of consciousness of individual wrongs in universal awareness of God's Love. Until then they must remain in unknown darkness.

"Thus love, which lies enfolded in every soul, as lotus leaves are found in perfect form within the undeveloped seeds prior to their germination, lies hidden in the breast of every brute, and only love resplendent can awaken it with gentle touch and warm it with God's rays; luculent and clear, sent forth from the Divine Bosom. So the germs of all that is, or is to be, dwell in the darkness, the Darkness that Breathes over the slumbering Waters of Life, replete with latent Spirit."

And then the ghostly troop began to fade away, and with it faded out the cavern and the rocks and crags, and faintly grew a phosphorescent glimmer that brought a dimly shining light upon the scene. A far-away tumult was heard that grew louder every moment — a rumbling noise approaching from the distance, a sound of shouting and of distant guns. And in the gloom appeared a mighty host of dim-seen shapes that struggled, fell, and rose again in flight; pursued by yelling hordes, barbaric. And sullen men of threatening mien on horseback led the army of pursuers; the War-Lords and the Captains of the fighting hordes; with mighty thunder of the drums of strife and clashing cymbals, sabres, spears; all calling to the festival of death and carnage. With blaring bugles, sounding the attack, retreat, enflanking movements, urging to the foul baptism of blood and mud, where gushing torrents of life's essence drain away in greedy earth, and kindly Man is made into a beast of brutal slaughter.

The sickle of a pale, wan moon shimmered over a field of battle that stretched for miles around, and Corpses piled and wounded bled and groaned in agony, as if that sickle of the moon were symbol grim of Death's sharp scythe, whose harvest grew as still the War-Lords cast their baleful, calculating glances round and gave gruff orders; and lurid flames of guns and cannons blazed upon the mowed down ranks and ranks of fathers, brothers, lovers, sons, destroyed in unappeasing greed. Bewildered victims; fighting, killing for an unknown cause their kindred from another land, who, too, the victims are and the agressors, at behoof of powerful masters, mad for gain and personal glory, which they cannot take away when Death calls loud their names and leads them to the land sinister, where with his grisly companies he reigns in nameless terror.

And every drop of blood the War-Lords spill must surely be redeemed somehow; with tears, or golden deeds of goodness; with pain and loss, with fasting and with prayer, with full awareness of the duty to one's brother, and with Service—endless—till all the stains are wiped away.

And as the din of strife arose and died away in whispering sounds, as if a million trees had shed their leaves that rustled in a wind of death, the Messenger and his companions stood in silence; watching that dread vision of useless agony; for victory and defeat alike are empty dreams.

Neteru-Hem turned to Ma-u and Ma-uti and said:—

"The thoughts of good and evil are like Light and Darkness which are identical in themselves, being only divisible in the human mind, and if has been told that Darkness adopted Illumination in order to make itself visible; and that Light is Matter, and Darkness Pure Spirit. Darkness, in its radical, metaphysical basis is subjective and absolute Light; while the latter in all its seeming effulgence and glory is merely a mass of shadows, as it can never be eternal and is simply an Illusion. So it is taught in the tenets of Eastern Occultism. But there is more to it than that and many of the teachings and holy books are masses of contradiction. In the Gospel of John, it says that 'the light shineth in darkness; and the darkness comprehendeth it not.' One explanation is that the word 'darkness' does not apply to man's spiritual eyesight, but indeed to Darkness, the Absolute, that cannot cognize transient Light, however transcendent to human eyes. We have here a mix-up of the principles of darkness from which sprang the material Kosmos with all its inhabitants, and this Darkness represents the material light as known to mortals, in contradistinction to the mortal concept of darkness, which represents sin and ignorance.

But there is a Greater Light, transcending all human concepts of Light and the Darkness of Chaos, and that is the ultimate goal of all *that* is created in the material and the nonmaterial.

When we read in the archaic narrative that the radiant child, Bright Face, Son of Dark Space, emerges from the depths of the Great Dark Waters and shines forth as the Sun, and that He is the blazing Divine Dragon of Wisdom, lifting the Veil, shutting out the Above, leaving the Below to be seen as the great Illusion, we must sense that BOTH that Above and Below are Illusions. Illusions so Supreme that the human mind and the human brain—its instrument here below—cannot conceive their Glory; much less the immeasurably greater Glory that IS beyond these Illusions. The awareness of this can only come by divine inspiration, under the guidance of those who are sent to bring a glimpse of the true Light to mortals. A sensing of the Un-nameable Great Thought behind the concealed Deity called Darkness, the Unfathomable Darkness, the Whirlwind, the Black Goose, or the Black Swan—all symbols of the temporary Manu, or God, of which fourteen reign supreme during one Day of Brahmâ; or of Brahmâ Himself, the Emanation of the Primordial Ray, the Vehicle of the Divine Ray, which otherwise could not manifest Itself in the Universe.

It is said that Father-Mother spin a web, whose upper end is fastened to Spirit, the Light of the One Darkness, and the lower one to its shadowy end, Matter. And this web is the garment by which man conceives God, as the Poet Goethe has said. Darkness is also called the Mother-Space, and the Mother of the Gods—Deva-Mâtri—as from Her Cosmic Matrix all the heavenly bodies of our system (Sun and Planets) were born. Therefore, we may consider that Darkness to be a physical, material darkness, just as the light—or its illusion to our physical senses— is a physical, material Light. This will become still more apparent when we learn that the Sons of Light clQthed themselves in the fabric of Darkness."

"Is it permitted to ask what happens when the hundred Years of Days and Nights of Brahmâ are over?" asked Ma-u.

"When that vast period is ended, my son, then all those spirits who have fulfilled the Laws of Love and Service will reach the threshold of the 'UNknown Darkness,' which, to them, will be the Great Day of Light; and for a period of time equal to One Hundred Years of Days and Nights of Brahmâ will they be absorbed in that Day; a time of rest and rejoicing after great travail."

So the Messenger and his companions crossed that great field of the battle of the shades of warriors and presently they reached a village of small, mean houses, huddled close together. Every house was closely shuttered and as they passed they saw the glare of anxious eyes within the cracks of doors and shutters. As the three passed along, one or two doors were softly pulled ajar, and when Ma-u turned round he saw the weird figures of thin old men, with shapes like attenuated goats and long and narrow wrinkled faces, with inquisitive pointed noses and little glaring eyes. Thin wisps of white hair hung lankly from their mean and shrunken skulls, and claw-like hands were gripping for support against the lintels of their doors, as, staring, they followed with cunning looks the Messenger and our friends.

"Who are these horrid people?" asked Ma-uti.

"They are the semblances of misers, still gloating over their useless gold. Come, follow me."

The Messenger strode to a door and knocked. With rattling chains and creaking bolts the door was opened, and a thin, quavering voice called out: "Who comes?"

Without answer the Messenger pushed wide the door and entered with Ma-u and Ma-uti, whilst the old man scuttled like a frightened weasel into a small, dark and dirty-looking room and made a hasty drive towards a rickety table, on which were several shining.coins of yellow gleaming sheen, visible within the dusk. Grabbing them anxiously, he hid them in a bag and placed this in a chest.

The three stood still and never spoke a word. And presently it seemed that the. old miser had forgotten them, and, sidling like a crab towards that chest, began to drag from its within bag after bag, placing them on the floor all around him. Muttering, he undid the strings that tied the bags and gloatingly put in his scraggy hands. But with dismay writ large upon his goat-like features, he drew forth the corpse of a child, that plainly had died of starvation. With howls of disappointment he went from bag to bag, and every one contained the corpse of a baby, a grinning skull, an arm, a leg, all given to corruption.

"My gold, my lovely gold, where is my lovely gold?" he sobbed, and wildly be began.to hunt in the dark comers, in the chest, under the table; crawling on the floor and peering, peering everywhere for that useless gold that was no more. His god, his idol gone and nothing left but anger, greed, despair and fury at his losses. With screams of rage he fled into the street and from every door poured forth another of these scraggy men, who mixed their lamentations, curses, execrations, with him who first found out his loss. With senile cacklings they accused each other of robbery and murder, and their raking talons dug angry furrows in their neighbour's cheeks, till with a mighty blast the struggling mob blew up and'like a mist dispersed, as if a strong north-wester blew the qualmy stench away from medieval city.

Now silence reigned again and everything seemed cleaner, despite the gloom of those dim regions. The village gone, the futile spites and greeds and empty hoarding of the useless wealth all done, though gold a noble metal, but only when employed for greatest good of all; while worse than bad when only satisfying few of worthless beings, whose only use for it is to hide it; dribbling over it in comers by a borrowed candle's light, whilst underneath their attics children starve and parents steal and go to jail, through trying in despair to get provender for their young. Thus the miser employs only the negative side of that which he so greatly treasures, instead of putting his wealth to positive productive uses, by making it the means of providing bread for his fellow-men by putting it into circulation. Sons of Ilda-Baoth they are, the Son of Darkness, and his mother, Sophia Achamoth, personifying the lower Astral Matter.

As the three stood in the silence, the horizon seemed to widen out in all directions, and in the faint light there appeared to lie a vast grassland, stretching for hundreds of miles into the far distance. A soft mist seemed to hang above the ground, and now this mist began to thicken and a restless movement from within spread across it like softly murmuring wavelets in the moonlight. This ripple now took shape and formed itself gradually into a huge flock of millions of white sheep. There they were, quietly grazing or looking up and chewing with sideways jerks of eager jaws. Some distance away there was a centre of agitation, and now a great platform slowly raised itself above the sea of woolly forms; and on that dais appeared a monstrous Goat with blazing eyes and shaggy, sharply-pointed horns above the evil head, and stamping angry hoofs that struck the floor with a hollow sound. And all the sheep, expectant, gazing mildly at that threatening figure. Around the dais a horde of smaller goats on guard, impatiently hustling, jostled the scatter-brained and bashful herd. Abruptly, the Goat rose to its hindlegs, stretched out a commanding fore-foot and sent forth a loud and piercing nicker.

"Baah", replied the sheep.

Again that Goat-call; louder.

"Baaaaaah", replied the sheep again.

And yet again that harsh, fierce call from the monster.

"Baaaaaaaaaaaaaaaah", once more the sheep replied.

Bewildered, Ma-u and Ma-uti looked at the Messenger; dumb with surprise.

"Behold a Dictator and his stupid Flock," said he.

"What is he telling the sheep?" asked Ma-u.

"He is not telling them anything in reality, for if he did, they—being only sheep—would not understand. But he is using a clever method of dealing with vast crowds, which is to shout aloud, with great determination, a simple word they can all understand. To this a mob will always re-act, having only sheeps' brains, which are used for feeding and reproduction of their kind."

"But are all sheep as stupid as this flock?" asked Ma-u.

"They certainly are, my son; but if any one of them should give any signs of being less sheep-like, the Dictator's bodyguard would soon use their sharp horns and striking hoofs and bring him back to normal sheep-behaviour; or else destroy him as an enemy of the flock. This is good discipline and much approved of by the rest, who do not like to see one of their brothers rise above the flock and so become their master."

"But what is the use of that great Goat to all these sheep?" asked Ma-uti.

"No use at all, my child; except that, being of a more aggressive order of beasts, the sheep will follow his commands; as sheep always like to do. They get a thrill at having such a fierce commander, who always promises them many fine things, such as sheep like to think of. This gives them the pleasure of great anticipation and it makes their Leader feel proud and generous."

"And does he ever keep his promises?" asked Ma-u.

"Why should he?" said the Messenger. "The sheep have very short memories and really do not expect that these promises will be kept; nor do they wish it, for every day the Leader promises something better, and all are very happy to have such a 'promising' Lord."

"But why are the body-guards chasing those black sheep over there?" asked Ma-uti.

"Ah," said Neteru-Hem, "being of a different colour, they are not considered to be of such fine descent as the white sheep; according to the Leader. Besides, a wise statesman, such as the great Goat, always sees that there are some amongst his people who can be blamed if anything goes wrong. The black sheep, being in the minority, serve this purpose very well, and give the other sheep a great sensation of superiority; which makes them more content and easier to control."

"I think the sheep are very silly," muttered Ma-u.

And now there was a movement in the distance, and a procession of elegant looking gentlemen, with top-hats and umbrellas, approached the great Goat's dais.

With many bows and genuflections and grave expressions on their faces, they solemnly placed rolls of parchment, heavy pendant seals on ribbons decorating them, at the feet of the great Goat; who nickered with disdain.

"Who are these people?" asked Ma-u.

"They are foolish statesmen from far lands, who come to treat with the Great Goat, lest he lead his sheep against them. They also bring him scraps of paper he loves to tear to bits and chew. This keeps him quiet and, for a time, at peace."

"But who is afraid of a few goats and a lot of sheep?" Ma-u wanted to know.

"My son, this is a matter of psychology," said the Messenger. "The great Goat, having a loud and angry voice, overawes these very polite but foolish statesmen. They think that, at the Goat's command, the sheep will attack in millions and destroy Civilisation; and so — to keep the peace, as they imagine — they pander to the Goat and his few satellites, and even give him power over other grazing-lands, with sheep too few to make resistance."

"But why do not these statesmen band together and so destroy that inept Goat. Would those sheep really invade other countries?"

"They do not want to band together, because the Goat knows how to promise as well as to threaten, and when he is in the right mood he can adopt a friendly countenance, at the same time bluffing and overcoming the witless brains of these poor'men. As to the sheep, they do not want to fight, but only wish to live in quietness on their fields."

"In that case, the statesmen are still sillier than the sheep," said Ma-u.

"Perhaps they will wake up one day," said the Messenger, "and then 'woe' to the Goats!"

"Oh, look!" exclaimed Ma-u," who are those funny creatures over there who run around in agitated circles, notebooks in their hands in which they scribble, hats on like parasols, flabby, pasty-looking faces, with cunning eyes as black as little currants, darting here and there?"

"Those are the editors, reporters and other men from Gutter Street; who, with distorted pens and twisted pencils destroy the sanctity of Truth, and all that sacred righteousness for which the ancient Messengers of God shed precious blood," said Neteru-Hem.

"With scares and rumours, lies, exaggerations, they fill their papers, so that the silly sheep at home shall buy and read—increase the circulation. So they make the sheep of different lands hate each other in their ignorance; and evil men, who live by selling guns and shells encourage such reports, in hope of war, to fill *their* money-chests with bloody gain."

"What horrid creatures," sighed Ma-uti.

"May their circulations so increase that all their veins shall burst," cried Ma-u indignantly.

"That is but empty play on words, my son," said Neteru-Hem, "and breathes a spirit of unwise thoughts. Remember that the goats and sheep, all foolish men, with or without umbrellas, pipes, or pruning-hooks, are but the wisps of an illusion which is so great that nearly all believe it's true.

"Behold:"

So saying, he waved his hand, and, like a puff of smoke the multitude of animals and those few men dissolved in air—were gone—and sweet peace reigned again.

"Such beings as you saw just now are but the shadows of the Light. Without those shades the pure in heart and wise could not be seen for what they are. There is an evolution that runs through the spheres above, just as below, and all the wise today were once as foolish. Eternal struggles towards supremacy, such as the wars in heaven, the ware of the Titans, the fights between Osiris and Typhon, the battle of the flames, are all symbolical of the eternal struggle towards the Light; and even the moons and planets, the stare and constellations involved in everlasting strife, as told in the old books. Gazing towards the Light from within the dark circle they will not cross, but must, in time to come, the shades of men dwell in Illusion; and too the shadow or the Astral form, to be annihilated if the Soul-Bird, the Divine Swallow, is to live for all Eternity in bliss, after Nuit, the Celestial Abyss is crossed. Meanwhile, these evanescent personalities dance, like a myriad sparks in the moonlight on life's ocean, just so long as the Queen of the Night casts her radiance and lustre on the running waves of Life, illusive. And, like a cat, whose eye reflects the solar light (the Goddess Bast of ancient Egypt), she watches in the dark, with bruising claw on head of Serpent of the Night, the everlasting enemy of Light.

"The shining moon, the Lady Nuit, the watcher in the gloom, aloft in heaven's Cupola, She sends her searching beams all round the globe and travels on her endless pilgrimage of angelic protection. Here is a mystery indeed!

"The Lady Nuit appears to some as darkling Goddess, who, standing on the spinning globe called Earth, bends down from East to West and shelters with her curve delectable the slumb'ririg Sphere. Her raven locks fall like a cascading waterfall of mourning, and like a curtain of black velvet they enwrap the Lands in atramentous dusk.

"For you to choose the symbol—Lady Dark, or Shining Maid of Light to fill the firmament.

"And both the shadow of the Unknown Darkness; the Self-Existent, of boundless Age, the One, concealed Deity, unknown for ever to the Shades in His Abode of Bliss.

"And when the Great Night commences, Mahct Pralaya, all this will end. You may read in Vishnu Purina that clouds, mighty in size and loud in thunder, will fill all space. Showering down torrents of water, the rain will last uninterruptedly for a hundred Divine Years and deluge the whole Solar System. Pouring down, in drops as large as dice, these rains will overspread the Earth, and fill the middle region and inundate the Heavens. The World is now enveloped in darkness; and all things, animate or inanimate having perished, the clouds continue to pour down their Waters, and the Night of Brahmâ reigns supreme over the scene of desolation.

"So it is told in the ancient Books, my children; and so it will come to pass.

"And all consciousness will be swallowed up by the Universal Intellect whose property is Wisdom.

"Before the rain the sky is full of omens. There will be heard strange sounds from every point, and dusk ascends the heavens. The Sun will pass away and no more cast his rays. The cold sets in, and spaces bare of life appear upon the land. The springs dry up, the rivers die, the ocean will be empty.

"And men and beasts shrink up each day, the planets halt and wither; so life and motion lose their force, and God Himself will fall asleep, His Task accomplished. Another Day is past and Night begins, until a distant mom shall dawn in rosy splendour. Meanwhile, the Eyes of the Sun and Moon and Planets are closed in sleep of dissolution.

"And Parabrahman, the Unknown, the Incognizable, who is not Ego, nor non-Ego, nor consciousness, not in Himself an object of knowledge, yet able to support and give rise to every object and existence which becomes an object of knowledge; He, the One Essence from which comes into existence a centre of energy, the Logos; He, the Verbum of the Christians, above, around, within, without, yea everywhere, and Light and Darkness His reflection.

"So all is black within the Night. Black doves, black ravens, black waters, black flames — invisible — the symbols of primeval Wisdom, flowing from pre-cosmic Source of All.

"The Angels of Darkness preside over that age-long Night, and reign full of unseen Glory, in mutable Radiance of immutable Darkness, unconscious in that Night."

Thus spoke Neteru-Hem, the Divine Messenger; and so ends the First Vision of Ma-u and Ma-uti.

ALEXANDRITE

In shifting colours, green and red,
Deceptive glamour shines
Upon the Face of Day or Night,
When Demons flit, or Devas
Benediction shed

VISION 2
DEMONS AND DEVAS

Silently Ma-u and Ma-uti stood beside the Messenger after he finished speaking, deeply impressed with what they had seen and heard.

A wan glimmer of light cast an eerie, unsubstantial illumination over the wide space where they waited expectantly for further instruction. Dead silence reigned everywhere; so great a contrast with that which had just gone before that the hush could almost be felt.

With hands clasped before him Neteru-Hem was mute also, as he too was waiting, deep in meditation.

Imperceptibly the Light began to change its hue to a lurid, murky, reddish tinge and it seemed as if it were alive and tremulant with unseen forces. A feeling of oppression made breathing difficult, there was a sense of foreboding, ominous, electric; which produced a feeling of inertness, difficult to overcome.

A slight tremor ran over the ground like a wind-made ripple across a field of com; and a faint rumbling sound was heard, impossible to place. The air felt warmer too; not a pleasing warmth, but as if a distant blast from a fiery furnace was wafted across space. A deeper rumble from beneath the soil could now be felt and traced from its source; and a softly-heaving movement of the ground made Ma-u and Ma-uti grasp each other in sudden fright.

"Hold each my hand, my children, and have no fear", the Messenger said, and eagerly the two did him obey; whilst with protective holy circle he made them safe.

Heavy clouds began to blot the paling stars and scurried across the face of heaven, and sudden gusts of wind increased the pressure of the elements, as if in sullen fits of temper, both air and earth stirred restlessly in easeless agony.

And now was heard another sound, this time from above, a rolling, sinister bombardment in the distant sky;

and sudden flashes lit the reeling rim of earth with grey-black clouds above. At rapid pace the storm approached, and suddenly a mighty heave of restless soil all round threw high the cracking land, accompanied by heavy crashes, as if a thousand fearsome monsters tried to escape from deep below. And jagged flashes pierced the clouds and dived in sudden brilliant splendour deep in loam and mire of agitated squirming sods.

And trembling rolls of mighty thunder split all the firmament with dreadful bursts, as if the tympanies of all the spheres, with one loud crash of crazy drummers, were smashed in shivering booms of mad delight.

Now, with a splintering, shattering roar rose high the whole of all the earth; raised in a mighty sweep to heaven, with rending cannonades of a shaking, blustering, vaunting uproar of the rocks and soil; tumultuous perturbation of unseen powers of the deeps; and in the distance rose a fierce volcano, shooting high aloft its fiery message of destruction, grim with booms and hollow humming; whilst from the rifts in writhing soil sprang up boiling, whistling streams of steam and seething watery jets and scalding vapours. And overhead the thunder rolled with droning roars, and from the clouds torrential streams of heavy rain descended on the tortured ground; the hills flung up, the mountains raised on high, as if the whole of Nature in a carnival of mad destruction held one final festival of wrath.

Dumb with terror did Ma-uti and Ma-u behold the fell upheaval; gripping the hands of Neteru-Hem, who silently and calm regarded the dreadful scene.

And now came added consternation, for as the destruction of that even plain took place, a multitudinous horde of formidable demon forces rode the clouds, flung far the gruesome lightning, dived in the burning glow of that volcano, shrieked loudly and violently swooped all round the sky in mad delight.

From out the soil rose up the demons of the earthquake, yelling hoarsely, running up the shaking hills and mountains that now raised mighty crests on high; pledging with raucous curses their kinsfolk from above.

And from within the protecting shell, Ma-u and Ma-uti, though fascinated, watched that scene with terror in their hearts. Borne on the wings of windy gusts great regiments of demons now rode in the sky; grinning with malignancy, they swept above the mountains. Thte rain still fell in torrents, glittering crimson in the light cast by the flames;. cascading rubies driven like vast walls, or garnet clouds, or waving blood-red curtains made of tinted crystals, shaking madly in the wind.

And still those rolling booms below and cracks above; a pandemonium so great that all the senses reeled.

"Thus were born in dreadful anguish lofty mountain ranges like the Alps, the Himalayas," said the Messenger. "Great Civilisations that existed when the earth was round and even—as was this even plain we saw transformed—were then destroyed, and millions upon millions of beasts and birds and humans wiped from off the earth in one dread hour. Those Beings in the sky and on the land you see disporting here in such delight, are but the denizens of the sidereal World, inverted Gods and Angels, made of Astral fluid. They are sons of Dark Space; what the superstitious call devils; and theirs the task of evolution of Earth's body, and the guiding of the mighty Forces that destroy or build. They are the entities that rule the World, but not humanity; and electricity is but one example of their nature, from which that unknown, useful, dreadful substance proceeds. Neither Gods nor Devils are they, but Nature's Forces, blind and strong, intent alone on their great task, not knowing suffering such as mortals fear. Their Masters rule the Cardinal points; are called the Mahâ-râjahs, four in number, and those accursed ones in the North and West cause all destruction such as you see here. But from the South comes healing and from the East all Wisdom flows.

"There are 'Four Winged Wheels', one at each Corner for the Four Great Ones and their Hosts, the Regents, they who rule the Cosmic Forces. Many names have been bestowed upon them and both the Kabalists and the real mystic Christians of John the Baptist and the Initiates of Christos state that Bahak Zivo, the Father of the Genii, was ordered to construct creatures. He failed and called in Fetahil, a purer spirit, who failed even more completely, just as the Lords of Light failed one after the other. These are symbolical teachings of the 'fall,' and thus we get the kingdom of the reign of Spirits and spiritual action, which flow from and are the product of spirit-volition, in contradistinction to the Kingdom of Souls and Divine Action. In the CODEX NAZARÆUS we learn how Bahak Zivo was separated from Spiritus, and the Genii, or Angels, from the Rebels. Then, the greatest of all—Mano—calls Kebar Zivo the Helm and the Vine of the Food of Life, and commiserating with the rebellious Genii, so foolish on account of the magnitude of their ambition, tells him that the Genii are the Princes, the Sons of Light, but that he, Kebar Zivo, is the Messenger of Life.

"So, in order to counteract the influence of the bad principles, Kebar produces seven other—the Cardinal Principles—in order to reestablish the balance between good and evil, light and darkness.

"In this way he produces the allegorical dual system we find in the early teachings, such as the Zoroastrian, in which lies the germ of dogmatic and dualistic religions of the future. An outline of the two 'Supremes '—God and Satan. In the various religious tenets we find these Angels and Demons changing place; examples are the fight of Indra, the God of the Firmament, with the Asuras—now degraded from High Gods into Cosmic Demons; the War in Heaven of Michael and his Host against the Dragon—Jupiter and Lucifer—Venus—Lucifer, now an Angel of Light, again debased to Satan.

"We find in the Chaldean Oracles, as well as in the teachings of St. Paul, the Doctrine of the Seven Cosmo-Creators of of the World, the World-Pillars, which are double; one set to rule the superior Worlds, spiritual and sidereal and the other to watch and guide matter. This is also the opinion of Iamblichus, who makes a distinction between the Archangels and the Archontes. An eternal above and below, Light and Darkness, good and evil; yet each completing the reverse side of each.

"Are, then, all these demons evil, and is the Astral Fluid of which they are made destructive to mankind?" asked Ma-u.

"No, my son, they are not evil to mankind, for they simply do not realize that there are such things as men; and evil lies more in the intention than the deed. As to the ambient and all-penetrating Fluid; this—detached from the Spiritual Sun's Splendour, an electro-magnetic ethereal substance, a vital and luminous caloric—is a living intelligent force which must be conquered by the mind, so that it may detach itself from earthly chains. If the mind fails to do this it will be absorbed into it again, and the same power which first released it, will draw it back into the Central Fire. Good and Evil are delusions of the earthly mind, symbologically they are represented by such pictures as the snake-emblem of Eternity of the Egyptians, when he encircles a water urn, his head hovering over the water which he incubates with his breath. This is a symbol of Kneph, the Eternal, Unrevealed God. Here, the Serpent is a good spirit—Agatho Daimdn, in opposition to the evil spirit, or Kakodaimdn. In the Pythagorean Triad, however, we have The God of the three aspects, and this is transformed, through the perfect quadrature of the Infinite Circle into the four-faced Brahmâ. 'Of Him Who Is and yet is not, from Non-Being, the Eternal Cause, is born the Being, Purusha,' as Manu, the legislator, says. And when the Being is re-absorbed in Non-Being, the cycle is completed, the work is done, and the Veil—the Mûlaprakriti of Parabrahman, will be raised, the Absolute Point revealed.

"And so there is a dual aspect to everything the senses realize. The Goddess Nuit, Isis, Diana, Hathor, demiurgal, at, once visible and invisible/different names for the same Divine Lady, had a dual aspect too, one Divine, the other Infernal. Semele, the wife of Jupiter and mother of Bacchus, is after her death carried to Heaven and reigns as Queen of the World, between Mars and Venus, or as Queen of the Universe, at whose name all the demons tremble, just as they do when the name of Hathor, Hecate, and other Infernal Goddesses is pronounced. In the Hierarchies of Demons we find Pulastya, a Son of God, who is made the progenitor of Demons, or Râkshasas, the temptors and devourers of men. We find Pishâchâ, a female Demon, who is the daughter of Daksha, also a Son of God, and she the mother of all the Pishâchas. But these Demons, so-called in the Purânas, are very strange beings, since all of them are shown as extremely pious, following the precepts of the Vedas and some of them being even great Yogins!

"In the Talmud you find Samaël, the Chief of the Demons, 'that Great Serpent with Twelve Wings that draws down after himself in his Fall the. Solar System, or the Titans.' His *alter ego* is Schemal, which really means the Year in its astrological evil aspect, with its twelve months, or Wings, of unavoidable evils in Nature. But in Esoteric Theogony both Samaël and Schemal represented a particular Divinity. And the Kabalist regards them as the Spirits of the Earth, the Personal God that governs it, and therefore identical with Jehova. Even the Talmudists themselves admit that Samael is a god-name of one of the seven Elohim. There is a secret meaning hidden behind all these allegories, known to the Initiated, who have the key.

"To the ignorant masses all these forces were gods, independent and supreme; they were demons to the fanatics, and to the Hermetic Philosopher they are either blind potencies or intelligent, according to which of the principles are under consideration.

"It is recounted that when the Demons were defeated in the Sacred Island — Atlantis — they fled to the northern shore of the Milky Ocean — the Atlantic Ocean — whence they addressed prayers and supplications to the 'first of Beings, the Divine Vishnu;' and the curious part is that they address him as the 'One with the Serpent-Race, double-tongued, impetuous, cruel, insatiate of enjoyment.'

"There are still peoples and tribes in America, Africa and Asia, whose religion is Demonocracy, or the worship of devils. It all depends on the point of view, and during the ages we find philosophers, such as Plato, who classifies the Demons in nine groups, namely: —

1. The Seraphim.
2. The Cherubim.
3. The Order of Thrones.
4. The Order of Dominions.
5. The Order of Virtues.
6. The Order of Powers.
7. The Order of Principalities.
8. The Archangels.
9. The lowest Angels.

The deposed Angels are Azares, Belial, Barbatos, who were all of high rank in Virtues.

    Bileth, Focalor, Phoenix, of the Thrones.

    Goap, of Powers.

    Purson, of Virtues and Thrones.

"Michael Psellus divides the Demons into six great groups or bodies.

1. Of Fire.
2. Of the Air.
3. Of the Earth.
4. Of the Waters and Rivers, causing tempests and floods
5. The subterranean, causing earthquakes and volcanoes.
6. The Shadows; ghostlike in appearance.

"Then we have the Demonography, or history and description of Demons in the writings of such authors as Wierus, Delancre, Leloyer and Bodin.

"And we must not forget the Demonius; a stone containing a demoniacal rainbow, which appears in it when rubbed and is useful in ceremonies in which the demons are invoked."

"How did these people acquire all this knowledge?" asked Ma-uti.

"By study of the ancient books, by instructions from the old Initiates, by inspiration and sometimes by imagination, my child."

While the Messenger had been speaking, the tumult of earthquake and storm had gradually subsided; the rain had ceased and the wind died down.

Gigantic mountains towered in the sky and were of rough and most fantastic shapes. Huge rocks and boulders hung precariously on narrow ledges and many of the demons were gleefully engaged in pushing them down the uneven slopes, where with thunderous crashes they bounced from point to point, until they became wedged in wide cracks, or came to rest on the lower parts of tortured soil.

Weird clouds were sailing in the heavens, reflecting the fires from the still erupting volcano, which, rumbling fiercely, threw out a mass of glowing stones and red-hot lava, which crept slowly down the slope.

"Is it safe yet to have a look around, Messenger?" asked Ma-u.

"Not yet, my son, the work is not completed," was the reply. At the same moment was heard a distant clamour high above, and a majestic Being appeared, in his hand a gleaming sword, riding on a pale horse, with mien of a great King, terrible to behold; Beleth his name.

A thousand trumpeters did go before him, blowing melodious and martial calls, and sackbuts gave a deeper tone, a basis for the higher sounds, a blend of rousing awe-inspiring music, thrilling every nerve.

And legion after legion of fearsome demons trooped in never-ending swarms behind him, until all that quarter of the firmament was filled with shouting dreadful forms. Some had lion's heads, or goose's feet, or tails of hares. Some had raven's heads, or heads of goats, or heads of cats or toads, or they were clad in the garb of fearsome warriors, or with a griffin's wings. Covered they were with scales, defended with huge teeth and fierce talons, sharp and poisonous; a marvellous spectacle of great legions, eighty-five in number.

And now arrived another troop of thirty legions, headed by Lerail, the great marquis of demons. Astride a giant crocodile, with hawk on wrist, he leads his fiery henchmen; crooked horns adorned their heads and in their hands are prongs of lightning, which they swing around in blinding circles.

Here comes another troop, led by Furcas, cruel Knight, with twenty legions of his mercenaries of hell. He rides a wolf and in his hand is a writhing viper, darting furious tongue and showing poisonous fangs, full eager to destroy. And all his soldiers are wrapped in flames, breathing sulphur-clouds, astride of serpents from the burning deeps, of frightful aspect.

Wild Morax adds his legions of monsters, thirty-one in number, and the shouting and the yells increase, as, flame in hand astride a black horse, this giant Earl and mighty President of evil gallops in the clouds, and circles wildly with loud shouts of devilish joy. Clad is he in crimson raiment, wearing on bold front a crown, and sallying along. His troop consists of demons with three heads, encircled with a fiery zone, and some have heads of dogs or snakes and bark or spit in anger.

And yet another ferine troop; that of Azares, First Duke under the Power of the East, with thirty-one savage legions. An infernal Dragon is his steed, and he swings serpent's tail aloft. His minions, strange and hideous, swarm around in dizzy circles. Black as pitch they are, with talons like the lion, claws like the wild bear, tusks like mastodons, sharp as rapiers. Bellowing with rage and gall they charge the rest, and ghastly battle threatens, until the chief, with sanguinary screams, rounds up his brood and whips them to submission.

But now a greater clamour still resounds, when other mighty throngs come storming forth and Lucifer himself arrives with legions near uncountable. Two-thousand-and-four-hundred legions follow this dread Lord, and now these multitudes fill all the sky in ring Tartarean, Stygian; and such a clamour rises now that all the welkin rings and shakes and the new-formed mountains tremble.

The fiery chariot of Lucifer pulls up, and with commanding gesture he projects on high a ball of burning black flames, and at this sign a space is made, central, wide and circular; while from above descends a group of Demon Dukes, Marquises, Counts and Earls, Knights and Prelates, Presidents of Calamities, They stand and wait expectantly and silence deep ensues, till suddenly with thunderous roar ten-thousand drums burst forth in tempestuous uproar, and now four Puissant Forms proceed towards the Centre. Borne on flaming Thrones from East and West, and North and South they come. In the form of a cross the four Thrones are placed back to back in pairs, so that each Lordly Monarch faces his own Cardinal Point.

Zimimar, on Throne of ebony drawn by polar bears, his sceptre a great firebrand, faces to the North. Of evil countenance is he and black of mien and threatening; from him comes all disaster, crime, iniquity and horror.

To the West is faced the Throne of Goap, the Prince of War and bloodshed, anger, lust and hatred. His Throne is red and drawn by leopards, and in his hand a lance with pennon black, to slay the innocent when chance does place them in his way. His glittering eyes dart cruel looks all round, aye seeking victims to destroy.

And Gorson, King of Southern climes, with bow and arrow on mauve Throne, is drawn by bulky elephants from place to place. His looks are mild, and on his brow a glistening crown of gold and pearls, denoting tears of happiness. But a mighty Lord is He, who can with one kind gesture grant all Happiness and Riches; or withdraw the same at will.

Now, lastly we behold the Golden Throne of Amaymon, King of Wisdom from the East. Great dromedaries draw His Throne, and milky white are they, the precious beasts beloved of Kings and Princes of the Desert Lands. Gloriously crowned, and Sage his Brow that glows with inner fires of wise profundity.

In front of each the Kings are rank on rank of Messengers with up-turned horns; some made of whitest ivory and hollow, and some of silver, brass, or gold, with which they sound their King's commands at his behest, when, blaring with loud blasts of trumpets he calls his winged Ministers.

And now a shattering roar resounds and at this savage utterance rise up the demons of the Earth, whose task it was to make the mountain-chain whose forming we have witnessed.

And, bowing deep, they make report of all that region and beyond; for when those mighty hills were raised, at other points of earth's fair face the lands were sunk, the waters have rushed in, and seas and oceans spread their tossing waves where once great Nations blossomed fair and wise, but soon forgotten.

Wild laughter sounds from the great multitudes who shriek with glee when the tales of death, destruction, suffering and loss are told; and with loud yells of mad delight the demon hordes disport themselves and leap with joy. Their grisly steeds rear up and gallop in confusion and add their barking, growling, hissing, thundering bellows to that grim festivity of execrable clangour.

But now, at a sign from the four Kings, bright Lucifer commands his legions to restore once more a semblance of tranquility, and that wild orchestra of demon, maniac fury is stilled again, and only the splendour of that glittering host is gleaming in a vast carouse of scintillating glister.

Now Zimimar, the Northern King, holds up on high his firebrand sceptre, and his trumpeters raise-up their horns and with a shivering roar there streams from out their mouths a swarm of small black demons which spread in all directions and settle on the hills, the valleys, and the mountains far and wide. These are the seeds of future deeds of evil, plagues, disasters, sent to teach the coming generations certain lessons, hard to learn, but if grasped with due humility and wisdom they will raise the aspirant to the highest pinnacle of bliss.

But Gorson, from his golden Throne, now shoots a trembling arrow wide, and at this sign resounds a long clear call of silver horns, whilst from their mouths stream out in rising glory glittering clouds of rosy fragile little demons, with gauzy wings that glisten splendidly in rainbow hues, and far and wide they flutter and descend all over the land; and southern zephyrs blow caressingly and waft a subtle perfume through the pellucid air. Here are the seeds of Love and Kindness and good deeds, to counteract the force malign of the dread Northern Monarch's satellites.

Thus strike the Gods themselves a balance in their Wisdom; guiding stumbling Man along his path of test and trial and reward.

And now a loud fanfare of brass, that hoarse and threatening precedes the warlike forms of tiny demons flying from the mouths of brazen trumpets, as Goap's Band from Western Climes blare out their challenge. Fiercely their Lord points with his lance towards the corners of the earth; in one wide sweep of mail-clad fist embracing all directions. With heavy drone of steely wings the seeds of war and strife, rapine and destruction soar high to heaven, and like a plague of locusts darken all the Land.

A solemn hush now falls on all when on his golden Throne Amaymon, King of Wisdom, slowly rises and with sonorous voice proceeds to read a proclamation from a heavy roll of papyrus, inscribed with mystic characters. It is a proclamation, with message sage, Divine with Knowledge of the Highest Gods, which only Gods can understand; and therefore Man, who has within his Soul all Intellect—prescience, which will in time unfold and make him One again with *THAT* from which he is descended.

Amaymon's sparkling crown sends rays of brilliant radiance within the air and lights with arcane fires the path on which Man shall wind his way to heaven, when death and life and war and love have been subdued with understanding of Celestial Holiness and pity. And all the demon legions that fill the Empyrean vault are dumb and hang their heads in shame, remorse and pain, when clear-rings out that Angel Voice with Message so supreme. With clarion call ring out his golden trumpets now, and all revive; forgotten is the Holy Word; bonds of restraint are broken, licence fierce holds revel high, and even all the Princes, Dukes and Earls and Knights are powerless to still that great explosion; wrath demoniacal; antithesis of all that draws to God, unknown, forsaken in Divine Abode; His House is empty—silent are the Mansions of the Soul.

The Demons of the East and South call on Astarte, with prayer of Old Phoenicia: 'O Virgin of the Universe, blesséd Mother and Lady of the Skies, stay this tumult unholy.'

But powerless is She, that Maid and Mother, worshipped through the Ages; impotent to still that furious mob, who now regret their pang of piety with boundless rage and burning lust to kill. And tearing, rending, clawing, screaming, that evil throng attack, and, in two camps divided, a dreadful battle in the sky ensues, and all the regions shudder in dismay

....
....

> Far in the East
> Approaches snow-white Gondola.
> Drawn by the figures of seven Angels
> It draws near, apace.
> A silent MAN sits in the bows,
> With Sorrow graven on His Royal Countenance;
> And sternly gazing at those heaving multitudes,
> He rises up—
> Yea!
> Jesus Christos, Son of God Himself—

Rebukes that Host
And raging of the Warriors
And at His stem command they cease—
And there is calm.

* * *

The heavens cleansed;
And but a single glowing Star
Doth shine in clear cerulean sky,
Surrounded with a Halo,
Where He, the MASTER,
Stilled that clamour.

* * *

Quite overcome by the prodigious phenomena they had just witnessed, their ears still ringing with the uproar of that mad contest and turbulence of overbearing violence, and that Majestic Figure, noble, exalted, Lordly in that One Mandate, that swept the upper regions clear of all iniquity, Ma-u and Ma-uti knelt at the feet of the Messenger and wept . . .

Gently he raised them up and told them that all danger was past and that now they were free to walk around and see the wonders of that vast upheaval.

"The demon spectacle you have seen was what the old philosophers imagined when they wrote their classifications of the different Orders of Spirits.

"The leading tenets of these doctrines can be traced to the Jews and early Christians; but in the Dark Ages the Moors of Spain, who were then the principal Philosophers, matured and developed these teachings and communicated them to the natives of France and Italy.

"In those days great schools of Magic were to be found in Salamanca, Toledo and Seville. There it was taught that from the Fallen Angels all knowledge and power might be obtained. They were masters of the abstract sciences, in alchemy, of the languages of mankind and the animals, of poetry, pneumatology, moral philosophy, magic, history, divinity and prophecy. They had power over the winds, the waters and the influence of the stars: to raise earthquakes, induce diseases, or cure them, and release souls from purgatory.

"The King of all the Demons was not Satan, but Beelzebub. Satan was considered by Wierus to be a dethroned monarch; Leader of the Opposition.

"Moloch was Chief of the Army, Pluto Prince of Fire, and Leonard Master of the Sphere. Then, there were the masters of the infernal courts, such as Adramelech, Grand Chancellor; Astaroth, Grand Treasurer; Nergal, Chief of the Secret Police; and Baal, Chief of the Satanic Army.

"Each State in Europe had its Infernal Ambassadors:— Belphegor, in France; Mammon, in England; Belial, in Turkey; Rimmon, in Russia; Thamuz, in Spain; Hutjin, in Italy; and Martinet, in Switzerland.

"There were also earthly representatives:—

"There was Moreau, magician and sorcerer of Paris, who represented Beelzebub; Pinel, a doctor of Salpetriere, represents Satan; Bouge represents Pluto; Nicholas, a doctor of Avignon, represents Moloch.

"Altogether there are in the infernal regions 6,666 legions, each composed of the same number of devils or demons. So those ancient thinkers built a universe of spirits, based on dim memories, of the still more ancient arcana. Never forget that thoughts like that take shape in a more or less solid form, according to the amount of thought-power expended upon them, or the intellectual strength of their creators.

"In the Stanzas of Dzyan we read that the third and the fourth Race took wives from the mindless, the narrow-headed, who were fair to look on. And then they bred monsters, wicked demons; male and female did they breed them. The Giants of the Fourth Race obtained the sovereignty of all the earth and defeated the Minor Gods; and the Gods of our fathers became our devils. This sort of thing often happened quite suddenly, as, for example, in the case of Seth, or Typhoon, who conferred on the sovereigns of the eighteenth and nineteenth Dynasties in Egypt the symbols of Life and Power. But in the course of the twentieth Dynasty this God, who was once universally worshipped and adored throughout Egypt, suddenly was treated as an evil Demon, and all his effigies and names were obliterated on all the monuments that could be reached.

It is told in the ancient teachings that when Brahmâ wished to create the world anew and construct progeny through His Will, he began by creating Demons, who thus take precedence over Gods and Angels. There is a deep esoteric reason for this belief, as the so-called Demons are the Self-asserting -and intellectually active Principle; are the positive pole of creation; and are therefore first produced. Just as in every ancient Theogony without exception down to the times of Hesiod, in the order of Cosmogonical evolution, Night is placed before Day; Darkness before Light; Chaos before Order.

"The rebellious Sons of Brahmâ. are all represented as Holy Ascetics and Yogis in the Aryan allegory. Nârada, a Son of Brahmâ, refuses to marry and is cursed by Daksha, who brings 10,000 Sons for the purpose of peopling the world, and Nârada is condemned to perish in his Angelic form and to become a maii; and thus these Gods were degraded into Demons. Many reasons are given why these Sons of Brahmâ. refused to become men; some refused because they had no Astral body, others because they had been Adepts of long past Ages; but in the end they sacrificed themselves for the salvation of these Monads which were waiting, and who otherwise for countless Ages would have to linger in human form, with only animal understanding. Thus these Gods endowed Man with a *conscious* immortal Higher Mind, reflected in the Lower Mind. Those men into whom the Gods projected their Divihe Selves became Arhats; those who received but a spark remained destitute of Wisdom; for the spark burned low; some remained without intellect altogether, for they were not ready.

"In Genesis you may read how the Sons of God become enamoured of the daughters of men; marry, and reveal to their wives the mysteries unlawfully learned by them in Heaven, according to Enoch; and this is the 'Fall of the Angels.'

"It is said that divine wisdom falls like lightning from Heaven, but this is only a symbolical synonym for inspiration and initiation. Each time that ah Angel decides that there is a man who has evolved sufficiently to receive that Initiation, there is another 'Fall' when the Spirit of that Angel descends upon that man. But that 'Fall' does not turn either Angel or man into Demon, but rather transcends both into more perfect realizations of their Divine Prerogative.

"We are taught that Logos is passive Wisdom in Heaven, and conscious, self-active Wisdom on Earth. It is the Marriage of the Heavenly Man with the Virgin of the World—or Nature as described in Pymander; the result of which is their progeny—immortal Man. This is in exact opposition to that dogmatic horror of fiction of Western Theology—that the 'Fallen' Angel is Satan. Therefore, the ancient doctrine teaches that the Angels and Divine Rebels preferred the curse of incarnation and the long cycles of terrestrial existence and rebirths, to seeing the misery, even if unconscious, of the beings who were evolved as Shadows out of their Brethren, through the semi-passive energy of their too spiritual Creators. If man's uses of life should be such as neither to animalize nor to spiritualize but to humanize self, to do so, he must be born human—not Angelic. So the Celestial Beings became sometimes voluntary victims in order to redeem Humanity, and the 'Fallen' Angels became part of humanity itself.

"It is taught, therefore, that the evil Spirit, Satan, and Samael, the Angel of Death, are the same; and that Jehovah (mankind, or Ja-hovah) and Satan, or the tempting Serpent are also one and the same in every particular. There is thus no Devil, no Evil *outside* mankind to produce a Devil. Evil is a necessity for progress and evolution, as night is necessary for the production of day, and death for that of life; so that man may live for ever in true spiritual intuition, intellect and Wisdom. This is the Secret Wisdom; and it is not necessary to worship Nebo, the Deity of the planet Mercury, or Hermes, or Buddha, called Kokab by the Jews, and Nabo by the Greeks; it is not necessary to worship this oldest God of Wisdom, as he was worshipped in Babylonia and Mesopotamia, to find this Wisdom; for it is hidden within all men's souls.

"It is said that 'Satan is always near and inextricably interwoven with man,' and in the Book of Jude it is written that: 'For even Michael the Archangel . . . durst not bring against him (Satan) a railing accusation, but said, The Lord rebuke thee;' and this is repeated in the Talmud.

"In the Zohar and other Kabalistic works we find that Satan is simply the personification of the abstract Evil, latent or active in man. And all beings, whether Angels or Demons, are governed by the Law; there is no escape; and both are inherent in man.

"Man must become proud enough to believe in the God-principle within him, brave enough to find release from evil at the price of suffering, strong enough to keep full control and Faith in darkness and agony, and to build himself a throne out of the pyre of his destruction. An apotheosis of self-sacrifice for the sake of his brothers, whom he can then lead onwards, and up the Golden Stairway with a strong hand, a pure mind, and unfaltering Love and Wisdom.

"There is no difference between the fallen and the upright, except in their functions; for all are derived from the same Divine Source. The Christians have failed to reconcile the Jewish Jehovah—whom they took as he was portrayed—with the Gospel of Light and Love. A Deity of darkness and submission cannot be the Father of that Son who brought Liberty to mankind by showing them the Way of Freedom and Illumination. That freedom can be won by subduing the Satan within and calling forth the

Angel, or, in other words, by overcoming and taming the material animal who obstructs the way to Light; or dispelling the clouds of ignorance, so that our thoughts take wings towards the Sun of Truth, majestic and sublime.

"Only then will the black-winged demons fold up their pennons and disperse their evil forms, as if dissolved in sighs of Zephyr's Music; drifting on the dreamy air of summer night."

As the Messenger finished his wise discourse, a great silence fell upon the hills and mountains, rocks and crags and stony valleys. No longer did the boiling springs below the crust rise up; and the volcano too had ceased to labour. A light spread o'er the firmament and each stark detail of the barriers and gorges, ridges and clefts, stood out in full relief.

The ground on which the Messenger and our two friends had stood to witness the strange scenes in the sky had not been lifted up in the turmoil of raging fury, but was bestrewed with splintered, uneven stones, shot off from rocky ledges when heaving in their torment. A purple haze hung in the distant dales and valleys, and above the summits and plateaus and shelving rocks there drifted multicoloured clouds, heavy with the ashes the volcano had flung aloft.

There lay this strange landscape; autochtonal, primitive in its pristine audacity of overpowering, brutal splendour. And centuries seemed now to glide away, soft-footed and unheard; and a gradual transformation took place.

The lofty mountain-tops were gradually bedecked with snow that drifted silently, until a line of demarcation stopped its spread. And great crevasses filled with glistening ice, that threw blue radiance afar; whilst little rills went trickling down the wrinkled mountain-sides and seams and reached the valleys' beds, to rush away in broadening curves to lower levels leading to the sea.

Changing lights and tints of blue horizon, orange and russet, grey lights on dark dim outlines; hovering shadows, the cloak of twilight, or the sparkling sun; or nights that faded to obscurity, mingled in a phantasmagoria of illusive images and optical illusions. And all the time the streams, the rivers, rivulets and rills, the winds, the sun, the rain, the air, were grinding down the unhewn rocks, until long swelling slopes shone in the sun-swept haze above, beswathed with virgin soil, arrayed in shining green. And trees with varigated foliage sprang up, and flowers hung from crazy ledges.

The seasons turned their ceaseless wheels of birth and sleep, of spring and winter; and tempest-twisted chestnut trees, and forests full of royal oaks, gnarled by time and howling storm, spread wide their searching branches, dense-foliaged, a canopy, of leaves, with lowering shades of monarchs of the forests.

Impenetrable woods rose darkly in the distance. A lonely, fringed blue gentian waves gently in the southern breeze, and gold-eyed celandines peep from between their heart-shaped leaves, whilst locust-blossoms, creamy white against the soft green moss, shine out among the thickets and along the hazel-bordered trails.

The monstrous shapes of tortured rocks that lay about as if a troop of Titans, slain in ghastly battle, jaws stretched out in a last scream of agony, with broken fangs and twisted limbs raised up to Satan, as if they howled and prayed for mercy, are now invested with festoons of brilliant flowers; with giant ferns that wave their tips of sculptured, rare perfection.

The stately ash-trees, mystic pines. and broad-leaved poplars, oaks with kingly mien, they stand on guard around. The slender-bladed grasses, grey and amber mosses, dainty plumes of golden rod, now form a cloak of beauty that o'er-spreads with sweeps of glory that hoary place of conflict on which the giants sleep.

The scenes of deepest peace are sometimes found around an ancient battleground, as if at that last dread encounter, when mind escapes from smitten body, and knees, unloosened, bend in final genuflexion, those enemies each knew the holy spark that dwelt within the other, and, with a sob of loving recognition fell; and lie in brotherly embrace at rest at last, all hate forgotten.

And honeysuckle, lilac, blue delphiniums, sweet-scented violets, bloom everywhere; and from their gentle, coloured shapes rise up in swift delight winged forms that flutter, dart and hover in the golden rays of Sun.

Whilst underneath the fragile ferns and over lichen-covered stones, anatomies of unknown things creep on mysterious errands.

Strange beetles, gold and bronze and red, hide under fallen logs and boles, or climb green trailing vines, as if they too would find the light; though creatures of the shadows. The scarabeous rolls his mystic ball that's filled with life; a symbol of the shining orb above.

On blackthorn bushes shine white stars enshrining tiny sparks of amber; and glowing spider-webs, in dazzling rainbow tints, suspend their tenuous nets from branch and twig, to catch the careless gnat or fly and bring provender to the spinners, who, with their tiny eyes aglow with death, sit, waiting in the dark.

In sunny meadows, open glades and glens and on the graceful breasts of sloping hills that undulating in the distance lie, the modest daisy raises up its sweet pale face so like a star in white, with golden heart; the loveliest flower in all the world; a magic symbol few can understand.

From where the grey splintered cliffs sheered down to deep dark groves and purple shadowy depressions, dropped babbling brooks to black ravines; and gushing springs flew down to moonlit lakes and glancing rivers; all rippling in the southern winds. And limpid, misty, eddying pools, surrounded by steep banks of green, lay shining under azure skies and faintly stirred, as if they dreamed in cool delight of soft caressing Zephyr's wings that gently touched their silver surface.

In thronging charm, cool swarms of purple crocuses, bluebells and primroses bestrew the bright green spots upon the hilly slopes, that seem like islands on the darker ocean of the forest trees in vastnesses of heavy timbered hollows. And in the birches gleaming white, curly-barked and graceful like sweet ladies, or in the rustling poplars, and the leaves and twigs of trembling aspen, the birds attend their nesting-places, or sing their songs of love.

See how the lark soars up like a winged thought of melody, and sails all o'er the pearl-begemmed plains and fields, before returning to his nest on earth to gather up fresh strength, to rise with airy curve aloft and pour out song seraphic at the rising sun.

So all the birds the Gods have made do sing their trilling quavers, to wake the dawning of the day. Their forms symmetric, motions full of grace, in plumage delicate, enchanting, in aery caravans float in the sky. They warble music in the trees, or on the sprays of flowering shrubs, that scent the morning with soft odours.

The royal eagle on her eyrie tends her young; the storks on cliff and cedar-top stretch out their wings and raise sharp beaks in greeting; the prudent crane, borne on the winds, sets forth on hunting expedition, and snow-white swans drift on the lake or river like angels of a dream.

The linnets and finches carol and flit, and softly-warbling redbreast answers shrilling ousel.

And then at eve the nightingale's sweet notes roll through the dark blue depths, lit up between the scattered leaves and mazy lacery of twisting boughs grotesque, with glittering argentry of summer moon. With drooping, sleepy wings the feathered tribes have gone to roost; the noisy hum of insects rings no more, and only philomel drops notes of liquid splendour in the drowsy solitudes of forests shrouded in the night.

* * *

High on the mountain crests, above umbrageous dales and dells, the cold chaste Queen of Heaven casts her silver radiance upon a mighty spirit-form, that sits upon a rocky throne be-tipp'd with silvery icy flame; a most majestic

Deva King, who watches in the silent night o'er his domain. And on the distant snowy summits and the hills and floating over woods and fields, and dark cool streams and pools, like forms appear, as if transparent films of mist and splendid iridescent glory of arduous incandescent fervour have condensed their lustre into shapes superlative in beauty; immaterial and sacred.

The highest poetry of speech or pen could never once succeed in a recital that would aptly show the purity of these inspiring shapes, ethereal, intangible; not shades or phantoms, but a race of pure intelligence and full of vital essence.

During the scene of transformation of the rugged, fierce landscape into one of the utmost beauty, Neteru-Hem, and Ma-u and Mauti had slowly strolled about, the latter enthralled with the splendour that was rising up all round them and in the far distance. But at the appearance of these Heavenly Beings, they were completely enchanted and wanted to know who they were and whence they came.

"These great Devas are some of the Dhyân Chohans, of which there are seven divisions. Of those, the Kumâras have most to do with Nature—and with humanity also. They are the Mind-Born Sons of Brahmâ-Rudra, or Shiva, the Destroyer, whilst Vishnu is the Preserver; and both are the Regenerators of Spiritual as well as of physical nature. To live is to die, and to die is to live, and so Shiva, the Destroyer, is the Creator and the Saviour of Spiritual Man, as he is the good gardener of Nature. His is the task to weed out the Cosmic and human plants, to kill the passions of the physical and to call into life the perceptions of the spiritual man.

"The Kumâras are known as the 'virgin ascetics' who refuse to create the *material* man.

"Those Devas you see here are the ones in charge of the waters, the woods, the hills, the mountains, and they are entirely benevolent and loving in nature. There are, further, the cloud and wind Devas, who paint those magnificent pictures in the sky at sunrise and sunset, or even in the middle of the day, or at night when there is a moon.

"There are, further, the Purânas of the Tairyagyonya creation, or fifth creation, who are the creators of the animals, birds, and fishes, and all that creeps on the soil, or flies in the air, or dwells in the waters or in the earth.

"Thus Brahmâ Himself creates the four Orders of Beings, termed Gods, Demons, Progenitors, and Men. The Progenitors are those Pitris who evolved the first Root-Race of Men, and there are seven classes of Pitris. This creation took place in what is termed the Seventh Creation, the evolution of the Arvâksrotas Beings, or man; the so-called Mind-Born progeny with the 'soft bones,' who in turn became the evolvers of the 'Sweat-Born,' who in later evolutions gradually evolved into Man as we know him today.

"The Nature Devas are only one of the ranks or orders of spirits who compose the Hierarchy which rules the Universe under God. There are vast numbers of them and they are again divided into three classes — the Bodiless, the Form Devas and the Passion Devas. The Bodiless ones belong to the first Elemental Kingdom, and are composed of mental elemental Essence. Form Devas are of the lower Elemental World, and while their bodies are composed also of the same Essence, they are connected with the second Elemental Kingdom.

"The Passion Devas are in the Astral World, and their bodies are composed of Astral Elemental Essence.

"These Devas are all glorious Beings of vast knowledge and power, calm, yet irresistible, and altogether magnificent in appearance, as you can see. The elements they belong to are the air, the earth, fire and water. They are the Rulers of these Elements, and I will show you more of these later, and also the Elementals, who are their subjects."

In the meantime the Devas presented a wondrous spectacle as they floated above the groves and rills, the fields and woodlands, the hills and mountains.

The Shining Ones were at their work of the evolution of the plants, the flowers, the trees; their auras radiating all around and stretching out in lovely colours like streamers, or moving clouds; and with these auras they touched the growing things; thus imparting to them their own vital forces. With radiant smiles they gazed upon Ma-u and Ma-uti, changing their auras' forms into lovely golden wings; or rose, pale blue, soft green, or into a veritable palette of all the tints beheld in mother-of-pearl. Sometimes they ascended in the air in conformation at rapid pace, and then, after circling high up, they formed into groups that like glittering meteors fell down and each group in so falling produced a note of trembling music. When several groups fell together, each in a different formation, a chord rang out and as it sounded there rose from out the earth a shining fiery pillar that rang with heavenly melody, so sweet that all the senses reeled in ecstasy.

It was a glowing column, stretching right on high up to the sailing fleecy clouds that slowly swam along. Vibrating with an elemental energy it whirled round and round whilst throwing vortex after vortex wide of brilliant coruscations, each particle a note of ringing minstrelsy, yet sweet and dulcet to the soul. Vaster and yet vaster did the pillar turn in swift gyration, and wider flew the glowing singing particles, till suddenly a great bouquet of jubilant streamers rose high up from out its apex and scattered in the heavens in a mighty chord, a symphony sublime, a burst of melody divine that filled the starry vault.

And now there came an interchange of radio-activity from group to group, dynamic, vital; and streams of coloured light flashed to and fro and set the firmament on fire with splendour inconceivable. And all the heavens rang with luscious, mellow themes, concordant and harmonious; triumphant, descant, ariose and sweet, as if a choir of angels chant in poignant rapture, ravishment, delight and ecstasy beatific.

A rain of liquid sparks descends all o'er the land, in colours pink and mauve and white and silvery blue; a pouring down from out these harmonies of pure delicious incantation—that conjures up a surging swell of animation; vitalizing all the earth.

Delirious with happiness, Ma-u and Ma-uti turned their shining eyes upon the Messenger and grasped his hands.

"Oh, thank you, thank you for showing us all these wonders," they said.

Lovingly the Messenger regarded the pair for a few moments and said: "Some of the Hierarchies of Devas of the First and Second Races have taught humanity the origin of everything on earth, and of the Cosmic Evolution of all things and beings, including physical man, right from the first beginnings up to the beginning of the Kali Yuga, about 5,000 years ago, which coincided with the death of Krishna, the bright Sun-God, the once living hero and performer. They taught the true history of the Races, from the First to the Fifth. The Sages of the third Race, the McLnushis, learnt it from the Devas and passed the knowledge on to the inhabitants of lost Atlantis; and it was given in the Senzar language, which was known to the Initiates of every Nation. These learnt this secret sacerdotal tongue from the Sons of Light in Central Asia, and parts of this knowledge can be found in all the sacred Books, such as the Chaldean Book of Numbers, the Pentateuch, the sacred volumes of the Egyptian Thoth-Hermes, of the Purânas in India, and the Shu-King, China's primitive Bible, in the Kiu-ti, the Siphrah Dzeniouta, and even in the Sepher Jetzirah of the Kabalists.

"The Devas are also known as the Anupâdaka, parentless, without progenitors. The mystery of the Hierarchy of the Anupâdaka is great, its apex being the Universal Spirit-Soul, and the lower rung the Mânushi-Buddha; and every soul-endowed man also is an Anupâdaka in a latent state. The ignorant early Christian Fathers regarded the Devas as evil, in common with the later Zoroastrians, whereas in reality they are the conscious intelligent Powers in nature; and not only have they to do with the evolution of the earth, but there are Devas connected with all the planets.

"All the Devas, as well as the Gods themselves, pass through several states of evolution, which are referred to as Immetalization, Inherbation, Inzoönization, and finally Incarnation. When they reach the stage of human evolution—as many of them have done—they become active forces and have to do with the elementals, the progressed entities of the animal kingdom, in order to develop gradually into the complete form of humanity. But they do not incarnate as humans until the Third Root Race, for in the First Race on earth they are ethereal beings, and in each of the subsequent Races and sub-races they became more and more encased in material matter; in the Second Race they are still of Giant stature, but ethereal, though more in the form of a human; until the Third Race they have acquired a perfectly concrete body, ape-like, and more cunning than spiritual. Later on, in the Third Race, they become smaller in form and more rational; whilst in the Fourth Race their intellect has greatly developed and they gradually acquire speech and language. Their primordial spirituality is eclipsed and overshadowed by nascent human mentality. So they have descended from the ranks of Gods to Man, and now commences the terrible climb back to God-hood; through suffering, trial, test and temptation, to initiation into the mysteries, whence they return laden with the treasures of experience; victory over the material; and wisdom fully developed.

"As it is said so beautifully in the Secret Doctrine:—'Sitting at the threshold of Light, he looks into it from within the Circle of Darkness, which he will not cross; nor will he quit his post till the last day of this Life-cycle. Why does the Solitary Watcher remain at his self-chosen post? Why does he sit by the Fountain of Primeval Wisdom, of which he drinks no longer, for he has nought to learn which he does not know—aye, neither on this Earth nor in its Heaven? Because the lonely, sore-footed Pilgrims, on their journey back to their Home, are never sure, to the last moment, of not losing their way in this limitless desert of Illusion and

Matter called Earth-Life. Because he would fain show the Way to that region of freedom and light from which he is a voluntary exile himself, to every prisoner who has succeeded in liberating himself from the bonds of flesh and illusion. Because, in short, he has sacrificed himself for the sake of Man-kind, though but a few elect may profit by the GREAT SACRIFICE.'

"It is through these 'Sons of God' that infant humanity learnt its first notions of all the arts and sciences, as well as of spiritual knowledge; and it is They who laid the first foundation stone of those ancient civilizations that so sorely puzzle our modem generations of students and scholars.

"So they lead men onwards, until by eating of the fruit of knowledge, dispelling ignorance, Man becomes like one of the Elohim. They are the guardian spirits of the human race, or, as Hermes says: 'those who dwell in the neighbourhood of the immortals, and thence watch over human affairs.'

"The Esoteric Doctrine teaches that the Devas are the collective aggregate of Divine Intelligence or Primordial Mind, and that the first Manus, the seven mind-born Spiritual Intelligences, are identical with them; they are the Lords of Light, who cast no shadows.

"In Lemuria and Atlantis the Devas assumed bodies to rule over the Races in these continents as Demi-Gods, or Angels. The Lemuro-Atlanteans were the first to have a Dynasty of Spirit-Kings; not of Manes, or Ghosts, as some believe.

"But as these Devas were Rupa, or material Spirits, they were not always good. One of the bad Devas was their King Thevetat, and it is due to the evil influence of this King-Demon that the Race of Atlanteans became a nation of wicked magicians. This led to war and the disfigured allegories of the race of Cain, of the giants, and of Noah and his righteous family. This war ended when Atlantis was submerged, which cataclysm again found echoes in the stories of the Babylonian and Mosaic Flood."

During the Messenger's discourse the dark-blue of the night sky had gradually paled; the stars had one by one gone out, but the white moon hung still above, like a withered flower. The creatures of the night had drowsily fled to their lairs, and a glittering dew lay laving upon the land. Soft swirling vapours melted in the East, and the early morning bee was darting buzzily from cup to cup of opening flowers collecting nectar for his brood. The glow-worms cast their shine no more, the crickets ceased their tinkling call, while clouds of pearly haze float silently above the woods and fields awaiting kiss of morning sun. A rosy light does touch the snow upon the mountain crests with soft caress, and in the azure dome above the Devas of the clouds commence their beauteous task. With fairy touch of rose, pale blue and apple-green, they tint the misty shapes, and tiny cloudlets like a swarm of multi-coloured birds swim in the firmament in mass formation. Soft mauve and golden, opalescent quivering of a thousand glorious hues, betipp'd with gold and violet, they drift along—a silent benediction from the heart of Angels.

The radiant forms of the Devas now amalgamate with all this glory in waves of ecstasy; and brilliant tinted feelers, like winding shreds and skeins of crimson silk, stretch out as if the Holy Breath of God had blown them all asunder.

"Why cannot all humanity see these Devas at; their work?" asked Ma-uti.

"Because they lack the Deva eye," said Neteru-Hem. "The inner senses, which were natural to the early Races, have atrophied during racial growth and the development of the outer senses. There once existed four-armed creatures, male-female in nature, with one head, but three eyes. The third, or central eye at the *back* of the head, gave them spiritual vision, and all the elements—to them—were full of wonders.

"After the separation of the sexes, men having fallen into matter, the third eye began to lose its power, and, when the Fourth Race had run half its course, it was closed entirely and the inner vision had to be awakened by artificial *stimuli*; the process of which was the secret of the Initiates or Sages. Then the third eye gradually petrified and disappeared altogether and became what is now known as the pineal gland, a small pea-like mass of grey *nervous* matter attached to the back of the third ventricle of the brain; it now almost invariably contains mineral concretions and sand, and nothing more. The inner vision can now only be acquired through training and initiation, save in the case of the natural and born magicians, or sensitives and mediums. During trances and spiritual visions it swells and expands; the initiate knows how to regulate it, and the aspirant who is pure in heart need not fear it. Unfortunately, the Deva eye exists no more for the majority of mankind; it is dead-and acts no longer, and the only witness to its *previous* existence is the pineal gland inside the brain. The two remaining eyes in the human embryo are also centred within the brain and grow from within without, instead of being part of the skin, as in the insects and cuttlefish.

"As in the case of the eyes, so all the human senses are developed from within to the without; the third eye retreated inward when its course was run. It was also called the eye of Shiva, and it is known that the reason for its loss was the mis-use the Fourth Race Men put it to, by making it the fane of every spiritual iniquity in the Land of Sin—as Atlantis was termed by the early Pioneers of the Fifth Race.

"In the ancient Books it is said about the fall of Atlantis that: 'The Kings of Light have departed in wrath. The sins of men have become so black that Earth quivers in her great agony... The Azure Seats remain empty. Who of the Brown, who of the Red, or yet among the Black [Races,] can sit in the Seats of the Blessed, the Seats of Knowledge and Mercy?

'Who can assume the Flower of Power (the Lotus), the Plant of the Golden Stem and the Azure Blossom? They of the Deva-hue, the moon-like complexion, and they of the refulgent (golden) face have gone to the Land of Bliss.'

"And so the Devas departed, and, their protecting hands being no longer over it, Atlantis sank beneath the waves in that great cataclysm two-hundred-thousand years ago."

And now the glorious King of Day came rejoicing from the East. With fluid gold beshining all created things and beings, and his ray-brush painting Earth with luminous irradiation — Efflux Divine!

The mignonette again spreads round its odour; forget-me-nots unfold by cooling stream; red berries gleam on dark green trees; tall sunflowers turn nodding heads in greeting to that higher light above; wood-anenomies, like stars, diffuse a soft sweet glimmer.

Along the river-banks marsh-marigolds crowd in yellow clumps, whilst water-crowfoot hides the darker water of the ponds with flowers set in tangled luscious green; and all is bright as at Creation's Day.

With thankfulness Ma-u and Ma-uti looked at the Messenger, as thus the second Vision ended with a Song of Gladness.

EMERALD

Green burns the Fire of Nature's Beauty,
On trees and grass in wood or field.

Essence of Life:

That's drawn from out the bosom of the Earth
By bright and warming Rays of Helios,

Father of Being:

To rest the eyes of human-kind,
And make a background
For the vivid colours of the flowers
That stand around, and raise
With fragile grace,

Their petals up to God.

VISION 3
ELEMENTS AND ELEMENTALS

As Ma-u and Ma-uti now beheld the landscape, it seemed as if a million sparkling jewels bestrewed the fields, the woods, the hills.

Here were the animated sparks that over-night descended from the vital streams of energy that flowed from out the Devas' auras. And now these scintillating drops of life began to swell, take shape, and there arose a host of fiery forms, some small, some larger, but very busy with their task of helping on the growth of grass and flower, tree and bush, or floating over pool and stream; or drifting on the southern breeze on gauzy wings resplendent.

Fantastically dressed they are, and little elfin faces peep out and peer from under pointed hoods and caps of gold and brown and red and blue; their eyes mischievous green and sparkling with life's joy. Some are transparent like a crystal and others look like little men, who busily bestir themselves with mien important. Here are tiny elves like angels, as they fly from bloom to bloom and kiss their petals softly. And gnomes with spades dig in the earth and fetch great gems and lumps of gold to hide in caverns in the hills, where treasures vast accumulate, to give delight to mortals in the far dim distant ages.

Suddenly, one of the little ones becomes aware of Nseteru-Hem and his companions, and all at once a hush fall over every group. With startled eyes they look, and then a softly sibilant twitter breaks out, whereupon some troops of little manikins come trotting from the bosky shaws and dells. They carry axes in their hands and with threatening looks come running towards our friends, until they see the Messenger.

Stock-still they stand and full of awe regard him, and then, with many bows of great respect come near and kiss his hand.

Two feet high axe they and dressed in russet brown, with dark green tall peaked caps and pointed shoes. A tremor of excitement runs over all the little folk, and one small crimson fairy, but one inch tall, now takes a running leap and lands on Ma-u's shoulder, there disporting himself with great delight. And swarms of tiny cherub forms flutter round Ma-uti's head and touch her locks with shining wings.

"Here you see some of the gentle beings that spring from poets' minds and from the dreams of Children; dim memories of ancient bliss in the celestial realms," said the Messenger.

"Are they real?" asked Ma-uti.

"Of course, they are, my dear," was the reply." Are not all thoughts things, alive or still, according to the inspiration that created them in bygone days?"

"Some have faces like flowers," said Ma-u," others look like timorous beasties, and some like butterflies and moths."

"That is according to the work that draws them," said the Messenger.

"They take their tasks very seriously; and if you have the Sight you see them in the trees, the rocks, a drop of rain, the rushing waterfall, or in the ponds between the plumes of reeds, and on the leaves and in the cups of waterlilies. And at the sound of music they come trooping out and dance; and when the artist is inspired to great creations, they guide his hand and eye and mix his paints, and every stroke of brush imprisons a wee fairy, that shines out from his master-piece in rays of beauty.

"And when the master-singer rings his golden streams of melody, they float upon the waves of that delight right into trembling souls of all his audience.

"They live in blocks of marble and of granite, until the chisel of the sculptor brings release; and for all time they stand in ecstasy that echoes in the hearts of men and brings them joy.

"More wondrous still: they are in every word that flows from the great pens of authors guided by the Master; and in every drop of ink a spark of glowing fire that spreads on virgin page in traceries of mystic characters, that even he can't always understand at time of writing."

"Are these lovely fairies everywhere, dear Messenger?" Ma-uti wanted to know.

"There are fairies and elementals everywhere,, my child, but they are not always so beautiful as those you see here; for a man, in ignorance, creates fairies and elementals of all kinds, and some are spiteful and can do harm if they are given the chance."

"How did they come to be in the beginning?" asked Ma-u.

"In Esoteric Philosophy, the elements of Fire, Water, Earth and Air, or the elements of Primary Creation as they are called, are homogeneous elements and not the compound elements as they are on earth; and every particle corresponds to and depends on its higher scale, on the Being to whose Essence it belongs. So the lower nature-spirits come under the domination of the higher ones, such as the Devas you have seen at work. The Devas are the collective aggregate of Divine Intelligence, and Vishnu is the Lord of the Elements and of all things. Therefore, the creation of the elements, out of which the elementals have sprung, goes right back to the time of the period of the first breath of differentiation of the Pre-Cosmic Elements, or Matter in Primordial Chaos. The Devas, of which there were seven classes, first appeared on earth as the Seven Powers of the Logos; in control of the seven Kingdoms — which are the Cosmic, the terrene, the mineral, the vegetable, the animal, the aqueous, and the human, in their physical, spiritual and psychic aspects and then they re-incarnated, mixed with matter, as great Sages and Instructors, who taught the Fifth Race, after having instructed the two preceding Races, and finally sacrificed themselves, to be reborn under various circumstances for the good of mankind, and for its salvation at certain critical periods. Every

Power among the Seven, once he is individualized, has in charge one of the elements of creation and rules over it. The elements, as the mothers of all creatures, are of an invisible, spiritual nature, and have souls; they are guided and informed by Spiritual Beings in the invisible Worlds, and behind the Veil of Occult Nature, and they all spring from the Mysterium Magnum. From the Primordial Substance, presided over by embodied Spirit, proceeds the unequal development of those qualities. From the Universal Mind is produced the origin of the subtle elements and of the organs of sense.

"In the Secret Doctrine it is taught that: 'in the exoteric interpretation of the Egyptian Rites, the soul of every defunct person—from the Hierophant down to the sacred bull Apis—became an Osiris, was Osirified (the Secret Doctrine, however, showing that the real Osirification was the lot of every Monad [or unit] only after 3,000 *cycles* of Existences).

'The Monad, born of the nature and the very essence of the Seven (its highest Principle becoming immediately enshrined in the Seventh Cosmic Element); has to perform its septenary gyration throughout the Cycle of Being and Forms, from the highest to the lowest; and then [up] again [and] from man to God. At the threshold of Paranirvâna, it reassumes its primeval Essence and. becomes the Absolute once more.'

"This circular movement of evolution is like a wheel; the whirlwind of God. Logos becomes a whirlwind and rotates back to Logos. There were great prophets and seers in the olden times who could behold this whirlwind and penetrate the mystery of Breath and Motion retrospectively. This rotary motion applies to everything in Nature, from the orbs of heaven to the smallest Monad. It is the law of vortical movement in primordial matter, and is one of the oldest conceptions of Greek Philosophy, whose first historical Sages were nearly all Initiates of the Mysteries, which they had from the Egyptians and the latter received them from the Chaldeans, who had learned these secrets from the Brâhmans of the esoteric school. Amongst the so-called pre-dynastic Egyptians were also present some of the great Teachers from Atlantis, who selected Egypt as their new country after their own Continent had disappeared beneath the waves. It was principally they who gave Egypt the means of rising from primitive conditions to a prolonged state of might and splendour and wisdom, such as the world has never witnessed since.

"Leucippus, and Democritus of Abdera—the pupils of the Magi—taught that this gyratory movement of the atoms, as well as the spheres, existed from eternity.

"Hicetas, Heraclides, Ecphantus, Pythagoras and his pupils, taught of the rotation of the earth; and Âryabhata of India, Aristarchus, Seleucus, and Archimedes calculated its revolutions as scientifically as the astronomers do now; while

the theory of the Elemental Vortices was known to Anaxagoras nearly 2,000 years before it was taken up by Galileo and others."

"How do these elements reach earth, apart from the projections by the Devas Messenger; are they projected by means of the Sun-rays?" asked Ma-u.

"Yes and no, my son; they also come by means of the Tiaou, which is the path of the Night-Sun of the Egyptians, who placed the inferior hemisphere, or infernal region, on the concealed side of the Moon. The human being, already existing, in principle in the elemental units, came out from the Moon, evolved through the whole cycle of existence and returned to his birth-place; to issue again thence when commencing his next cycle. This is a triple mystery; astronomical, physiological and psychical. The Moon is the symbol of reincarnation. Osiris says: 'O sole radiant beam of the Moon! I issue from the circulating multitudes; open me the Tiaou.'

"When the Dhyânis were commissioned to create man in their image, they threw off shadows as delicate models for the Nature Spirits to work upon. So they made the latter man—physically—out of the dust of the earth, and his creators and fashioners were many. And so the elemental essences became material and composite elements as we know them. With every Race, man became more material, and the Soul stepped back to make room for the Mind—that principle which incarnates to learn all knowledge in its successive cycles of evolution; from mineral, through the vegetable cycles of evolution; thence through the animal and elemental kingdoms to man; making ready to return to his original Source through the Heavenly Man."

"And what happens then, dear Messenger?" asked Ma-uti.

"It is taught that when Matronitha, the Mother, is separated and brought face to face with the King, in the excellence of the Sabbath, all things become one body. In other words, when all is reabsorbed once more into the One Element, the Souls of men become NirvcLnis, and the elements of everything become again what they were before—Protyle, or Undifferentiated substance. Nirvana and Sabbath mean the same thing. It means Rest, but not annihilation or extinction of the consciousness, or of the personal awareness of the Soul; nor does it mean inactivity for those who have earned the Blessings of Nirvâna. It is a period of absence from strife, such as we know on earth when we are endeavouring, by trial and test, to become worthy of that Holy Day of Re-Union with all those who have fought and conquered the snares of the material in times past.

"Sabbath does not mean seventh *day* only, but seventh period of any length of time consisting of seven parts."

"What is the Undifferentiated State of the Elements?" asked Ma-u.

"The Undifferentiated State of the Elements is the same as Chaos, which the Ancients called senseless, because—Chaos and Space being synonymous—it represented and contained in itself all the elements in their rudimentary state. Æther is the Fifth Element and the synthesis of the other four, and the Essence of Æther, or the Unseen Space, was considered divine, as being the supposed Veil of Deity, and therefore the medium between this life and the next. The Ancients taught that when the directing active Intelligences—or the Gods—retired from any portion of Æther in *our* Space, then that portion was left in the possession of *evil*, so called by reason of the absence from it of *good*.

"Æther and Chaos are the two primeval and eternal principles of the Universe, namely: Mind and Matter. Æther is the all-vivifying intellectual principle, and Chaos a shapeless liquid principle, without form or sense. The union of these two principles produced the Universe, or the Universal World, with the first Androgynous Logos, whose body was made from the former chaotic Matter and whose Soul from Æther. Chaos, from this union with Spirit, obtained *sense* and shone with pleasure, and so was made Protogonos, the (first-born) Light. Primitive religion was something better than mere speculations about physical phenomena and some very elevated principles were hidden under the transparent veil of such natural divinities as thunder, wind, or rain. The Ancients knew how to distinguish the corporeal from the spiritual elements in the Forces of Nature.

"The four-fold Jupiter, as well-as the four-faced Brahmâ, the aërial, the fulgurant, the terrestrial and the marine God, the Lord and Master of the four Elements, may stand as the representative for the Great Cosmic Gods of every Nation. In spite of Hephaestus-Vulcan as the God of Fire, or Poseidon-Neptune as the Sea-God, and Pluto-Aidoneus as the Deity of the Earth, the Aerial Jove was all of these; for Æther had preeminence over the Elements from the first and was the synthesis of them all. But there are several kinds of Æther!

"You may read in the Secret Doctrine that: 'Tradition tells of a grotto, a vast cave in the deserts of Central Asia, whereinto light pours through four seemingly natural apertures, or clefts, placed crossways at the four cardinal points. From noon till an hour before sunset the light streams in, of four different colours, as averred, red, blue, orange-gold and white, owing to some either natural or artifically prepared conditions of vegetation and soil. The light converges in the centre round a pillar of white marble with a globe upon it, which represents our earth. It is named the grotto of *Zaratushta*.'*

"Included under the arts and sciences of the Fourth Race, the Atlanteans, the phenomenal manifestation of the Four Elements, which were justly attributed by these believers to the intelligent interference of the Cosmic Gods, assumed a scientific character. The Magic of the ancient Priests consisted in those days in addressing their Gods in their own language.

"The speech of men of the Earth cannot reach the Lords. Each must be addressed in the language of his respective Element.' So says the Book of Rules, in a sentence which will be shown pregnant with meaning, adding as an explanation of the nature of that *element-language*:—

'It is composed of *sounds*, not *words*, of sounds, numbers and figures. He who knows how to blend the three, will call forth the response of the superintending Power' [the Regent-God of the specific Element needed].

"Thus this 'language' is that Of incantations or of *mantras*, as they are called in India; sound being the most potent and effectual magic agent, and the first of the keys which opens the door of communication between Mortals and Immortals. He who believes in the words and teachings of St. Paul, has no right to pick out from the latter those sentences which he chooses to accept, to the rejection of others; and St. Paul teaches most undeniably the existence of Cosmic Gods and their presence among us. But such attunements have only to do with material conditions, and not with the purely spiritual evolution of, mankind.

"When Plato put in the mouth of the Highest Principle (Father Æther or Jupiter) the words: 'The Gods of the

---

* Spelt in this manner here.

Gods of whom I am the *maker, as* I am the Father of all their works,' he knew the spirit of this sentence as fully as St. Paul did, when saying: 'For though there be that are called Gods, whether in Heaven or in Earth, as there be Gods many and Lords many'.

"Both knew the sense and the meaning of what they put forward in such guarded terms.

"There is but one Element considered from a metaphysical and esoteric point of view, and the Root of it is the Deity. In esoteric teachings we are told that there are seven elements in all, five of which have already manifested; the last one to do so being the Æther, which is that principle which permeates everything. Plato said that the Four Elements are those which compose and decompose compound bodies—Fire, Air, Water and Earth. These are the symbols of the invisible Cosmic Gods; worshipped by the ignorant, respectfully recognized by the wise. The Elementals, or Nature Spirits, are the phenomenal sub-divisions of these principles, of lower grades than the Elements themselves.

In both the Egyptian and the Hebrew Temples there was a gigantic curtain, supported by five pillars, which separated the Holy of Holies—now the altar in the Christian Churches—from the profane. Only the priests were allowed to enter. The four colours of this curtain symbolized the four principal Elements, whilst the five pillars signified the divine Wisdom man can acquire by the right use of the five senses, with the aid of the four elements.

"The Symbols for the four elements are always the same in each country, or with each nation, when traced to their source. We find the God of Fire symbolized by thunder, as Jove or Agni; the God of Water symbolized by the fluvial bull, or some sacred river or fountain, as Varuna, etc.; the God of Air is symbolized by the hurricane, cyclone, or tempest, as Vâyu and Indra; and the God or Spirit of the Earth, who appears in earthquakes as Pluto, Yama, and many others. These Cosmic Gods are found in every cosmogony or mythology.

"The Greeks had the Dodonean Jupiter, representing all the four elements and the cardinal points, known in Rome under the pantheistic title of Jupiter Mundus; in modem Rome he has become Deus Mundus, the One Mundane God. And it is argued that the Dodonean Jupiter was identified with Dis, or the Roman Pluto; with the Dionysus Chthonius, the Subterranean; and with Aidoneus, the King of the Subterranean World; whilst in the *Codex Nazaraeus* it could be shown that Jehovah is based on Aidoneus and Dionysus—the Iurbo-Adonai as Jehovah is called, for in that *Codex* it is written: 'Thou shalt not worship the Sun, who is named Adonal. whose name is also Kadash and El-El, and also' Lord Bacchus.'

"Baal-Adonis of the Babylonian Jews became the Adonaï by the Massorah, the later Jehovah.

"Jupiter Aërins or Pan; Jupiter-Ammon, and Jupiter-Bel-Moloch, are all of one Cosmic Nature and correlations with Iurbo-Adonaï."

"What is the difference between the Divine Principle, or Soul, of these great Nature Spirits and the Soul of Man? asked Ma-u.

"The Divine Essence, or Fravarshi, which the French know as Ferouer, is the same in the Nature Spirits, or Gods of the Elements, in the sky, fire, water, plants, animals and man, even—in a dormant state—in the material Kingdoms. In Zoroaster's Vendidâd it is said: 'Invoke, O Zarathustra! my Fravarshi, who am Ahura Mazda, the greatest, the best, the fairest of all beings, the most solid, the most intelligent . . . and whose Soul is the Holy Word—Mâthra Spenta.'

"The Fravarshi is the inner, immortal principle, or the Ego (higher mind) which re-incamates, that existed before the physical body of whatever kind, and survives them all. For this reason does Ahura Mazda tell Zarathustra to invoke his Fravarshi, or the true and impersonal Essence of Deity, *One with Zaraihusjtra s own Atma,* Soul, or Christ Principle, and not the false and *personal* appearance of Ahura Mazda.

"But in reality the *Soul* itself never incarnates, although it hovers round, and is closely connected with, the living body.

"There is a radical unity of the ultimate essence of each constituent part of compounds in nature—from star to mineral atom, from the highest Dhyân Chohan to the smallest infusorium, in fullest acceptation of the term, and whether applied to the spiritual, intellectual, or physical worlds—this unity is the one fundamental law of Occult Science. The Magnus Limbus, or Yliaster of Paracelsus, is the source from which all that is has sprung, and the little Limbus is each ultimate being that reproduces its form, and that has itself been produced by the greater. The little Limbus thus has all the same attributes and qualifications as the greater, and both are of the same potentialities; as father and son have each a similar organization, both coming from and returning to the same source; as the great Dragon of Wisdom is born of Fire and Water, and into Fire and Water will all be reabsorbed with him.

"As to the elementals—they are guided by the sure and unerring hands of the Rulers, Devas, or Angels, and so produce the phenomena of light, heat, magnetism, growth, decay, and so on. They manipulate the formation of minerals, the growth of crystals, the development of plants and animals, and the awakening within them of the first germ of consciousness, which can be distinctly noted in such creatures as the protistic Monera, half plant, half animal."

"Will the Devas hear the prayers of men and give them their protection?" asked Ma-uti.

"The Nature-Spirits, Devas, or Angels, are sentient Beings, of whom whole Hierarchies exist, each having a definite mission to perform. They guide and control the whole Kosmos and are no more, no less, than the agents of Cosmic Laws. They vary infinitely in their respective degrees of consciousness and intelligence. Each of these Beings either *was*, or prepares to become, a man. They are perfected, when not incipient men; and in their higher, less material, spheres differ morally from terrestrial human beings only in that they are devoid of feeling of personality and of the *human* emotional nature, which are two purely earthly characteristics. When perfected men, they are free from these feelings, as their spiritual element is now free from the weight of the fleshly bodies; when incipient men, never having had earthly bodies, they have no sense of personality, emotion and Ego-ism.

"Only the Adept, who keeps his spiritual and physical qualities entirely separated, can be sympathetic to the prayers of mankind. The only individual sense of all the rest of the elemental forms rests in their Hierarchies; not in the units. They are neither ministering, protecting, or punishing entities; such as the 'Harbingers of the Most High', or the 'Messengers of Wrath' of any God created in man's fancy. It is foolish and useless to appeal to their protection, or to believe that their sympathy may be secured by any form of propitiation, for they themselves are but the slaves of Cosmic Law; just as man. It is said that man can neither propitiate nor command the Devas; but by controlling and subduing the lower personality man can become as one of them, even during his 'terrestrial life."

"How many Dhyânis did become men?" asked Ma-u.

"The three classes of the Arûpa Pitris, forming one third of all the Dhyânis, were doomed by the Law of Evolution to be incarnated as men. They were endowed with intelligence, which is a formless breath, composed of intellectual — not elementary — substances. Some were known as Nirmânakâyas, and they appeared on this globe in the third Manvantara, or Third Root-Race, as Kings, Rishis and Heroes. They were ethereal Beings, following the incorporeal, or Arûpa Men; they had form, but no solid substance. There were whole Dynasties of these Divine Beings, those Kings and Instructors in arts and sciences of the Third Race, and their teachings were as far above our present sciences as elementary arithmetic is removed from Geometry. They were not supernatural, but super-human, or inter-human intelligences.

"It was the Golden Age, when the Gods walked upon the Earth and mixed freely with the mortals. It was the dawn of man's consciousness, and man in those days had no beliefs that could be called religion. Had they not their bright Gods of the Elements around them, and even within themselves? Their childhood was nursed and tended by those who had given them being, and called them forth to intelligent life. When the Gods departed, or became invisible, the later generations ended by worshipping their Kingdoms — the Elements."

"How did the Kings of the Elements teach the first Races, Neteru-Hem?" asked Ma-uti.

"Each element had to do with one of the five senses, and so Æther has to do with sound and hearing; Air with touch; Fire or Light with colour and sight; Water with taste; and Earth with smell.

"In this order man's physical senses were evolved and he was taught to use them. As the Dhyan Cbohans (or Devas) proceeded from the First Cause, mankind emanated from these active Agents of the Kosmos.

"Thus we find two kinds of men on earth; those who are the incarnated Dhyânis, and those who are the descendants of the peoples of the Third Root Race, whom the Arûpa Pitris gave being by constructing men in their own image. And there is a mystic signature written upon the brows of the former, by which they may mutually recognize each other inwardly.

"Up to now man has become aware of five elements, the last being Æther, which is not yet fully known — as it will become later, towards the end of the Fourth Round of the present Race, when it will become visible and rule supreme over the others during the whole of the Fifth. The remaining two elements are as yet absolutely beyond the range of human perception; for there are seven in all. These two last elements will appear as presentiments during the Sixth and Seventh Races of this Round, and will be fully known in the Sixth and Seventh Rounds respectively. The ancient teachings of the Seven Rounds of Earth's history and evolution, and the various Root and Sub-Races can be found in the Secret Doctrine, and provide sufficient material for lifelong study; I can only hint at them here, my children, for there are so many other things I have to show you."

And now the heavens and the winds began to thrill with sounds melodious, as on the shining wings of Zephyr from the South there drifted glittering throngs of fairy forms besheened with rainbow tints; and lovely voices rang in golden tones and silver; as if Kwan-Yin and Vetch, melodious Cow who milked forth sustenance and water, with potency of occult sound of nature and the Æther, called forth illusive form of Sien-Tchan, the Universe, from out of Chaos and the Seven Elements. And from Tien-Sin, which is the Heaven of the Mind, came forth the elementary Germs with which the world became bestrewed, as if with multitudes of glittering gems And all the seven colours of the prism rose swiftly up in clouds from earth to sky, and shone; and all that symphony of Sound and Light *becoming* blended into sparkling net that overspan the earth with glory wide, until Creation swooned with God's delight.

Here are the elemental groups at work of building each their own domains of plant or sinew, horn or nerve. How carefully the Deva? guide their labours, so that each department shall harmoniously blend with each, and build the Temples large or small in which the spirit dwells, and eke the spark and lower mind.

Their shapes and forms?

Each is a unit, formless, but intelligent and plenary with strength divine.

Invisible to mortal eye, but potencies from God's own Breath; a mystical Arcanum this; the tools that make the forms of all that lives on earth, or in the deeps; or blows upon the winds as birds, or moths, or butterflies; or rustles in the mighty trees, or nods upon tall stems; or waves in fields of com; or whispers in the reeds that lave their graceful feet in silv'ry streams.

The elementals in their myriad forms dwell everywhere; to science they are known as atoms, molecules, electrons; and hosts of other names. The seer knows them as they are, the Sages of the olden times learnt all their secrets; long forgotten now by most and veiled from vulgar gaze.

The poet sees them with an inner vision and tries in vain to tell the glories that his soul beholds.

They dwell within the hearts of flowers, or in the sheen of iridescent insect's wings. They sparkle in the eyes of laughing maidens and linger on their dimpling cheeks.

'They are the scent of roses and of the odorous may; and with their fairy-brush they tint the blooms, the fruits, the leaves and grasses, that with their joyful message raise up the hearts of men to Paradise.

And now Ma-u and Ma-uti did see further wonders, for in the sky appeared the glorious form of Lucesius, or Jupiter, the heavenly Father of the Greeks and Romans. Jupiter Triumphator, who in his hand holds flinty pebble wherewith to throw his fulminating flashes, when, as Jupiter Tonans, his thunderous roars resound in answer to Porsena, calling loudly on the sender of the prodigies; Jupiter Fulgurator, who storms and raves; or Pluvius, whose drenching rains refresh the soil and swell the floods with life abundant.

There shines the Prince of Light, all dressed in white, his sacred colour, within his silver chariot with four white steeds. Beside him heavenly Juno, forming radiant pair; the guardians of married bliss. Their consuls also dressed in white, and priests with snowy caps surround them; and flocks of birds do wheel and tumble, and soar and dip to presage the events of future happenings; the messengers of the bright God.

And in the distance rises smoke of sacrifice, as in the days of old the ides of every month saw on the altars mighty rams, and on the kalends female lambs as offerings to Jupiter and Juno; and invocations to the pair, and Janus, did ascend unto their thrones on high.

Far down, from out the bowels of the earth and the volcano, rise up the sounds of hammer-beats on steel; where Vulcan, or Hephaestus, God of Fire, and Son of Zeus and of Hera, works at his anvil with its twenty bellows. And in his workshop are produced things exquisite and fine and wondrous to behold. The clamour ceases and, the sides of that volcano cleft in twain, there comes the God himself with Aglaia, his wife, the youngest of the Charites. Of ugly mien is he and crooked, his wife abright Goddess of Beauty. His retinue of Cyclopes, grim and strong, and of the Brontes, Steropes, and Pyracmon surround the limping form of the fierce God; rejected and thrown from Heaven once by Zeus, the Lord, himself; when Thetis and Euryome received him in their grotto that surrounded was by Oceanus, there to dwell for nine long years. Now he is on his way to palace in Olympus, that shines like the stars and is imperishable.

His work and that of his attendants done; the preparation of the lower depths completed, so that earth's bright contours be further rounded.

And now the rim of earth towards the West sinks down and frightful chasms do appear, full awesome to the soul. A distant roaring fills the air, and towering walls of Ocean's floods draw near apace to fill the deeps and scatter high upon the rocks in scornful clouds of spray.

And high above the towering rollers, shouting with exuberance and joy, comes Neptune, or Poseidon, brother of Zeus, Son of Cronos and Rhea; whose kinsfolk, Hades, Hera, Hestia and Demeter, vied with him to rule that glorious Kingdom of the Sea, which fell by lot to him.

His horses, of which he himself is the creator, with brazen hoofs and golden manes, come galloping o'er the tossing waves, which at his approach are stilled.

Amphitrite, his lovely spouse, is with him, as, with trident held aloft, he scatters rocks or stills the turmoil of the inundation. The great Leviathan and playful Dolphins swim around his chariot, and all the monsters of the deep do homage to their King and Queen.

ELEMENTS AND ELEMENTALS

Loudly does the ocean roar its music of the mighty breakers, bursting on the shore with wild profound eternal bass, and booming tympanies and drums, in boundless vast omnipotence. Pure, unpolluted emblems of the Infinite, thundering on the patient shore in awful grandeur; a paragon of elemental might and beauty. The rippling waves and rolling billows now bring corallines and painted shells and precious stones and lay them at the feet of waiting strand; and wondrous creatures from mysterious caves below the surf creep on the sands; bewildered riches from the treasure chests of azure deeps.

Now comes fair Demeter, Goddess of Earth, and Persephone, bedecked with Zeus' flowers; ravishing daughter of fairest mother, not yet despoiled by Pluto, but like a lovely rosebud, sweet and pure, with breath like nectar and ambrosia; where'er they tread the fruits of earth spring up in great abundance, and com, the gift of Demeter, strives upwards to the animating light. And she, the good Goddess, with garland golden made of heads of com and blood-red poppy as her sceptre, beholds with gentle glance her glorious kingdom, stretching far and wide.

"These are the Rulers of the Elements of old," said Neteru-Hem. "The worship of the Ages has given shape and form to them, and still they roam the earth, and visible they are to favourite few whose eyes can pierce the veil that shields the higher Worlds."

"Are these Worlds very high above us?" asked Ma-uti.

"Nay, my child, a higher world is not higher by reason of its location, but because it is superior in quality or essence. It exists on a higher rate of vibration and intermingles with our own human, or earth atmosphere. Verily, the Gods still walk the earth and mix with men. There are conscious ethereal Entities, as invisible as the Ether in these higher worlds, of immaculate nature and purity; they are those who have completed the cycles of human evolution and are the elect of past races of men. They are called the Flags, the Guardian Angels, the Ancestors, the Pitris, the six-fold Dhyan Chohans; and are, in fact, men, minus the physical body.

"It is a true mystery to those who reject the existence of intellectual and conscious spiritual Beings in the Universe, and who limit full consciousness to man alone, and that only as a function of the brain. Only the right comprehension of the primeval evolution of Spirit-Matter and its real Essence, can elucidate the mystery of the soul's destiny.

"The Universe is a product of the imagination of Nature or God; but its processes can be guided to a certain extent by the will of the Adept. As God uses the Universal Mind's imagination to create the planets, the seas, the mountains, and all the rest, so can the imagination of the Adept's mind use the elements of matter to manifest certain material phenomena, by making visible the invisible elements of matter and giving them form and substance. The Universal Mind, the mind of the Adept, the mind of the man on the lowest rung of evolution, they are all the same, in different grades of perfection; and the elements and elementals are at the disposal of each, according to their powers. But there is also the teaching which states that no form can be given to anything, either by Nature or by man, of which the ideal type does not already exist on the subjective plane, and that no form or shape can possibly enter man's consciousness, or evolve in his imagination, which does not exist in proto-type, at least as an approximation. Fpr this reason it will now become clear to you, that all human forms and all objects in the Universe must have existed in Eternity as Astral or ethereal prototypes. According to these models the Gods, or Spiritual Beings, brought them into objective being and terrestrial life, and evolved the protoplastic forms of the future Egos from their own Essence. Even these Gods could not *create* or *invent* new forms of which the proto-types were not already extant in Eternity; and for the same reason the mind of man cannot invent any being, form, or condition, which does not already have existence in the Kosmos. This proves that all the Hierarchies of Gods, Angels, Spirits, Elemental, Heavenly Mansions, Elysian Fields, no matter how seemingly fantastic in conception, *do* exist—or else the mind of man could not conceive them.

"In the Limbus, or Ideos of primordial matter, the only matrix of all created things, the substance of all things is contained; and this applies to all thoughts also, for thoughts are things and have substance, weak or strong, according to the strength or weakness of the thinker's will and imagination. From the primordial substance proceeds the unequal development of these qualities of mind, and is produced the origin of the subtle elements and of the organs of sense.

"Pymander states that: 'God is not a mind, but the cause that the mind is; not a spirit, but the cause that the spirit is; not light, but the cause that light is.'

"As man is composed of all the great elements—Fire, Air, Water, Earth, and Æther—the Elementals which respectively belong to the Elements feel attracted to man by reason of their co-essence. Each man has one Element which predominates in him; and if a man has a preponderance of the earthly element, the Gnomes will lead him towards the assimilation of metals, money and wealth; and so it is with the rest of the Elements in connection with man. Man is ruled by the Elements, but he can rise above them and become their master.

"It is further said by Paracelsus that:—'Animal man is the son of the animal elements out of which his soul was born, and animals are the mirrors of man.'

"If we substitute the word 'life' for 'soul,' we shall find that this statement is correct, and that it contains a clue to our own status in comparison to that of the higher Beings."

"Why is it necessary to use mantras, or incantations, in order to speak to the Elementals?" asked Ma-u.

"Because Sound is a tremendous Occult Power, a stupendous Force, if used for material reasons. It may be used in such a way by the Adept that the Pyramids would be raised in the air, or that a dying man would be revived and filled with energy and vigour. The reason is that Sound attracts the Elements and draws them together, and when this is done by the Adept he can utilize these elemental forces in such a way that he seems to produce miracles; yet, all he does is to direct these potentialities with Occult knowledge.

"The essential power of all the Cosmic and terrestrial Elements enables them to generate within themselves a regular and harmonious series of results; and to achieve these results it is necessary that there should be intellects who can direct these powers. If that were not so and the elemental forces were allowed to generate without direction, there could be no harmony. Therefore, the intellect of the Gods, as well as of man, can utilize the elemental forces in a directive manner, and the medium is *Sound*, manipulated by manifesting *Mind*, for the elements are centres of force as well as spiritual beings whose very nature is to ACT under direction. And to the Seer the higher Elemental Powers appear under two aspects: the subjective—as influences, and the objective—as mystic forms, which become Presences; Spirit and Matter being One. Spirit is Matter on a higher plane, and Matter is Spirit at the lowest point of its cyclic activity; and both are ILLUSION.

"All are derived from the Absolute—which is that Light which condenses into the forms of the Lords of Being. From these downwards—formed from the ever-consolidating waves of that Light, which becomes on the objective plane gross matter—proceed the numerous Hierarchies of the Creative Forces; some formless, others having their own distinctive form, others again, such as the lowest elementals, having no form of their own, but assuming every form according to their surrounding conditions. From this One, Absolute, Spiritual Basis are built the countless basic centres from which proceed the universal, cyclic and individual evolutions during the active periods, or Days of Brahmâ.

"The Races of Man have developed coordinately, and on parallel lines with the four elements; every new race being physiologically adapted to meet the additional Element: Our Fifth Race is rapidly approaching the Fifth Element, or Æther; which has more to do, however, with the spirit than with physics.

"During the final centuries of the Third Race, or the Lemurians, the beings of that Race could live with equal ease in water, air, or fire, for they had unlimited control over these elements. These were the Sons of God; not those who saw the daughters of men, but the real Elohim. It was they who imparted Nature's most weird secrets to men, and revealed to them the ineffable, and now *lost* word. The last remnant of this Race lived on an island in a vast inland sea, which has since dried up and is now known as the Gobi Desert. We are told that this island still exists as an oasis in the Gobi Desert.

"Beyond the five elements of Fire, Air, Water, Earth and Æther, are the secret and incomprehensible Origin of the Elements and the Universal Mind.

"The seven Elemental Powers are symbolized in the seven large stars of the Great Bear, and the Hindus place their seven primitive Rishis in the Great Bear also, and call this constellation the abode of the Saptarshi, Riksha and Chitra-Shikandinas. Their Adepts claim to know whether this is only an astronomical myth, or a primordial mystery, having a deeper meaning than appears on the surface.

"The earliest forces recognized in Nature were reckoned as seven in number. They became the seven Elementals, demons, devas, or divinities; and it was understood that there were seven elements in man."

During Neteru-Hem's final words on the nature of the elements and elementals, there had gathered together great multitudes of Beings, representing the ancient beliefs in the elemental Gods and Goddesses, who had to do with the forces of nature in divers ways.

The merriest of all this host is in the fair form of Dionysus, or Bacchus, the God of Wine; who visits people in their sleep, when ailing, and reveals to them the remedies that will aid to set them once again upon the road to health and joy. He was the Son of Zeus and of Demeter, once changed into a ram by his Father and carried to Mount Nysa's nymphs, who tended the young God within their caves, and were rewarded for their labours by being honoured as Hyades, among the stars in heaven.

Surrounded is the God by riotous throngs of Pans and Satyrs, who chase the Mimalones, Bassarides, and Bacchantes, who in raging madness of enthusiasm dance with heads thrown back, hair dishevelled, striking audacious cymbals; whilst some wave in the air their thyrsus-staffs entwined with ivy and crowned with cones of pine. Some swing their gleaming swords or play with serpents, who circle round their graceful limbs; and violently do they jump or run with shining eyes agleam with wild emotion; as once they did when on Mount Cithaeron, or Parnassus, the Bacchic festivals were held; when the bright God had fought the Amazons and drove them from Ephesus to Samos, and slew them at Panæma.

Here comes he, riding on an ass, with Ariadne, his beloved; and all the Graces, Lenae, Maenades, Thyiades, in dithyrambic choruses perform; and Sileni and Centaurs, bedecked with vines and laurels, asphodel and ivy, storm around; and tigers, lynx and panthers fawn about the pair divine.

And there is Pluto; oft called Dis; the grim God of the lower worlds; yet can he give the wealth of all the world to mortals if he so desires. With lowering eyes, in saturnine derision, he glares upon the frolicsome and joyful groups; till Eros, God of Love, the fairest of the Gods, who rules the minds of God and man, comes riding on his lion; and darksome Pluto slinks away. The Son of Zephyrus and Iris has great powers, for he can break the thunderbolts of Zeus, the great Lord Himself; deprive bold Heracles of arms, and play and sport with fearsome monsters of the deep. His arrows in a golden quiver, and his torches none dare touch with impunity. Some of his golden arrows kindle love; but others, leaden, blunt, produce aversion in a lover. He tames wild beasts such as the lion, tiger, ram and hare; the Rose is his Sacred Symbol. He rises in the air with golden wings and flutters like a shining bird. And Psyche, his beloved, keeps him company and floats on wings of butterflies beside him, like a holy breath or Soul Divine; whilst Venus-Aphrodite, Goddess of Love, looks up and sees the happy twain with eyes of jealousy; though Mars in glittering mail and helmet waits her coming in the myrtle grove.

High in the air there drift mysterious sounds, delectable and sweet, as if a choir of angels hummed celestial tunes. This is Æolius, Son of Poseidon and of Arne; ruler of the winds he keeps enclosed in sacred mountain in the Isle of Lipara. Like minstrelsy of sighing harps, his voice floats through the atmosphere, and softly strokes the inner ear with gentle touch of beauty. It raises up a vision of the Muses in a ring, and memories of quaint old Pastorals, and the great plane-tree by the fountain, whereunder sits mild Callirhoë, who listens to the Songs of Innocence. It makes the soul harmonious and seems to lead it to the consecrated walks in venerable woods where dwell the shades of ancient bards, whose songs' deep meanings do abide beneath the spreading limbs of monarchs of the woods and groves; a viewless mystery, but full of potency of melting eloquence.

And from far Calamine, the lake with floating islands, come flying all those heavenly shapes of maidens on the drowsy hum of Hyblæan bees—for bees are only nymphs metamorphosed—and sweet Melissa, who discovered use of honey, with swarming, golden, honey-laden clouds of insects swimming, swirling, through the waves of air around her head, emitting soft aroma of wild thyme from Syria's fields and fertile hills whereon the luscious herbage grows. And Marcia, and other nymphs and maidens far too numerous to name, now join the multitude of Gods and bright Goddesses.

Ilithyia, Goddess of birth; Pomona, who guards the blushing fruits of trees; and Fornax, ripener of corn; Hecate, who can give wealth and wisdom, victory and good luck; Hygea, who brings health, with serpent whom she feeds from alabaster cup; Edusa, who protects the children and who blesses food and drink and sleep; and Flora, Goddess of the flowers of the Spring; and Furina, from sacred grove; they all add grace and dignity and glamour. And as bright Helios, the Sun-God, rides along his course towards the West, from golden throne far in the East to distant rim of Oceanus, his horses fed upon the herbs that' grow and thrive within the Islands of the Blessed, there now come great processions of still further Gods from out the ancient times, and twilight comes apace; for presently the Sun-God will embark on his golden boat, that fashioned was for him by the God of Fire, Hephaestus, and after sunset he will sail from West to East in time to make another Day appear on the horizon of the Morning-Land. And in the crepuscular light we now see Gaea, who holds the key of all the mysteries, and from whose form arise the vapours that produce divinest inspirations. The first of Delphic Oracles she; invoked when taking oaths; black sheep her share of sacrifice. And Ganymede, most beautiful of all the mortals; changed was he into an eagle when transported to the heavens by the Gods to fill the cup of Zeus, like Zeus' daughter and Hera's: Hebe, personification of youth, who can restore full vigour to the aged, and used to fill that cup with nectar, food of Gods; and Echidna, half maiden and half serpent, black-eyed mother of Chimaera, the hundred-headed dragon guarding still the fruit of Hesperides. They join with Hermione, as beautiful as golden Aphrodite; and Inachus, who rises from the river; he, the oldest God, or Hero, out of Argos. And Echetlæus, the mysterious Hero who with ploughshare slew barbarous hordes and disappeared; and Laodice and five fair maidens, but just returned from Delos where they carried sacrifice.

And as the Sun stands hesitant amidst the roses in the Western sky, the tops Of mountains still enamelled with his magic brush, there comes Apollo, God of song and music, inventor of the flute, who did receive the lyre from Hermes; and with his playing on the phorminx now he does delight the Gods.

Accompanied is he by all the minstrels of Arcadia, whilst by his side stands Marsyas, Athena's flute in hand, emitting of its own accord most beauteous strains of melody. And, as the strings of the Cithara twang and ring and shadows slowly fall, from out the sea-foam near the strand there rises Anadyomene, fair Goddess of the sea, entranced by that delicious sound of descant harmony, so dulcet in the evening air.

And harps' glissandos, clanging, shimmering cymbals, each beat of which sends clouds of gold-dust up above the players, tinkling, thrumming tambourines, and golden trumpets, splintering the air with alto-tones that gleam and glitter, supported by the rolling deep-voiced tones of solemn tympanies, now swell the chorus with delight.

And all the interwoven melodies and themes do blend in truly god-like fashion, which makes the nine sweet Muses jubilate and bless the fair performers in that Paradise of descantry amidst the sighing leaves of listening trees that softly dream in evening's breath of placid air, as if the rhythmic arias and songs symphonic gave added life and happiness unto their masséd leafy shapes.

All the tumultuous throng is still and lists with beating hearts to that melodious celebration, that leads right to the edge of th'infinite, so that the soul may gaze upon the face of the First Cause; if only for a moment; sweet with pangs of longing to return to that fair bourne, upon the shores of God's Eternity.

So sped the time: the shadows deepened, and still those luscious harmonies rang forth . . . until a discord, weird and spectral, rode upon the air and broke the charm.

A sudden hush . . . and once again that ghostly sound was heard; and then the vast concourse of Gods and Graces dissolved away, as if that phantom call was voice of Death himself, before whose dreaded summons all that lives is paralyzed with fear.

Once more that grisly note, but louder in the silent Night, as on soft wings there floated in the air the ghostly form of hooting great white owl; detested by the Gods bf Light as messenger of darkness.

The only other sound was that of Pluto's sneering, mocking laughter, as from the nether worlds he rose again to take his part in the black Sabbath of the Witches, that soon was to commence . . . .

Ma-u and Ma-uti looked in consternation at the Messenger's serene countenance as—at the end of this third Vision—he bade them sit upon a fallen tree-trunk, at the edge of the great forest that now stretched far behind them in the darkness of a moonless night.

BLACK OPAL

*When lambent flames glide searching in the dark
Abodes of sorcery and sin, and flicker, gleam,
and twinkle full malicious: lascivious tongues
of passion lick the pendant sullen lips
of hideous fervency and lust.
Oh, Sons of Light! destroy that monstrous
crew of wickedness; iniquity that soils the verdant
earth with sly pretence and counterfeit of
Love Divine.
And sidelong glances under beetling brows, satanic,
out of dev'lish eyes, besmirch the bloom of
innocence, that lies like peach-down on the cheeks
of radiant youth.
Alas! . . . too often do foul demons in the guise of
men, in wanton rollicking, bereave sweet
purity of all that holiness with which the
Angels sent it into incarnation.
A bitter lesson I Earned in thoughtless play
of long-lost ages; learned with scalding tears,
that flood despairing eyes in agony,
and deep regret.*

VISION 4
WITCHCRAFT

In front of the dark forest lay a vast rolling plain, rising up to wooded hills, with mountains on the far horizon. The only light came from the stars that shone within the blue-black firmament.

Ma-u and Ma-uti watched the sinister form of Pluto stride slowly towards the hills; his figure a blot upon the shadows of the night.

From the far distance sounded a long drawn-out note, mysterious and menacing, and at this signal Pluto raised to his lips a horn and sent forth shrilling blast, whereupon a choir of eerie howls and yapping broke out afar and rapidly approached.

Anon was seen a troop of wolf-like animals, galloping towards Pluto, and upon reaching him they fawned around with slavering jaws and heaving sides; eyes glowing wickedly in red and green through quenching gloom. No other sound is heard, but the faint whimpering or the low moans of these brutes, now and then raising to a fierce growl, when a touch of wind sets the leaves of the forest shivering in the trees. A low command from Pluto, and the beasts are silent and cower down at his feet, and the stillness becomes almost audible.

From afar come half-sounds of plodding steps a-whispering through the night, and the moving figure of a man is discernible as he slowly walks along towards an unseen destination. Pluto keenly watches him for a few moments and the animals seem frozen with expectancy, for their sharp ears and eyes have also discovered the wanderer.

Breathlessly, Ma-u and Ma-uti watch the weird scene and gasp with sudden fear as Pluto raises his arm and points to the man; whereupon the wolves start silently in pursuit.

Some instinct seems to give him warning, for they see the pale face of that man as he looks round, and, seeing the loping shadows of the beasts approaching on the plain, he suddenly begins to run towards the forest, hoping to climb a tree to be out of reach of the pack; but too late. Before he can reach the wood they are upon him, and his dreadful cries of agony ring out, as with rending, tearing claws and fangs they kill him, and, snarling angrily, fight amongst themselves for his flesh and blood.

"Oh, dear Messenger" sobbed Ma-uti, as Pluto, shaking with silent laughter walked away, "Could you not have saved the poor man? His terrible cries for help, and the growling of these beasts, will haunt my dreams!"

"It was but a memory of a happening in the past, my dear," said the Messenger. " These wolves you saw are really men, who, by means of a form of witchcraft, transfer themselves into semblances of animals, in order to indulge their low instincts by drinking blood of man or beast and eating their flesh. Even the Gods themselves have from time to time changed their shapes; as Jupiter did when he changed himself into a bull; Hecuba, who became a bitch; Actæon, who changed into a stag; the comrades of Ulysses, who were transformed into swine; the daughters of Prœtus, who believed they were changed into cows. In a poem by Marcellus Sidetes you can read how a madness attacked men in the beginning of the year, chiefly in February, when they retired to cemeteries at night, living in the manner of dogs and wolves. Herodotus tells that the Neuri, who were sorcerers according to the Scythians, change themselves once a year into the forms of wolves, and they continued in these forms for several days, after which they resumed their former shapes. Ovid tells of Lycaon, the King of Arcadia, who, on entertaining Jupiter, set a hash of human flesh before him, whereon the God transformed him into a wolf, 'hoary, his countenance rabid, his eyes glitter savagely, . . . the picture of fury.'

"Pliny tells that on the festival of Jupiter Lycæus, one of the family of Antæus was selected by lot, and led to the brink of the Arcadian lake, into which he plunged, whereupon he was transformed into a wolf. If after nine years he had not tasted human flesh he was allowed to resume his human shape.

"Agriopas relates that Demænetus, after having assisted at an Arcadian human sacrifice to Jupiter Lycæus, ate of the flesh and was at once transformed into a wolf, in which shape he prowled round for ten years, after which he recovered his human form and took part in the Olympic games. St. Augustine, in his *De Civitate Dei*, declares that he knew an old woman who was said to turn men into asses by her enchantments.

"The belief in were-wolves is world-wide, and they are supposed to haunt the Norwegian, as well as the German forests, whilst Oriental literature is full of stories connected with them.

"In Norway and Iceland it is believed that men can enter animal bodies, whereby their natural strength becomes doubled or quadrupled, as they acquire the strength of the beast in whose body they travel, in addition to their own. Their own body lies in a cataleptic trance meanwhile. The only parts of the man which do not change are the eyes, by which he can be recognized when in the animal body. He may become a bird, a fish or a wolf, and he takes on all the characteristics of whatever animal he enters.

"According to the Norwegian teachings, there are two ways in which a man can change into an animal. The first one is to take the skin of an animal and cast it over the body, after which the transformation is complete. The second method is more complicated: Here the mind has to leave the human body and enter that of the animal, as already mentioned. But there is still another method, where, by means of incantations a seeming transformation is made in front of spectators. The latter are merely hypnotized by this means and believe that a transformation has taken place, whereas in reality the individual in question remains unaltered.

"When the mind of a man enters the body of an animal, the man's intelligence accompanies it, but he takes on all the ferocity of—say—a wolf as well, and becomes full of rage and malignity.

"In the Völsung's Saga it is related how the mother of King Siggeir changed herself into a she-wolf and appeared night after night in a forest where Sigmund and his nine brothers were imprisoned in a row under a great piece of timber, which had been cast across their feet. Every night she devoured one of the brothers, until only Sigmund was left. Signy, his sister, then sent a trusted man to Sigmund, with instructions to smear his face with honey and fill his mouth with it. When, on the tenth night the she-wolf appeared again to devour Sigmund, she licked the honey off his face and then thrust her tongue into his mouth. He thereupon took hold of her tongue with his teeth, whereon she sprang up, setting her feet against the piece of timber in order to tear herself away. But he held firm and ripped out her tongue by the roots, so that the she-wolf died.

"A comparative study of Norse mythology will give an idea of how the were-wolf myth may have arisen: It was the custom of the warriors to wear animal skins of such beasts as they had slain, and so give themselves an air of ferocity, calculated to strike terror into the hearts of their foes. We hear, for instance, of Harold Harfagr, who had in his company a band of berserkir, who were dressed up in wolf-skins. In the same manner the word *berserkr*, was applied to a man possessed of super-human powers, subject to excesses of diabolical fury, and it was originally used to designate those doughty champions who went about with bear-skins over their armour.

"The bersekr was much feared, and an object of aversion to the peaceful inhabitants of the countryside, as it was his avocation to challenge quiet farmers to single combat. It was law in Norway that if a man declined to accept a challenge he forfeited all his possessions, even to his wife; he being considered a coward, not worthy of the protection of the law; and every item of his property passed into the hands of his challenger. If he accepted and was slain, his conqueror also came into possession of his property! These berserkir also amused themselves by joining any fair, or merry party and snapping the backbone, or cleaving the skull of anyone who displeased them; thus keeping themselves in practice too.

"In this way it can be well imagined that popular superstition went hand in hand with the dread of these wolf- and-bear-skinned rovers, so that in the end they were believed to be endued with the force, as well as with the ferocity, of the beasts whose skins they wore.

"But it is firmly established, too, in the history of the Northmen that berserkr rage was also a species of diabolical possession. They worked themselves up into a state of frenzy, in which a demoniacal power came over them, impelling them to acts from which in their sober senses they would have recoiled. They became insensible and invulnerable to pain, and acquired super-human force when in a rage. No sword could wound them, no fire burn them, and only a club could destroy them, by breaking their bones or crashing their skulls. During their rages their eyes glared as if a flame burned in their sockets; they ground their teeth and frothed at the mouth; they gnawed the rims of their shields and sometimes bit right through them; and as they rushed into conflict, they yelped like dogs or howled like wolves. Only baptism could extinguish their rage, and as Christianity advanced the number of berserkir decreased. After a fit of the berserkr rage the men were so enfeebled that they had to take to bed.

"The word *Vargr*, a wolf, had a double significance in Norse; it also signified a godless man, and it stood for 'restless' too. This word *vargr* is the English word 'were' in were-wolf, and *garou* or *varou* in the French word *loup-garou*. In the life of St. Hildefons the *loup-garou* stands for 'devil' and in nearly every language we can trace the connection between the word *vargr* and were-wolves, devils, witches, outlaws, scoundrels; whilst in the Salic Law there is an order which reads: 'If anyone shall have dug up or despoiled an already buried corpse, let him be a vargr.' With regard to the Scandinavian form of were-wolf, it is said by Baring-Gould that ' the whole superstructure of fable and romance relative to transformation into wild beasts reposes simply on this basis of truth—that among the Scandinavian nations there existed a form of madness or possession, under the influence of which men acted as though they were changed into wild and savage brutes, howling, foaming at the mouth, ravening for blood and slaughter, ready to commit any act of atrocity and as irresponsible for their actions as the wolves and beasts with whose skins they often equipped themselves.'

"The manner in which this fact became invested with supernatural adjuncts as already described, the double meaning of the word *'vargr,'* and above all, the habits and appearance of the maniacs, therefore provided sufficient material for the ignorant to build up their myth of the were-wolf, which spread over the whole world.

"Literature is rich in examples of men turning themselves into were-wolves, such as the story of the lady in Livonia who doubted the possibility of this happening. One of her servants at once volunteered to prove his ability in this direction. He left the room, and in another moment a wolf was observed, running away from the house. The dogs were set upon him and tore out one of his eyes. Next day the servant re-appeared minus one eye.

"Müller, in a dissertation published in Leipsig in 1736, relates the story of a certain Albertus Pericofcius in Muscovy, who was wont to tyrannize and harass his subjects in the most unscrupulous manner. One night, when he was absent from home, his whole herd of cattle, acquired by extortion, perished. When he returned he broke out into the most horrible blasphemies, exclaiming:—'Let him who has slain, eat; if God chooses let him devour me as well.' As he spoke, drops of blood fell to earth, and the nobleman, transformed into a wild dog, rushed upon his dead cattle, tore and mangled the carcasses and began to devour them. Of these circumstances there were not only ear, but also eye-witnesses.

"There is a similar story of a nobleman near Prague who robbed his subjects of all their goods, and even took the last cow from a poor widow with five children; but as a judgment all his own cattle died. He broke into fearful oaths and was transformed into a dog; his human head, however, remained. St. Patrick is said to have changed Vereticus, King of Wales, into a wolf, and St. Natalis transformed a whole family in Ireland into wolves, who for seven years lived in the forests and bogs, howling mournfully, and appeasing their hunger upon the sheep of the peasants.

"Rhanaeus divides the were-wolves into three sections, which he classifies as follows: —
1. They execute as wolves certain acts, such as seizing a sheep, or destroying cattle; not changed into wolves, but in their human frames and with their human limbs, yet in such a state of phantasy and hallucination that they believe themselves transformed into wolves, and are regarded as such by others, suffering under similar hallucination; and in this manner do these people run in packs as wolves, though not true wolves.
2. They imagine, in deep sleep or dream, that they injure the cattle, and this without leaving their couch; but it is their master (the devil) who does, in their stead, what their fancy points out or suggests to him.
3. The evil one drives natural wolves to do some act, and then pictures it so well to the sleeper, immovable in his place, both in dreams and at awakening, that he believes the act to have been committed by himself.

"Fincelius relates that in 1542 there was such a multitude of were-wolves about Constantinople that the Emperor, accompanied by his guard, left the city to give them severe correction, and slew one-hundred-and-fifty of them.

"Spranger speaks of three young ladies who attacked a labourer, under the form of cats, and were wounded by him. They were found bleeding in their beds next morning.

"Nynauld relates that in a village of Switzerland, near Lucerne, a peasant was attacked by a wolf; he defended himself and smote off a fore-leg of the beast. The moment that the blood began to flow the wolf's form changed, and he recognized a woman without her arm. She was burnt alive.

"Witches who transform themselves into animals are said to have no tails when so transformed. When thrice addressed by their baptismal name they resume their human form.

"A were-wolf may be known — when in human shape — by his broad hands and short fingers; and there are always some hairs in the hollow of his hand. Such men can also take on the forms of goats, white dogs, white hares, bears or hyenas.

"After death lycanthropists become vampires, and the power to become a were-wolf is obtained by drinking the water which settles in the foot-print left in clay by a wolf.

"In Ceylon, Tibet, China, and all over India, the belief in the transformation of a human being into an animal is prevalent. There is the story of the enchanted Brahmin's son, who by day was a serpent, by night a man.

"The son of Indra was an ass by day and a man by night.

"In Abyssinia it is believed that gold and silver-smiths transform themselves by night into savage beasts. They are distinguished from other people by wearing gold ear-rings, and ear-rings have been found on hyenas after they have been shot or speared.

"Joseph Acosta relates, in his National History of America, that the ruler of a city in Mexico, who was sent for by the predecessor of Montezuma, transformed himself, before the eyes of those who were sent to seize him, into an eagle, a tiger, and an enormous serpent successively.

"The Naguals, or national priests of Guatemala, have the power to transform themselves into lions or tigers."

"What is the real reason for a man becoming a werewolf?" asked Ma-u.

"There are two reasons," said the Messenger.

"The first is a form of insanity; but one also finds in the lower-evolved human beings, and very often in young children, an innate prediliction to cruelty. There have been, and are, many men who revel in inflicting torture on animals and on their fellows. The history of crime abounds with dreadful examples of the intense pleasure it gives some men to kill.

"Lycanthropy is a ghastly and revolting disease, and so remote from all our ordinary experience that it is not surprising that the casual observer should leave the consideration of it as a subject isolated and perplexing, and be disposed to regard as a myth that which the feared investigation might prove to be a reality. Moreover, man, in common with other carnivora, is often actuated by an impulse to kill and by a love of destroying life. This is proved by the crowds that used to enjoy public executions; by the lust for war; by the pleasure some children derive from torturing insects or small animals.

"Louis XI of France, for instance, caused the death of 4,000 people during his reign; he used to watch their executions from a neighbouring lattice. He had gibbets placed outside his own palace, and himself conducted executions. Think of Nero, of the early Christian martyrs, of Ivan the Terrible, of the cruelties of the pirates, of the mass-murders in Russia during the last revolution, of Caligula, Alexander Borgia, or Robespierre and the French mobs; of the ' noble ' Hungarian lady who, about the year 1600, had 650 girls beaten to death or burned alive, or cut to pieces.

Neteru-Hem said that one of the reasons why the witches believed themselves transformed was that they used certain narcotic drugs which induced a state of hallucination. He continued: "Transformation into beasts forms an integral portion of all mythological systems. We read of the Gods of Greece who changed themselves into animals so that they could carry out their designs with speed, security and secrecy. In Scandinavian mythology Odin changed himself into an eagle, and Loki into a salmon. As the Ancients believed — and rightly so — that animals had souls, or rather, minds, it was possible for the minds of men and animals to change places; and so the doctrine of metempsychosis was evolved, and it became possible for the mind of a savage and bloodthirsty man, like Lycaon for instance, to be degraded into the body of a wild beast; the mind of a timorous man entered into a hare, and drunkards and gluttons became swine. To the Buddhists identity exists in the soul alone, the body of man, beast, or bird, is only a temporary garment for the mind, and Buddha himself passed through various stages of existence as man or animal.

"Butler regards the members of the body as so many instruments, used by the soul [higher mind] for the purpose of seeing, hearing, or feeling, just as we use telescopes, or crutches, which may be discarded without loss or injury to our individuality. Vaughan calls the body a cage in which the soul is imprisoned, therefore, it is possible for the soul [the mind] to change the cage for another one. It is necessary to distinguish always between the principles of soul and mind; higher and lower mind. The soul *never* enters a body, but the higher or lower mind both do; in fact, the lower mind *is* the body.

"When Loki, the Northern God of evil, went in quest of the stolen Idunn, he borrowed of Freyja her falcon dress, and at once became a falcon. Thiassi, who pursued him as he left Thrymheimr, took an eagle's dress, and so became an eagle.

"The magicians of the Finns and Lapps often fall into a cataleptic condition, whereupon their minds leave their bodies and travel in the body of any animal most suitable for their purpose.

"In one of the ancient Sanskrit books appears the story of a King who was so amused at the antics of a clown at a fair, that he engaged him as his court fool and installed him at the palace. As this clown was apparently a person of low intelligence, apart from having a crooked body and contorted limbs which made everybody laugh, he was allowed to wander about at will, and be present at even the most secret council meetings. So it came about that the fool was present when the court magician instructed the King in the secret of how to make his mind leave his body and enter into any other body he wished.

"One day the King, accompanied by the fool, rode through a forest and there found the body of a holy man who had just died. In order to test his powers, the King left his body and entered that of the holy man. No sooner had he done so than the fool left *his* body, and. entered that of the King, and proceeded with all speed to the palace, where he was received with all the honours due to the King himself.

"But soon the Queen and the courtiers began to notice that all was not as it should be with His Majesty, and they wondered. A short time after, the King himself, in the body of the holy man, made his way to the palace and succeeded in obtaining an audience with the Queen, to whom he related the true state of affairs. They talked the matter over and hatched a plot, whereby they hoped to induce the fool to leave the King's body, so that its rightful owner might take possession again. The King—in the body of the holy man—therefore hid himself behind some curtains, whilst the Queen summoned the false king to her apartments. When he arrived the Queen asked him why a beautiful parrot that was in the room was unable to learn to speak. Everyone who had tried to teach it had failed; was there no way at all in which that bird might be taught? The fool, in his vanity, said that he could easily make that bird talk, and, leaving the King's body, entered into that of the parrot and began to show off. No sooner had he done this than the King left the body of the holy man and entered into his own, and immediately the King and Queen went for the parrot and wrung its neck!

"Could the fool not have left the parrot's body and entered' into that of the holy man?" asked Ma-uti.

"Being only a fool, he was not quick enough to find out where the body was hidden behind the curtains," said Neteru-Hem. "Moreover, this story is only an illustration of how the ancient peoples thought that the doctrine of metempsychosis would work out. It is a fanciful presentation of a real law, which is made use of in various ways by sorcerers and witches who have the necessary knowledge.

The stories about transformations deal principally with three kinds: those of the swan, the wolf, and the serpent; and the individual who knows how to change his shape into such, or other animals, is regarded with superstitious reverence as being of a higher order — of a divine nature.

"In Christian countries, however, such magicians were considered to be deserving of the stake, being the devil's own Spawn; and all stories of transformations fell into bad odour, and any miraculous powers, not sanctioned by the church, were attributed to the evil one.

"The ancient peoples regarded the forked and writhing lightning as a fiery serpent with god-like powers, manifesting himself to mortals in this way.

"The North-American Indians also regard lightning as the great serpent, and the thunder as his hissing. The German peasants, as well as the Greeks, call lightning the glorious snake. Anyone who could transform himself into a serpent was, therefore, considered to be a God.

"The dragon had the same origin; for he is nothing else than the thunderstorm, which, rising at the horizon, rushes with expended winnowing black pennons across the sky, darting out his forked fiery tongue and belching fire, whilst his eyes flash in anger, and with his lashing tail he overthrows pines and beeches; snapping them as if they were thin rods. '

"To the Greeks, Typhceus, the whirlwind or typhoon, has a hundred dragon or serpent heads, and he howls like a pack of wild dogs. He ascends to heaven and makes war on the Gods, who fly from him in various fantastic shapes. In modem Greek and Lithuanian mythology the dragon becomes an ogre, or a gigantic man; or he walks on two legs, sloughs off his scales and wings, talks, flirts with a lady and marries her. But he retains his evil disposition and his magic powers.

"The swan-maidens we can find in the ancient Indian Vedaic mythology. They dwell in the Æther between earth and sun and are called the Apsarases. They are fond of changing their shapes into swans, ducks, or sometimes human beings. The souls of heroes are given to them for lovers and husbands.

"Similar tales are found in Persian, Greek, Latin, Russian, Scandinavian, Teutonic and other literature. Even amongst the Samoyeds and American Indians such stories are told. Everywhere mythology, sorcery, magic and witchcraft are closely interwoven and produce a fantastic pattern, into the woof and warp of which run many threads of the ancient wisdom of the Magi.

"Apart from insanity and inborn cruelty, lycanthropy occurs under hypnosis, self-induced or otherwise. The use of certain drugs *does* free the mind from the shackles of the body; this has nothing to do with the *soul*. The mind can also be released by projection of the so-called astral self or body. This is a form of extension of consciousness; for the mind has the power to fix itself on any spot or locality, or being, removed *any* distance from the body. By the use of special exercises the mind can be trained to *project* in this way, and make its presence felt in no uncertain manner when sufficient efficiency has been attained by practice.

"In this way it is possible for an accomplished black magician to influence human beings to a certain extent, and animals to quite a large extent. Not only can he influence them, but take part in their sensations, whatever they are.

"In just the same way do witches take part in the unholy revels of the black sabbath. Their bodies lie at home or elsewhere in a state of catalepsy, and their minds take wings and issue forth on their ghastly errands. Their thoughts being so strongly fixed by the power of their minds, take form and become visible. If these witches have not attained full power, it is only the clairvoyant who can see these forms; but it is possible for some witches or magicians to make their thought-forms visible to people without clairvoyant gifts, They become 'Princes and Powers of the Air' which, under certain conditions, can be seen by anyone.

"Witchcraft is not confined to witches riding astride broomsticks, or turning themselves into black cats. Such is mere superstitious trash, although it is possible for a spirit-force to assume the shape of a black cat, should its fancy lie in that direction!

"The exercise of *magical* power is the exercise of *natural* power, but superior to the ordinary functions of Nature. This is not a violation of natural laws but a science, based on a profound knowledge of the occult forces and of the laws governing the visible or the invisible worlds."

"Where can one find the books in which these occult secrets are revealed?" asked Ma-u.

"These secrets cannot be found in books, my son; they were never put in plain writing, but always written down in such a way that only with the help of the real Adept, or Master, one can apply the key that opens the door to the occult Arcana. Neither Zoroaster, Buddha, Orpheus, Pythagoras, Confucius, Socrates, nor Ammonius Saccas, wrote any of these secrets down. Such knowledge is a double-edged weapon and unfit for the ignorant or the selfish. And not only that, but there was an added danger in the terrible persecutions the disciples of occult lore suffered from in the past. During a period of 150 years, no less than 90,000 persons were burned in Europe for alleged witchcraft. They were tracked like wild beasts by the ' Christian ' clergy, who saw in the dissemination of such knowledge a great danger to their soft 'livings,' and were therefore determined to stamp it out ruthlessly. In Great Britain alone, from the period of A.D. 1640 to 1660—a mere twenty years—3,000 persons were put to death for compact with the Devil.' There are still priests today who would gladly avail themselves of any laws permitting them to carry on with the 'good work,' for amongst these good Fathers one can yet find the most ignorant and savage 'defenders of the faith,' as they see it in their lack of perception, or for the reasons stated before."

"When the animal shapes of the transformed beings become visible to a seer, what does it portend?" asked Ma-u.

"It may mean that that person is obsessed," said Neteru-Hem. "It may be that he sees elementals, such as the horses and soldiers which were still heard at Marathon 400 years after the battle, as Pausanias writes. Many victims of obsessions, such as the afflicted persons of Salem and other historical witchcrafts, are incited to suicide and other crimes when they see the forms of dogs, cats, pigs, and other animals enter their rooms, biting them, and talking to them. Others see horses with so-called heavenly riders; or yellow birds which sit on their shoulders and whisper dreadful things into their ears. All such spectral animal forms are elementals, manifesting all the worst traits of depraved human nature, without themselves being human. These elementals act either on their own behalf, or at the behest of sorcerers or witches who know how to control them; but all are bad and dangerous to the uninitiated, who often go into raptures when describing their astral visitors. They forget, or do not know, that such visions come from without instead of from the within. Coming from without they should always be distrusted, for it is only *within* that we can find the truth. The Astral World without can be entered by the use of certain magical arts and practices, and an element existing without can attack a person and utterly scatter and destroy him and break him down, as a forest is stricken by a hurricane. Such an element can strike in a thousand places at once, without being visible; or it can select one man or woman at the command of the sorcerer's traced signs, or his voice. It can attack even the Adept, should he be momentarily off guard; only that in such a case he would be quickly rescued by his Brothers."

"But how can an Adept, with his vast knowledge and divine power, ever be hurt by a mere elemental force?" asked Ma-uti.

"The reason is, my child, that the Adept seldom thinks of himself, and so may neglect to surround himself with the protecting shell which no negative condition can ever penetrate. His work is that of Service to Mankind, and whereas he will do all that is possible to protect and guide others, less enlightened, he will forget his own protection against the evil he so often has to circumvent. In the earth's atmosphere there are hosts of spirits, as you have already seen; there are the invisible but tangible magnetic vampires, the subjective Daemons, the blood-dæmons of Porphyry, the larvae and lemures of the ancients. Moses, the great Egyptian Initiate, who knew them so well, enacted cruel, murderous laws against witches who were possessed by these beings; but Jesus, in his divine justice and love to humanity, healed such persons instead of killing them, by driving these elementals away. Against the wisdom of Moses and Jesus, we find the ignorant opposition of most churchmen, who put down witchcraft as mere superstition. Witches and sorcerers, or wizards, are human beings who have a bad spirit within them, and this also applies to lunatics and criminals. If one can only succeed in releasing such spirits, so relieving the one obsessed, a cure can be effected; provided the victim or patient remains under expert observation for a time. Generally the victims are mentally weak, and this defect has to be repaired by careful and patient instruction and guidance. St. Paul knew how to command evil spirits to leave the body of the obsessed, and in the Kabala it is said that one should shut the door in the face of the daemon, who will then run away as if pursued. This means that you must not give such spirits a hold on you, so that they can obsess you, and the best way to avoid them is to refrain from evil practices which attract them, for such practices form an atmosphere of sin congenial to these beings. The demental spirits are also afraid of swords, knives, or anything sharp. We find an illustration of this in Homer, when Ulysses evokes the spirit of his friend, the soothsayer, Tiresias. Preparing for the ceremony of the festival of blood, Ulysses draws his sword and in this manner he frightens away the thousands of dementals attracted by the sacrifice. The soothsayer himself does not dare to approach either, so long as Ulysses holds the dreaded weapon.

"In the Æneid we read that Æneas prepares to descend to the Kingdom of the shadows, and as soon as they approach its entrance he is warned by the Sybil who guides him, whereupon the Trojan hero draws his sword and clears himself a passage through the dense crowd of flitting forms.

"Psellus tells how the elemental who had taken possession of the body of his sister-in-law, was driven out by a magician named Anaphalangis, who threatened the elemental with a naked sword until he was finally dislodged. He further states that the elementals are sensible to pain when struck by any hard or sharp substance; for the elemental in possession of a human body Sees, hears, and feels in the same way as when not in such a body, and pain inflicted upon the body he temporarily Occupies hurts the elemental as well.

"It has been said that whilst the witch is the ignorant instrument used by the elementals, the magician, on the other hand, is their master, and these spirits must obey his commands. This is true.

"The amulets prepared by a master magician, for instance, are extremely powerful, as was proved in the case of the Spanish prisoner who was condemned to be shot in 1568 by the Prince of Orange at Juliers. He was tied to a tree and fired at, but was found to be invulnerable.

Thinking that he wore armour beneath his clothes they stripped him, but all that they found was an amulet. After that was taken away from him he fell dead at the first shot.

"There is also the well attested story of the Abyssinian sorcerer, who allowed himself to be shot at for a small fee by a party of Frenchmen. Although the muzzles were but two yards away from his body and at times five shots were fired at him simultaneously, he was never once touched; and when a German in the party pressed the muzzle of his gun against the body of the sorcerer and then fired, the weapon burst into fragments and the man walked off unhurt.

"Plotinus, when asked to attend the public worship of the Gods, replied proudly that it was for the spirits to come to *him* (for he was their master).

"Iamblichus asserted and proved that it is possible for our minds to hold communion with the highest intelligences; he always drove away any inferior spirits from his theurgical ceremonies, and taught his disciples to recognise them.

"Proclus taught that there was a magic password that would carry a person from one order of spiritual beings to another, higher and higher; till he arrived at the absolute divine.

"Jesus declared man *the Lord of the Sabbath*, and at his commands the terrestrial and elementary spirits fled from their temporary abodes. This power was shared by Apollonius and many of the Brotherhood of the Essenes of Judea and Mount Carmel, the predecessors of our present-day Sages, some of whom have these same powers also.

"The ancient Sortilegium, or divination by means of Sortes, or lots, was a form of witchcraft once widely practised by the clergy, and even St. Augustine sanctioned it, provided it was not used for worldly purposes; and so it was with the sainted Bishop Gregory of Tours and many other famous Churchmen."

"How do the wizards obtain knowledge of witchcraft, dear Messenger, and what is their principal means of power over the elemental?" demanded Ma-u.

"They obtain their knowledge by initiation from their masters, and their most powerful weapon is a certain Word. A real sorcerer, or witch, cannot die until he has passed on this word to a disciple. This is a well known fact, and when a sorcerer is dying, and there is no disciple near to whom he can pass on this Word of Power, he lingers on in agony. No one who knows the truth of this will come near him, for he can find release by passing on the Word to anyone. It is known that a doctor committed suicide after a dying sorcerer had whispred the dread Word into his ears. The wizard wanted release from his torment, but the doctor could not bear the knowledge of that secret Word; and he shot himself an hour after he had been told.

"It is not so long ago that even Royalty availed itself of the services of sorcerers, such as the apostate Jacobin priest, who had won the gratitude and protection of Queen Catherine de Medici, on account of his unparalleled skill in killing people at a distance for his pious mistress; and by torturing with various incantations their wax simulacrae. When her son, Charles, was dying of an incurable disease, her henchmen celebrated the devil's mass by decapitating a young child, after giving it the holy white wafer, and then placing the palpitating head on a black wafer upon the altar. The devil was then charged to pronounce an oracle; but without avail, for Charles died—and Catherine remained the faithful daughter of Rome!

"Pope Sylvester II was publicly accused by Cardinal Benno of being a sorcerer and an enchanter; for he used a brazen 'oracular head,' of the same sort as was made by Albertus Magnus.

"Popes Benedict IX, John XX, and Gregory VI and VII, were all known as magicians.

"In the Record Office of the House of Rolls, in the Cromwell papers, can be found accusations of witchcraft against Cromwell and Cardinal Wolsey.

"At the same time Torquemada, the confessor of Queen Isabella, burned over ten-thousand persons and had eighty-thousand tortured; all in the space of fourteen years.

"At Lisbon, in 1601, a trained horse, which could tell the spots on cards, was burned for witchcraft together with its trainer. Thus did holy church protect its flock from the 'wicked' wizards, and kept it pure.

"But it is also interesting to remember Luther's story of the fish-pond, near a convent in Rome, in which over 6,000 skulls of infants were found when it was cleared out one day. The church must not spill blood!

"And the Portugese Jesuit, Macedo, discovered the origin of the Inquisition in terrestrial paradise; alleging that God was the first who began the functions of an inquisitor over Cain and the workmen of Babel.

"History abounds with examples of witchcraft practised for or by the powerful ones; and killings of idiots, hysterical women, or people whose property was worth confiscating after they had been 'purified' by the flames.

"In the writings of the Jesuit Anthony Escobar (Theologiae Moralis) the secret instructions state that it is lawful to make use of sorcery, which is a science acquired through the assistance of the Devil, provided that the Devil's actual help is not depended upon when this science is put into operation. As the sin by which this knowledge was acquired has passed away, the knowledge itself remains, and becomes virtue! It is further stated that divination, by astrology and palmistry for instance, may be devoid of all sin, for in both the stars and in man's hand his proclivities may be read, and a forecast of his future made. At the same time the Fathers teach that the devil is the genius who deals in witchcraft and sorcery; which is a doctrine taken from the Jewish Pharisees, who made devils of the Pagan Gods, such as Mithras, Serapis and so on; and the Roman Catholic Church denounces the former worship as commerce with the powers of darkness; and the witches of the middle ages were thus but the votaries of the proscribed worship.

"The Albigenses, descendants of the Gnostics and Waldenses, as well as the whole of the Protestant world, came under the same imputation. The church does not distinguish between dissent, heresy, and witchcraft.

"Luther and Calvin were as intolerant as the Popes with regard to religious liberty, and what *they* were pleased to consider as witchcraft. Whole districts of Germany were in this way depopulated, and the statute books became encrimsoned with bloody legislation in Sweden, Denmark, Germany, Holland; Great Britain, and the North-American Continent. Whenever a man was found who was more liberal, or more intelligent than his fellows, he became at once liable to arrest and death. Young children were burned alive or whipped at the church-doors on Sabbath days, and there was no cruelty the vile imagination of the fanatic can invent that was not practised in the name of the Lord of Love and Mercy."

"What is the principal ingredient in sorcery?" asked Ma-u.

"The principal ingredient is always blood," replied Neteru-Hem, 'for blood begets phantoms, and its emanations furnish certain spirits with the material required to fashion their temporary appearances.'

"Eliphas Levi rightly says that 'blood is the first incarnation of the universal fluid; it is the materialized vital light. Its birth is the most marvellous of all nature's marvels; it lives only by perpetually transforming itself, for it is the universal Proteus. The universal substance, with its double motion, is the great Arcanum of Being; blood is the great Arcanum of Life.' ' Blood,' says the Hindu Ramatsariar, 'contains all the mysterious secrets of existence no living being can exist without. It is profaning the great work of the Creator to eat blood.'

"Paracelsus says that with the fumes of blood one can call forth any spirit he wishes to see; for with the assistance of its emanations the spirit can build itself an appearance, a visible body. This is the kind of sorcery with which the Hierophants of Baal produced objective and tangible apparitions; and they made deep incisions all over their own bodies in order to obtain the necessary material. The same practices are followed today by a certain sect in Persia, when, after frantic dancing, they cut themselves until all their garments and the floor are soaked with blood. Before the end of the performance every dancer has a spectral companion, who whirls round with him.

"The Thessalian witches sometimes used the blood of a black lamb, or an infant, to evoke the shadows.

"The Yakuts of Siberia say that bloody sacrifices assist the gods to perform their work in a better manner."

"Is the Word you mentioned just now really of such great importance in witchcraft?" asked Ma-u.

"Not only is it of the greatest importance in witchcraft, but in all other branches of Occult Knowledge, my son. In White Magic the Word is also passed on. Moses ' lays his hands ' upon his neophyte Joshua, in the solitudes of Nebo, and passes away for ever. Aaron initiates Eleazer on Mount Hor, and dies. Buddha promises his mendicants before his death to live in him who shall deserve it, embraces his favourite disciple, whispers in his ear, and dies; and as John's head lies upon the bosom of Jesus, he is told that he shall tarry until he shall come. Passing from Seer to Seer the Word flashes out like lightning, and while carrying off the old initiate from human sight forever, brings the new initiate into view."

"Behold!"

At this word a series of fires sprang up in the night, forming a circle in the midst of which was a cleared space in the centre of a forest. By the fires sat a throng of black people, who with staring eyes beheld a fearful scene.

A naked mulatto woman whirled around in mad frenzy, a number of garments which she had shed one by one lying around her, whilst several negroes, evidently priests of the black rites, chanted incantations, each having the finger of one hand raised stiffly upwards, and a number of native drummers beat out a weird and throbbing rhythm on their instruments. Faster and faster the dancer turned, foaming at the mouth and tearing madly at her skin with nails that dug deep furrows, from which the blood spurted in streams.

Now the priests sacrificed a white and a black fowl, by cutting off their heads and pressing out the blood from the writhing and fluttering bodies. A number of small green snakes crawled about the dancer and a huge serpent came towards her, and under the action of the drums' rhythm began slowly to coil itself around the woman's limbs, climbing higher and higher in spite of her contortions. Giving a loud scream she fell down in an epileptic fit, whilst the serpent slowly crushed her. With wild yells the whole assembly then rose to its feet, beating their breasts, and, each male grabbing a female, ran bellowing into the forest, whilst the rest of the scene slowly faded away.

"This is the picture of a form of voodoo rite, as practised by the. black sorcerers of Cuba and Haiti," said the Messenger. "It is the misapplication of arcane knowledge: and this is sorcery. When rightly used this knowledge is true magic, or Wisdom.

"All races of Man differ in spiritual gifts as well as in colour, or in other characteristics. Among some people we find natural seers, others have natural mediums, still others are addicted to sorcery such as you saw just now, and they transmit this knowledge from generation to generation, with a range of psychical phenomena more or less dire. The real thaumaturgist can cause himself to disappear by surrounding himself with a cloud, or he can seemingly take on any shape he wishes, or appear at long distances away from where his physical body really is, by making his astral form visible in projection. By skilful manipulation of the breath, the sorcerer can throw spells and enchantments and even kill people near or far. In 1611, a priest named Gaufridy was burned by the Parliament of Provence for seducing a penitent at the confessional, by *breathing* upon her, and thus throwing her into a delirium of sinful love for him. There is the famous case of Father Girard, a Jesuit, who, in 1731, was tried in France for the seduction of one of his parishioners by blowing upon her, so that she became instantly affected with a violent passion for him. She also had ecstatic visions of a religious character, stigmata, and hysterical convulsions, and this kept on for months, until at last she recovered her senses. The sorcerer is a public enemy of the worst kind and should be exterminated whenever his guilt is proved . . . or cured by experts.

"Sorcery, incantations, and the like are regarded as fables by the ignorant; yet from the Institutes of Justinian down to the laws against witchcraft of England and America—obsolete, but not repealed even today—such practices, even when only suspected, were punished as criminal. We can still read how the Emperor Constantine sentenced to death the philosopher Sopatrus for unchaining the winds, and in this manner preventing the grain ships from arriving in time to end a famine. Nor does this prevent Christian writers from advising prayer during storm and danger, and believing in the efficacy of such prayers.

"When the Atlantean giants and sorcerers were destroyed, the great Aryan mystics concealed the truth, astronomical, physical, and divine under various allegories, and ever since these days only the comparatively few Adepts have known what lies really hidden behind the phenomena known as witchcraft and sorcery. The Easter Island relics are the mysterious and astounding memorials of these giants and are true representations of the type and character attributed to the Fourth Race Men. Together with the giant statues of the holy men found in central Asia, they present us to-day with a picture of the descendants of the Gods through the Rishis—Heaven's first-born; the Easter Island Men being a brood of mighty wizards, the other Sons of God; mementoes of the eternal strife between good and evil."

"Are the names of these sorcerers of Atlantis still known, dear Messenger?" asked Ma-uti.

"In the Zohar there are allegorical references to such beings," replied Neteru-Hem.

"There you find allusions to the Ischins, chained to a mountain in the desert, which means that these spirits are being chained to the earth during the cycle of incarnation. There is Azazyel, one of the chiefs of the transgressing Angels, mentioned in the Book of Enoch, who, descending upon Ardis, the top of Mount Armon, bound himself by oath to loyalty to the other Angels who refused to incarnate as men. It is told that Azazyel taught men to make swords, knives, shields, and magic mirrors; Amazarak was the teacher of sorcery and herbal secrets; Amers taught the solution of Magic; Barkayal taught Astrology; Akibeel, the meaning of portents, signs and omens; Tamiel taught Astronomy; Asaradel, the motion of the Moon. These seven were the first instructors of the Fourth Race of Man. In the Book of Ezekiel the history of the Atlantean sorcerers and their ultimate fate is clearly revealed. Search the Scriptures!"

"Do the sorcerers use any magic symbols, dear Messenger?" asked Ma-u.

"The esoteric sign of human sorcery, also called the symbol of Kali Yuga, is the five-pointed star reversed, with its two points, or horns, upwards, thus: ⛧ ; in this manner it is used in ceremonial black magic. In the olden times the Jews were perfectly acquainted with sorcery and various maleficent forces, but they knew little of the real divine Occultism as a rule. Their great prophets like Daniel and Ezekiel *did* know, but the average Jewish prophets cared little about anything which had no direct bearing upon their own ethnical, tribal and individual benefits. Likewise, the Jesuits have turned the secret knowledge of the ancient mystery language of the Adepts, with its seven keys, which once was in the keeping of the highest initiated Hierophants of antiquity, into a system of sorcery. It is true that they possess only fragments of this language, but even so these remains contain a peculiar and dangerous power which the sorcerer can utilize to the detriment of mankind. From this esoteric, or mystery language, every theology has sprung. Each of its seven keys unlocks one of the seven mysteries of Nature. Its secrets were fully known to the High Priests of Egypt, but, from the fall of Memphis, Egypt began to lose these keys one by one, and in Chaldea only three were known in the days of Berosus. Only in India, China and Tibet, can be found men today who still have knowledge of all the seven sub-systems and the key to the entire system of this language. It was partly a system of exact science, geometrical, numerical and astronomical, and it was looked upon as of divine origin and revelation. Upon it the measurements of the Great Pyramid were based, and the programme of the Mysteries and initiations of which the Pyramid again is the everlasting record and the indestructible symbol.

"The knowledge of the astrological aspects of the constellations contained in this system gives the occultist the greatest facilities to perform what are called 'magic' feats; and on the 19th day of the second month, the 17th day of the eleventh month, the 7th day of the third month, for instance, the future of an individual can be seen, with all the coming events marshalled in their correct order."

"How were the sorcerers, or giants, of Atlantis finally destroyed?" asked Ma-u.

"The story of the destruction of the Atlantean sorcerers is very similar to that of the story of Exodus as told in the Old Testament.

"It is told in the ancient books that the 'Great King of the Dazzling Face' was sad, seeing the sins of the Black-Faced. This means that the White Forces had now arrived at the moment when the iniquities of the sorcerers could be tolerated no longer. The Great King sent his air-vehicles to all the chiefs of the pious nations and tribes with messages to prepare to leave Atlantis as soon as possible, for the Lords of the Storm were approaching. The Gnomes and Fire Elementals were preparing their great magic. 'Let all the sorcerers be sent into magnetic sleep so that they will be unaware of their approaching doom, and avoid pain and suffering in the end. But let their destiny be fulfilled and the Kings of Light return.'

'When the waters moved, the nations had already crossed the dry lands, and their Kings led them East and North. Meteors showered down upon the lands of the Black Forces, but still they slept on. The nether Lords waited for their orders so that they could arrest the elemental forces at work, but their masters, the black sorcerers, slept on, and no orders came. The waters then rose up and covered the face of Atlantis from one end to another. When the sorcerers awoke at last and called for the elemental Lords, it was too late, for they had gone. Some of the sorcerers, awaking before the others, pursued the fleeing peoples for three lunar months, but perished before they could reach them; the soil sinking under their feet and the Earth engulfing those who had desecrated her. Thus it is told in the ancient books, and in this manner were the Atlantean sorcerers wiped from off the face of the Earth. The old books also tell us of the terrible battles between the Sons of Darkness and the Sons of Light; in Atlantis as well as in Lemuria. These sorcerers knew how to change their forms, and in the stories of the amours of Poseidon we read how he became a dolphin to win Amphitrite; a horse, to seduce Ceres; a ram, to deceive Theophane, and so on. In the person of Poseidon we can discover the genius of the Spirit and Race of Atlantis, and also of the vices of the sorcerers."

"What then *is* sorcery, dear Messenger, and how do the witches produce their phenomena?" asked Ma-uti.

"Sorcery, Black Magic, and Witchcraft, are controlled by the *will* of the Wizards," said Neteru-Hem.

"They project from within themselves a magnetic fluid which they have learned to mould, shape and direct in a perfectly conscious and scientific manner. In a way it is similar to the projection of certain wave-lengths from a wireless broadcasting station. Only, in this latter case the receiving instrument has to be perfectly *built up* and *attuned* before it can receive those wave-lengths and make them visible or audible. The sorcerer, on the other hand, controls the will of his subject by force, so that it shall be subservient to his commands and suggestions. There is a similarity to hypnotism here; but hypnotism of a more powerful kind. When the witch-doctors of such tribes as the Mulu Kurumb as of Nilgiri, or the Dugpas of Sikkim and Bhutan, or of any other tribe or people, wish to destroy their victims, they do this by employing their fully trained wills for that purpose. Their wills act with absolute certainty and are not dependent on the amount of nervous impressionability of their subjects; but the witch-doctor having chosen his victim, and having placed himself *en rapport* with him, the witch doctor's 'fluid' is sure to find its way and reach its goal. If the subject is meant to die, he dies; if he is meant to perform some act, he will perform it; if he is meant to behold a vision, spectacle, or person, he will see it. There is no possible defence against the potency of the wizard's will, unless another and stronger will comes to the rescue and saves the patient. There are no haphazard methods employed, such as those used by the European 'experimenter,' who has no conception of the kind of forces with which he is contending.

"This knowledge of witchcraft and the methods employed by the expert is as old as the world, and has been used from the days of Atlantis and Lemuria in this cycle, or Day of Brahmâ; and it has been used in previous cycles too, under similar conditions. In a lesser degree it can be said to be employed whenever a strong will exerts its influence for bad on a weaker one. It is true that magic is a two-fold power, for it can easily be turned into sorcery; all that is necessary is an evil thought. The symbols of magic and occult science have all a dual power, and their employment is fraught with danger; especially if the student or experimenter is not under expert guidance. There are many students of the occult whose mental capacity is incapable of discerning the right path from the left, and the key to the symbols, or teachings, can only be given by the Adept by word of mouth. The many works that deal with the higher forms of magic, which anyone can read and experiment with without the guidance of a teacher, are a real danger to the uninitiated. They can easily lead to sorcery and black magic and bring untold woes to the student and his family; the end of many of such unguided persons has been the mental home—or worse. Let no one doubt this, at his peril!

"This applies especially to the mystic characters, alphabets and numerals found in the Great Kabala. The misuse of the Wisdom contained in these symbols has led mankind into its present bonds of slavery.

"Plato, the great initiate, tells us in Phaedrus:—'Before man's spirit sank into sensuality and became embodied through the loss of his wings, he lived among the Gods in the airy spiritual world where everything is true and pure.'

"Since that Golden Age the sorcerers have used for their own nefarious purposes the secrets contained in the Runes, the writing of Kischuph, the Ephesian and Milesian letters, the book of Thoth, and the dreadful treatises of Targes, the Chaldean, and his disciple Tarchon, the Etruscan. They have perverted the Science of Correspondences, the mysteries of the Pentagram, the Tetragrammaton, the Elemental Pyramid and the various crosses; and they have pulled down the branches of the Tree of Life and made of them a bon-fire, the flames of which threaten to destroy all that is meant by the sacred words, 'Light, Life, and Love.'

"Divine miracles are produced by the same causes that generate effects of sorcery. Intense will and desire result in conscious or unconscious magic. The only difference rests on the good or evil effects aimed at, and on the actor producing them.

"In addition to the will there are other aids to the sorcerer, such as the incantations, magnetic passes, philtres, and so on, of which we read in the Greek Ms. entitled *Philosophumena*, the author of which is supposed to be St. Hippolytus of the Greek Church.

"In the time of Ramses III of Egypt, there was the case of a man named Hai, a shepherd, who wanted to acquire power. He obtained possession of a book in which the formulae of Ramses Meri-Amen, his royal Master, were written. By means of these formulae he succeeded in getting magical power, reading the future, and committing all sorts of horrors and abominations conceived in his mind., At last he was discovered and ordered by the judges to die according to the order of Pharaoh, and according to what is written in the lines of the divine language. In other words he was destroyed by means similar to those he had employed for his evil purposes.

"In the Temple of Khous, at Thebes, the Temple of the God who has power over the elementaries, was an inscription—since presented to the National Library of Paris—in which there is found a complete romance of Magic.

"The difference between the Astral shells of the departed, the elementary demons, the planetary and the real Gods, was fully known in Egypt, and those wicked sorcerers who employed this knowledge in their dark pursuits were invariably killed upon discovery.

"Philo states:—'The Mysteries were known to unveil the secret operations of Nature.'

"The prodigies accomplished by the priests of theurgic magic are so well authenticated and the evidence— if human testimony is worth anything at all—is so overwhelming that, rather than confess that the theurgists outrivalled the Christians in miracles, Sir David Brewster conceded to the former the greatest proficiency in physics and everything that pertains to natural philosophy.

"Herodotus, Thales, Parmenides, Empedoclus, Orpheus, Pythagoras, all went, each in his day, in search of the Wisdom of Egypt's great Hierophants, in the hope of solving the problems of the Universe. Psellus says that: 'Magic formed the last part of the sacerdotal science. It investigated the nature, power, and quality of everything sublunary; of the elements and their parts, of animals, of various plants and their fruits, of stones and herbs. In short, it explored the essence and power of everything.'

"Excesses of power, abuse of knowledge and personal ambition, very often led selfish and unscrupulous Initiates to Black Magic, Sorcery, or Witchcraft; and it was Black Magic that led finally to the abolition of the Mysteries, as we can read in Mommsen's Roman History. As early as 560 B.C., the Romans had discovered an Occult Association, a school of Black Magic of the most revolting kind; it celebrated mysteries brought from Etruria, and very soon the moral pestilence had spread all over Italy. More than 7,000 Initiates were prosecuted, and most of them were sentenced to death. Later on, Titus-Livius shows us another 3,000 Initiates sentenced during a single year for the crime of poisoning."

The Messenger finished his discourse, and silence fell upon the three as Ma-u and Ma-uti meditated for a while on all they had seen and heard.

And it seemed as if a procession of shadowy forms arose upon the plain before them, and a weird light began to shine, illuminating the scene in a ghostly manner. Plainer and plainer became the shadowy shapes, until a succession of living actors performed a series of strange feats, illustrating in a remarkable manner the principles of magic and witchcraft discussed by Neteru-Hem.

There appeared the strange figure of Simon Magus, the great magician, making a man out of air and causing him to appear and disappear at will. Or he pierced stones with his fingers, as if they were made of clay, or turned them into bread. Anon he changed himself into a ram, or he flew in the air like a bird; and with a wave of his hands produced a heap of gold. Two-faced he was, like Janus, and at his behest a marble statue came to life and walked around.

There was the Bohemian sorcerer, Zyto, who made fat pigs out of bundles of straw, and caused antlers to grow on people's foreheads when leaning out of windows to watch their neighbours, so that they could not draw their heads in again! A wicked-looking old hag sat muttering by a pool, beating the water with her finger in the name of her Master. In the sky above black clouds gathered, which the witch drove presently towards the cornfields of one of her enemies, which later could be destroyed by a hailstorm descending from these clouds.

Sitting on a fallen tree they beheld the majestic figure of Pythagoras, holding converse with his trained eagle. Dressed in the bodies of dead men they saw a number of demons, for demons, being the source of death, they can have no human bodies of their own, but have to steal them from the grave. There were also female forms of such elementals, and little demons with two horns on their foreheads; the offspring of incubus and succubus-demons and humans; the results of abnormal sin.

And riding upon staves and brooms, reeds and cleft sticks, distaffs and shovels, oxen, goats or dogs, came a great throng of witches, young and old.

They were those, deeply versed in the black arts, who knew how to attend the Sabbath in person, whilst at their homes they had left a double of their bodies, seemingly asleep. They lit a foul and horrid fire, and their president, the devil, sat on his throne in the shape of a huge and dreadful goat. Approaching him they did homage; some bending their knees as suppliants, others with their backs turned, some kicking up their legs so high that heads bent back and chins pointed to the sky. They offered him black candles, or infants' navel cords, and a terrible noise proceeded from them, many running around like mad beings-—which they certainly were. The majority were women, but there were men also. Tables were placed on which a host of serving demons placed food; but when the guests began to eat, the food was so bitter and obnoxious that they could not retain it; at which the devil became so angry that he could hardly refrain from tearing them to pieces. Black wine was also served from filthy drinking horns, but there was no bread or salt. The scene became one of great confusion.

Then followed dances in circles, always turning to the left, and these dances gave no pleasure, but brought great labour and fatigue as of the utmost toil. Each had his familiar spirit with him and blasphemous sentences were uttered in which Beelzebub himself is acclaimed the creator, giver, and preserver of all; and when addressing him they turned their faces to the ground, turned their backs, and approached him in a crab-like manner.

Up in a tree sat a herdsman playing the pipes to which the witches danced. As the dance proceeded, the witches crowed like cocks, clucked like hens, mewed like cats, barked like dogs or bleated like sheep. Others lowed, neighed or grunted, and the whole produced a hellish uproar, to the delight of the devil and his demons, who ran about amongst the crowd and stabbed the witches with pronged forks, to make them howl the louder. And gradually the mob increased in numbers and there appeared the fiery demons of the upper air, the aerial demons of the middle air, the terrestrial, the water-spirits, the subterranean, the lucifugous — who abhor and detest the light — and they appeared in many forms as dogs, cats, oxen and horned owls. They shrieked and groaned, or screamed with high-pitched whistling sounds, such voices as those of the bad elementals of the Egyptian priests, attached to tombs or statues, or objects of evil worship.

Around the fires that burned upon the plain sat wizards and witches, absorbed in their task of burning human corpses to collect the fat for magic salves, and to burn the bones to powder with which they sprinkle fields and orchards of their enemies so that the crops shall fail.

Others were making poisonous lotions, waters, powders, oils and unguents, with which to kill or bewitch for unholy gain.

And Pluto — in the shape of a fierce black man, a very Prince of Evil — once more appeared; and all the devils, demons and the witches gave him worship, fell to the ground and grovelled before him, tearing at themselves with their own teeth.

The dreadful form of Pluto swelled out and grew until it filled the sky. It rose and floated high above like a black cloud, and from the cloud his harsh voice rang forth like thunder, whilst lurid lightning split the air. A dreadful roar — — — and all that multitude of sin was blown away like a heavy cloud of dust towards the corners of the earth . . . .

Only a brooding silence remained within the ghostly light, and Ma-u and Ma-uti regarded the White Messenger, still seated upon that tree-trunk from which they had witnessed the strange scenes and listened to the teachings of the Fourth Vision.

SARDONYX

The false and fitful glamour of deceitful denizens
Who swarm within the Astral gloom
Is now revealed; and shown to be
But low mendacious perfidy and witchery,
Which in Cimmerian regions loom
Upon horizons dark with treachery,
Where lurks stark madness and despair.
* * *

Oh, that the Fires of Logos would descend
From out the Cosmic Æther, and destroy
In one great Holocaust that brood
Of foul iniquity!
* * *

Or raise it up to God with pity's hand;
Or, if not willing, tear and rend
The monstrous Gangs that do employ
Their caitiff wiles upon the good
And innocent with deadly turpitude, and lend
Their knavish aid to sinful men on earth,
Who, under guise of inspiration, betray the Faith
Of simple seekers: striving after Light —
But only finding dismal Night,
And lies they are unable to perpend

VISION 5
SPIRITUALISM

"What is this weird light, dear Messenger?" asked Ma-uti.

"It is the light of the Astral World, my child. The spectacle you have witnessed was of an Astral nature, and the scenes that presently will follow are also partly on the Astral Plane. You will learn what spiritualism really is, and what are the forces and conditions used by the elementals when they produce the so-called 'Psychic Phenomena' at spiritualistic séances.

"As I have already told you, White and Black Magic are subject to the same Laws. Sorcery and Witchcraft are forms of Black Magic, and Spiritualism is a form of sorcery or witchcraft. This does not necessarily mean that all Spiritualists are Black Magicians. Far from it. Among Spiritualists are found the most sincere and honourable people one can wish to meet, and they would be shocked if they could only realize that their practices *are* a form of Witchcraft. They would be still more shocked—and terrified—if they knew what happens during some seances, when a great deal of power is available which the elemental forces use for their own purposes. If spiritualists could only see the monsters attending some seances, Spiritualism would soon die out; for all clean-minded people would flee from those abominable magical rites in which the Elementals delight. Happily, the average 'circle' meeting once weekly for 'developing' purposes, is quite harmless. Due to the weak mentality, the low rate of psychic unfoldment and the poor physical vibrations of the sitters, there is very little real power available for the Elementals, and the worst that happens at such meetings—*if* anything happens at all—is a little leg-pulling, or harmless horseplay; by the lower elemental beings, who delight in playing all sorts of stupid pranks on the members of the 'circle.' "

"This seems rather a hard verdict on the poor Spiritualists," said Ma-uti. "If they should come to hear of this they would be terribly cross and very offended, I think."

"Not necessarily, my dear child," replied Neteru-Hem. "Never forget that no single being is ever forced by the Sons of God to accept the Truth if he is not ready for it, or does not want it. All have free-will to accept any teaching, or reject it. When force is applied in any way with regard to a teaching, this teaching becomes dogma; and it is far better to believe in nothing at all — if that were possible — than to be dogmatic. Dogma stultifies the brain and mind, for it prevents people from utilizing their God-given freedom of thinking, or believing, if you will, (which is not the same thing). Dogma turns men from being the true sons of the Father, into unthinking slaves and machines. Besides, an honest opinion or a true teaching can never offend the *wise* man. It only turns into a furious beast the mindless person, or the dogmatic, or the wilfully blind, who generally have *financial* reasons for preventing the Truth from becoming known. The same applies to the zealot or the fanatic; but as all such beings have many bitter lessons to learn before the scales can fall from their eyes, they must be tolerated with love and compassion by the wiser ones, who have probably been through the same phases of experience themselves in the past."

"And what if they turn and rend you?" asked Ma-u.

"In that case we have to remember the everlasting example of the great Master Jesus, the Christos; who prayed for his torturers and freely forgave them their thoughtless cruelties and persecutions of Him."

"How, then, has it happened that the Spiritualists have erroneous conceptions of the work they are doing?" asked Ma-u.

"The reason is that all these Spiritualistic phenomena are of an *Astral* nature. The actors — supposed to be the spirits or souls of the departed human beings — are the elemental inhabitants of the *Astral* World, or they are thought-forms projected by humans on the earth-plane, manipulated by the elementals, who also use the vital force of the mediums *and* the sitters — it is called ectoplasm. These manipulated forms are supposed to be the shapes or Astral bodies of departed humans, who are now thought to come back to earth in order to prove existence after bodily death; and the elementals use shapes, or elementaries, or thought-forms, in order to deceive people into believing that the departed ones are still alive and aware of their kin and old friends. Actually, the apparitions have no connection whatever with those who have passed on. The elementals build these forms and speak through the medium's voice—*if* the séance is not a fake altogether—and the elemental entity inhabits that, shape during the séance and manipulates it as if there were a genuine human soul or mind in that temporary body. The thought-forms I mentioned just now appear as shapes, more or less substantial. If strong in thought-power they may even look solid to the sitters. If no shape appears at all and only the medium's voice is heard, it is sometimes very difficult to tell whether the inanities proceeding from the medium's mouth are his or her own thoughts, or the thoughts of the sitters, or even the thoughts of the elementals. Only the true clairvoyant can tell.

"The so-called *apports*, the levitations, the moving about of tables, trumpets, and other material things, are all the result of the manipulations of the vital forces of those present by the elementals. Sometimes the combined thoughts of the sitters will produce a form or a phenomenon, just as the combined thoughts of an assembly of witches may produce a shape in the form of a demon.

"With regard to researches in Spiritualism by men of science, we have such famous names as Crookes, Wallace, Flammarion, and Conan Doyle, who have devoted many years to spiritualist investigation. They all come to the conclusion that, even if the materialization of spirits did not prove the identity of the persons who were supposed to be represented, in any case these phenomena were not the works of mortals. Such opinions are correct, of course. When there is a séance conducted by genuine and intelligent people, with a medium who can *really* get *en rapport* with the elementals, the results are due to manipulations by 'spirits'; — that is: elemental powers in the Astral World. This is true. But to say that these 'spirits' are the departed human beings they purport to represent 'on a higher plane,' is to labour under a misapprehension. The *Souls* of the departed cannot penetrate into the dense material atmosphere, or manifest at a spiritualistic séance. This is quite impossible; for these departed souls, having no form or. substance — although they have complete memories of *all* their connections with their second halves, the higher mind in various human incarnations, and complete awareness of their surroundings and selves — they cannot under *any* conditions manifest on the earthly, material plane, without being chained, as it were, to a *body*, with a *mind* and its *vital essence* and a *brain*. Having none of these material attributes, there is no material appearance possible. This must be plain to every thinking person. When materializations occur during séances, therefore, they are *not* made by the *Souls* of the departed, but are merely clever imitations of the same, acted by the elemental forces on one of the Astral planes — which can be either a material plane of a lesser or grosser density than the earth plane. The elementals love this sort of play-acting and are highly entertained when the 'sitters' believe that these materializations are the real spirits of those whom they represent. They obtain all the details necessary to build up their spirit-forms from the subconscious memories of the sitters. A typical example of this is the series of spiritual phenomena witnessed by Madame Blavatsky when she was on a fourteen days visit to the Eddys.'

"She there saw 119 materializations and all the details connected with these spirit-forms were correct. In a letter of October 14th, 1874, to the Daily Graphic of New York, she describes some of these spirits, such as a Caucasian boy, who played at her request the Lezguinka, a Circassian dance; an old Persian in the national dress of a merchant; a gigantic warrior of Kurdistan; an old Russian woman, whom she recognized as an old servant; a powerful negro, whom she knew as a conjuror from central Africa; and lastly, an uncle of hers.

"Each of these persons had been personally known to her at some time or another. The details for making up their semblances were obtained from her own memory, although she herself did not realize this at the time. In later years she changed her opinion, as will be shewn later.

"In an article in the "Spiritual Scientist" (Boston) of October 14th, 1875, she humorously refers to the 'mighty army of Indian controls,' and 'Miscellaneous Guides' of our bright 'Summerland,' and she mentions the elementary Diakka, *Esprits matins et farfadets,* and other such-like unreliable and ignorant denizens of the spirit-world, arraying themselves in pompous, world-known and famous names, who foist upon bewildered witnesses, or sitters at séances such deplorable, unheard-of slip-slop trash, and betimes something worse, that more than one person, who previously was an earnest believer in the spiritual philosophy, now suddenly and silently takes to his heels. She also mentions the invisible, mysterious worlds swarming with beings, the true nature of which is still an unriddled mystery to everyone, though their existence has been proved by millions of wise people through countless ages. Spiritualism, in the hands of an Adept, becomes Magic, for he is learned in the art of blending together the laws of the Universe without breaking any of them and thereby violating Nature. In the hands of an experienced medium, on the other hand, Spiritualism becomes unconscious sorcery; for, by allowing himself to become the helpless tool of a variety of spirits, of whom he knows nothing save what the latter permit him to know, the medium opens, unknown to himself, a door of communication between the two worlds, through which emerge the blind forces of Nature lurking in the Astral Light, as well as good and bad spirits. The Adept controls the spirits instead of being controlled by them. The inspired Sybils and Pythonesses of olden times were mediums too, but they were entirely guided by their High-Priests and these were initiated into the Esoteric Theurgy and Mysteries of the Temples. These High-Priests were Magicians of an elevated order, and all the secrets of their Theology, which included Magic, or the art of invoking ministering spirits, were in their hands. For these reasons the oracles of olden times were of a true and sacred nature, and far removed from the rubbish pronounced by most modern mediums in these 'enlightened' days, due to the pranks and capers of their controlling elementals.

"If similar attempts were made in ancient times by illegal mediums, outside the Temples, such mediums were judged to be obsessed or possessed, and according to the Bible 'they had seven devils in them' and were put to death. Such mediums, who are without the proper guidance of an Adept, deserve our pity, for it is quite possible for the elemental forces to compel them to cheat when under control. They become the helpless tools of unprogressed invisible beings, full of malice and wickedness. It is a more dangerous thing to play with the mysteries of life and death than most spiritualists imagine, says Blavatsky; and this is absolutely true.

"It is not without good cause that the authorities of the Roman Church are so opposed to Spiritualism; *they* know the dangers attending these practices, and in the *Catholic World*, Vol. IX, p. 290, it is stated that: 'The Church has declared that the practices of Spiritism, evocation of spirits, consulting them, or holding communication with them—that is, necromancy—to be unlawful, and she prohibits it all to her children in the most positive manner.'

"It is no manner of use to deny spiritual phenomena, as has been materialism's *easy way out* by ascribing to epilepsy the divine entity of the Socratic *Daimon*, Cicero's *Divinum Quiddam*, or the ghost of Caesar; or by saying that the prophetic oracles of the Jewish *Bath-Kol* are due to heridetary hysteria! This is mere unsupported assertion and false pretence.

"There is a further confusion of terms when elementaries and elementals are discussed and mixed up indiscriminately. Elementaries are earth-bound human spirits, and elementals are nature spirits. The elementaries are those human spirits who—*according to the Kabalists*—have irretrievably lost every chance of immortality.

"Communication between the Minds—or even Souls of the departed is possible if the human being on the earth-plane knows" how to *reach out* to the worlds where these Minds and Souls dwell between incarnations. But this is not for the average human being; and it requires strict training under expert guidance during many incarnations before such contacts can be made. They can never take place in the séance room which is filled with elemental spirits, through 'inspirational' mediums or 'spirit' guides. But communication between pure mortals and pure Souls *is* possible; just as it is possible between bad men and bad spirits. And I am afraid that ignorance of the technique of communication with pure Souls must also be classified as BAD, for if an ignorant person meddles with divine principles, he commits an evil action and draws evil results—in the form of evil or ignorant elementals—towards him. He becomes then a Sorcerer; or, if female, a Witch!

"For the Holy Communion between pure mortals and Divine Souls we require the *Cosmic Mediator; not* the passive, ignorant, and gullible medium, who does not know how to distinguish between good and bad spirits, elementaries, or elementals.

"By Spirits, I mean the Sons of God, and it is only the Highest Adept who can contact these Holy Beings.

"It is therefore debasing the term Spirit when the Spiritualists apply it to the impure, or imperfect beings who produce the majority of their phenomena.

"In the 16th chapter of the *Mahâbhârata, Harivansha Parva,* you can read of the raising of Spirits and other spiritual phenomena. Now compare how East meets West in the teachings of Manu, Kapila, and other Philosophers of ancient India, when we consider what A. R. Wallace, F.R.S., said in his *'Contributions to the Theory of Natural Selection,'* and *'On Miracles.'*

"[Having] ... 'been led, by a strict induction from facts, to a belief—firstly, in the existence of a number of preter-human intelligences of various grades; and secondly, that some of these intelligences, although usually invisible and intangible to us, can and do act on matter, and do influence our minds—I am surely following a strictly logical and scientific course, in seeing how far this doctrine will enable us to account for some of those residual phenomena which Natural Selection alone will not explain. In the tenth chapter of my *'Contributions to the Theory of Natural Selection'* I have pointed out what I consider to be some of these residual phenomena; and I have suggested that they may be due to the action of some of the various intelligences above referred to. I maintained, and still maintain, that this view is one which is logically tenable, and is in no way inconsistent with a thorough acceptance of the grand doctrine of evolution through Natural Selection.'

"In India there are no séances dependent upon 'conditions' of darkness, or 'harmonious circles,' and Indian phenomena are never sporadic and spontaneous (apart from the independent apparitions of ghosts), but they depend entirely upon the will of the operator, whether a Holy Yogî, a Sâddhu, or a Jaddugar, or sorcerer. These phenomena are often the counterparts of what are termed *miracles* in the Bible.

"In the *'London Spiritualist'* of January 18th, 1878, Dr. Peebles states:—'I have met not only Sinhalese and Chinese Spiritualists, but hundreds of Hindu Spiritualists, gifted with the powers of *conscious* mediumship.' He quotes a Hindu gentleman, by the name of Peary Chand Mittra, of Calcutta, who blesses God that his 'inner vision is being more and more developed' and that he talks 'with spirits.' But when Dr. Peebles termed these people

'Spiritualists' he was under a misapprehension, for no Hindû is a Spiritualist as we understand the appellation in the Western World. A Hindu does not believe in continued conscious existence—as do the Spiritualists—though he assigns for the holy, sinless soul, which has reached Swarga, or heaven, and Moksha, a period of many millions and even quadrillions of years. The Hindû believes in cyclic transmigrations of the soul, during which there must be periods in which the soul loses its recollections as well as the consciousness of its individuality. The Hindûs believe in 'Bhûts'—which are the earthbound spirits, or elementaries, who, having become wicked devils, are liable to be annihilated any day under the potent curses of the Brahmân exorciser. Human beings are often obsessed by a Bhût, and the most loving couples are often parted when the woman is attacked by such a Bhût; who never attacks men. In the same letter quoted just now Dr. Peebles gives a very happy definition of what constitutes an Indian medium; he says: 'Some of the best mediums that it has been my good fortune to know, I met in Ceylon and India. And these were *not* mediums; for, indeed, they held converse with the *Pays* and *Pisachas*, having their habitations in the air, the water, the fire, in rocks and trees, in the clouds, the rain, the dew, in mines and caverns.'

"Madame Blavatsky says: 'This proves that these mediums who were *not* mediums, were no more Spiritualists than they were mediums!' *No*, the Yogi, having successfully served his apprenticeship during his years of meditation and probation, suffering the most cruel privations in order to become utterly insensible to heat or cold, hunger or thirst, and to overcome the dominion of the fleshly body, and to elevate the material Mind into the higher vibrations of the Astral worlds, by means of existing outside the body instead of within—the Yogi, I repeat, can assume control of the elementals and elementaries only when he has first attained complete sovereignty over himself. He is horrified when told that the Spiritualists actually *invite* these beings to their séances and allow them to take control of a medium, when it is certain that their mere presence alone is a pollution. You see—these wise Yogin *know* the powers they are dealing with, whilst the Spiritualist is ignorant of their dangers.

"The ability of the supercorporeal entities to float the bodies of mediums through the air—as in the case of D. D. Home, for instance—or the moving about of all sorts of objects, light or heavy, the controlling of mediums or sensitives so as to enable them to speak strange languages, paint pictures, or play upon unfamiliar instruments—all these things have been known for many milleniums of years—and even millions of years—but such phenomena were never ascribed to the powers or presence of disembodied *humans* by the wise ancient Hierophants. They too knew how to produce these phenomena—but they had the entities who performed them under *control*. They also knew that there were two sides to these occult wonders— good and evil—and they did all that was in their pow'er to prevent the ignorant from meddling with these dangerous potencies. The time for a revival of such prohibitions is more than ripe; it would prevent much unhappiness.; it would protect people from unscrupulous swindlers, who batten on the sorrows of those who have been bereaved of the *bodily* presence of their loved ones,by pretending to draw these released Minds back into the material (which in itself would be a cruel action if it were possible); it would protect the genuine and sincere medium from terrible dangers—which are not always immediately apparent on account of their insidious nature—and it would put a stop to the sensation-mongering mob of hysterical perverts, who flood the world with an endless stream of stupid lies and unwholesome imaginations.

"We need more illustrious investigators, like those with the eminent names I mentioned before, and we want those investgators to make public their findings and bring them to the notice of the authorities, so that more effective legislation could be put into operation, in order to deal with all those human vampires who now reap a rich reward from their unhealthy practices. It serves no purpose to fine a few old women here and there, who pretend to tell you your future for a few shillings or pence. We need strong laws, enforced by *wise* men, who can deal with all the occult miscreants and who understand the occult science as a *Science*, and do not regard it as a heathen superstition — as it is now regarded by many who do not know better. This will take years to accomplish, but the need is very great indeed."

"Are the terms 'elementary' and 'elementals' modem ones, dear Messenger, or were these beings known as such in ancient times?" asked Ma-u.

"The term 'elementary' is very old indeed, my son," replied Netem-Hem.

"Kunrath refers to the four classes of elementary spirits in his Amphitheatrum-Sapientiae Æternæ, and explains that these are disembodied vicious men, who have parted with their diving spirits and become as beasts.

"Eliphas Lévi uses the term elementary when he speaks of the evocation of Apollonius of Tyana by himself. The greatest Kabalistic authorities who lived before Christianity say that if a man has a criminal mind, his' astral body — which holds him prisoner — seeks again the objects of his earthly passions and desires, which he wants to resume as when he had an earthly body. He torments the dreams of youth and bathes in the vapours of spilt blood and wallows in places where bestial people foregather. He watches over the treasures he has buried or hidden, and tries by all means to create for himself material organs by materializations, so that he can 'live' again. Finally he loses all memory and the astral body also dies sometimes and *he* with it, and for ever. There is no rebirth for such beings. The term elemental is of later date, although the principle of these nature-spirits has always been known to the ancient authorities. In the King James' version of the Bible you can read of the destruction—or annihilation—of the wicked. This bears out the teachings of the ancient Kabalists and the generations of Sages who preceded Christianity.

"There has never appeared at any Spiritualistic séance, a being who could truly state that he had risen so high in the celestial realms that he had become what is known as a Son of Eternity, with a Soul so highly evolved that IT had reached the state of perfect bliss experienced in these realms and become co-existent with the formless and actionless ever-present time; where there is neither past nor future, but one infinite eternity of NOW.

"Has there ever appeared at such séances a being who could tell us even as much as our own *Master Within* can whisper to us in moments of divine initiation or inspiration?.NO! When an *Honest* 'spirit' is asked at such séances a question which can only be answered by one truly inspired by Divine Wisdom, he answers that he does not know.

"There is one class of Elementaries whom Lévi describes as 'neither souls of the damned or guilty; these elementary spirits are like children, curious and harmless, and they torment people in proportion as attention is paid to them.' These beings he regards as the factors which produce all meaningless and useless physical phenomena at séances. They are also at the disposal of the vicious earthbound human elementaries, if such are attracted to a séance. These can use the former in combination with the emanations of the sitters and the medium, and in this way they can build up materialized 'spirits.' At times a cadaverous odour can be noticed when a materialization takes place. In such cases we are confronted with necromancy, where the phosphoric emanations of putrified corpses are used by the medium, who, in this way evokes vampires."

"Can anyone learn to become a medium?" asked Ma-uti.

"Mediums are generally so from birth, my child; they have a peculiar psychological constitution which allows the elementals to take control of them. But as there is in many persons a latent mediumistic faculty, this faculty can be developed by attending Stances for that purpose. Some of the most famous mediums of modem times have been developed in this manner.

"The belief in continued existence after death prevails amongst all peoples. Father F. de Bobadilla asked the Indians of Nicaragua, soon after the Spanish Conquest, what they believed happened when a person died. They told him that: 'when men die, there comes forth from their mouth something which resembles a person and is called *Julio* (in Aztec yuli — to live). This being is like a person, but does not die, and the corpse remains here.' (This is, of course, the 'Astral Body.').

"The engraved frontispiece of *Death and the After Life*, by A. J. Davis, shows what is entitled the *Formation of the Spiritual Body*. It is the picture of the death-bed of an old woman, out of whose mouth issues a luminous appearance, which is her own rejuvenated form.

"The Hindûs believe that the spirit of the departed sits for ten days on the eaves of the house where it died; and two plantain leaf-cups, one full of milk and the other full of water, are placed on the eaves, so that the spirit may drink and bathe. During those ten days the spirit-body is gradually built up. According to A. J. Davis, this building up of the spirit body occurs at the moment of death; and the Clairvoyant sees the formation of that body in almost the same way as the Hindûs believe it is formed, namely, head, face, neck, shoulders and the rest of the body down to the feet. The image is bright and shining and a little smaller than the physical body, but without any disfigurements. When this new body is complete, the fine thread that connects it with the human brain snaps — and it is free to accompany its guardian to the finer spheres. The Aztecs again say that 'when the deceased has lived well, the *Julio* goes up on high with our Gods; but when he has lived ill, the *Julio* perishes with the body, and there is an end of it.'

"The Finns and Laplanders also say that when the physical body dies and decays the spirit receives a new one, which the Shaman alone can see.

"Herbert Spencer, in *Fetish-worship*, says that the savage *Mandans* place the skulls of their dead in a circle. The widows know the skulls of their dead husbands and the mothers those of their dead children. Nearly every day they visit them and bring them of their best food; and they talk to those skulls in the most loving manner, and seemingly receive answers.

"These few examples must suffice.

"How the elementary and elemental spirits can mislead one, even the most experienced Spiritualist is shown when we remember the story of the Russian lady, the *personal* experience of the Editor of *The Theosophist*; quoted in Vol. Ill, No. 6.

"This lady was afflicted with mediumship in her early youth, and controlled for about six years by a 'spirit,' who came evening after evening and wrote automatically through the child's arm; covering reams of information about that spirit's life and family, and about a son who committed suicide. Later on it was discovered that neither the lady—impersonated by that 'spirit'—nor her son had died. Yet, the handwriting was perfectly reproduced and the same as that of the lady herself; and the facts quoted in these writings were all correct, except the death of the principal lady and her son.

"There is sufficient evidence of a similar nature to fill a library of books; but the Spiritualists ignore these proofs, and prefer to be hoodwinked in the same way as has been done for many years past. Read the complete works of H. P. Blavatsky (Riders) for an endless succession of such true stories, analyzed by that remarkable woman.

"It is the same with spirit-photography. The genuine, unfaked photographs of what are supposed to be these 'spirits' exist in large numbers. There can be no doubt about the honesty of the mediums, sitters, and photographers in such cases. But they are *not* photographs of *spirits*, but photographs of the semblances of these 'spirits' as they were during their life-time, and not as they are after they have sloughed off the earthly body. These photographs are the reflections of what is already indelibly impressed upon the mind of the sitter, or sitters, or medium; they are pictures of those images abiding in the aura of one or more of those present, and *as such* they are genuine phenomena. Thoughts are things, and if the thought is strong enough the sensitive plate in the camera will reproduce it. Regard the vagueness of most of such photographs; the rigidity of the subjects; the sameness of the pose and position in nearly all of them; all wrapped up in the traditional ghost-wrappings or clouds of the stage, or of amateur theatricals. Very often the supposed likeness is so vague that it might fit almost anybody. The fact of the matter is that they are objective copies from subjective photographs impressed upon the ether of space, and, as such, constantly thrown out by our thoughts, words, or deeds.

"When the *theories* of the Spiritualists are compared with the *facts* of Occult Wisdom, we come to some interesting conclusions.

"The theories are the result of untrained observation and wrong deductions on account of insufficient training in the Mysteries. After beholding many wonderful phenomena at séances, the most intelligent spectators work out for themselves a fairly consistent theory of how these things happen. On comparing notes with one another, they will find that others have come to similar conclusions. Then they feel convinced that their views are correct and issue forth to proclaim these discoveries. But—what they have witnessed can be compared with the spectacle we behold at the theatre from *before* the footlights. We have not yet been introduced to the stage-manager or the producer, and we see only what they wish us to see. What goes on behind the scene is hidden from us; and the play itself is an illusion to our senses. It is only the person initiated into these illusions, having full knowledge of the apparatus behind the curtain, who can know how the effects are made possible; and he will have an entirely different view-point with regard to the stage-technique and the marvellous tricks, feats and effects which dazzle the spectator. Thus, the initiate has *facts* at his disposal, and the spectator only *theories*.

"The spiritualistic medium has generally a well-defined preconception of what he thinks he *ought* to see or hear, or make contact with in any way you like. In most cases he will see or hear just that and seldom more. But the trained seer can place himself *en rapport* with *real* entities and see and hear truly—without preconceptions—what takes place in the spiritual worlds. He can thus contact elementaries, elementals, or the spirits, minds, or souls of human entities on higher planes. Thus spirit will reach *up* to spirit, never *down*; for, as. I have already stated, the spirits dwelling in the higher spheres cannot descend into our material and dense atmosphere on earth. Moreover, the medium can only see and hear what the particular spirit with whom he makes contact sees and hears. When on the Astral plane that spirit lives in a Paradise or Dreamland of its own making, surrounded by all the things and beings it loves, or for which it has a longing. The discarnate spirit (mind) of a European will find itself in an entirely different dream-region from that which a Red-Indian, a Polynesian, or a Chinese spirit would behold. Moreover, the fact that a medium is conscious of contact with a discarnate spirit makes that spirit not necessarily aware of this contact. It is possible to obtain knowledge of the spirit-world without the spirits being aware of it. The mind of the medium becomes assimilated with that of another personality and thinks, speaks and writes as the departed one would have done on earth; a synchronization of the two minds, in other words. Should the medium obtain a true picture of such a spirit clairvoyantly, this does not mean that he has seen it as it was on earth; he may have seen a *semblance* of it in the Astral light; especially if the passing over took place many years ago. Furthermore, the untrained medium, or the medium who is not under the guidance of an expert, such as the ancient High-Priests were, or as the modem Adept is, will inevitably colour any contact with the conceptions of his own mind. Therefore, we never receive a true picture or message in such cases.

"A bereaved sitter at a séance can unconsciously place a medium and a discarnate spirit *en rapport* on account of the strong longing for renewed contact with the lost one in the mind of the sitter. But here again the spirit itself is not necessarily aware of this. It must not be forgotten that immediately after the final separation of the spirit from the deceased human body (which often takes place several *days* after the death of the body itself), this spirit sinks into a state of unconsciousness or sleep. It is borne around on magnetic currents and swayed about like a dead leaf in the wind. So it may pass within the range of vision of some seer, or the medium in question; or its reflection in the Astral light may be caught by the inner eye of a clairvoyant. As a rule the trained seer will know from the position, or aspect, of the spirit he beholds, whether it is in a dream-state or subjectively or objectively conscious of its surroundings and self; and the spirit-form may assume an animated or even transfigured appearance, according to its degree of spirituality or purity. Against these possibilities we have the danger of the passive state of the medium being the cause of its coming under the dominion of the elementaries and elementals.

"The uninitiated theorize and generalize and are therefore empiricists; the trained Occultist is a Scientist. He *knows* the forces he is contending with and has no need to speculate about them and so build up a fanciful structure that rests on air and has no foundations;

"For thousands of years hundreds of real initiates have explored the unseen worlds. The results of their explorations have been recorded and collected and discrepancies eliminated by fresh verifications. These facts have been generalized and the laws governing them deduced therefrom and again verified by experiment. Therefore, it must be admitted that Occultism is in every sense of the word an exact science, whilst the conclusions of the untrained seer can only be empiric. It is just as ridiculous and vain to question the work and science of the mathematicians, for instance, as the Work and science of the trained Psychists; but Spiritualism in the hands of the amateur of Occultism can never become a science.

"The objective phenomena of Spiritualism are the results of the activities or interventions of Elementals, or half intelligent nature forces, and elementaries or shells, retaining very little of the personal memories, but in which the more material or animal instincts survive. The latter survive the body for only a limited time; gradually all consciousness departs and they disintegrate. The purer the personality, the less their vitality; the coarser the human being from whom they were separated, the longer their survival, and the greater their chance of finding their way into the séance room. No real good can come of any intercourse with these beings. Even if not actually wicked, they are always imperfect and weak and their influence can never be elevating. Moreover, it is wrong to encourage such remnantis into activity or to feed them upon the vital essences coming from the sitters, thus galvanizing them into a fictitious renewal of their existence. Association with these beings can never benefit mankind in any way, and sometimes it causes great harm.

"Of such nature are the 'angel' guides of the Spiritualists. Idle dreams and speculations; the *succubi* and *incubi* of medieval times are now the spirit 'wives' and 'husbands' of modem days! Since Spiritualism—as such—began in the 19th Century there have been thousands of good, pure and honest men and women, who, but for the cultivation of the evil capacity for reception of impressions by elementaries, might have lived useful lives leading to higher things, but who through the gradual pernicious influence of these low, earth-bound natures, have sunk from bad to worse. Often they meet with a premature end on account of constant heavy losses of their vital essences which are soaked up by these 'spirits'; and cause not only their own ruin, but the ruin of those near and dear ones who have become the innocent victims of these entities and the dreadful atmosphere surrounding them when they followed home the weaker members of once happy families.

"Once a person comes under the dominance of the elementaries, his or her very nature changes completely. We see a loving wife and mother turn into a very fiend towards her husband and children; utterly callous and indifferent to their wellbeing. We see homes that were once happy and harmonious entirely devastated and mined beyond redemption. This influence can turn a good man into a demon and a good woman into a fiend. They become completely lazy and filthy and neglect their homes and kin as well as themselves. Many are driven to suicide or have to be locked up in mental homes. Oceans of tears have been wept by their relations, and untold misery caused by the evil influences of these foul spirits. And still the séances go on; mediums freely advertise for new clients; 'investigators' keep on following the dangerous roads that so often lead to the total loss of all they hold dear."

"And what happens to those who commit suicide, dear Messenger?" asked Ma-u. "Can they be helped in any way?'

"Eliphas Lévi says:—'You may help the poor deserter of life with prayer—but that prayer must *be one of action*, not words. See whether he has not left something undone ... and then try to accomplish the deed for him, and in his name.'

"In answer to this Madame Blavatsky says: 'The Kabalistic theory is, that a man having so many years, days and hours to live upon earth and not one minute less than the period allotted to him by fate, whenever the Ego gets consciously and deliberately rid of its body before the hour marked, then must it still live, even as a disembodied suffering soul. The *Ego*, or the [negative] sentient individual [Higher Mind] is unable to free itself from the attraction of the earth and has to vegetate and suffer all the torments of the mythical hell in it. It becomes an elementary spirit; and when the hour of deliverance strikes, the Mind, having learned nothing, and in its mental torture lost the remembrance of the little it knew on earth, is violently ejected out of the earth's atmosphere and carried adrift, a prey to the blind current which forces it into some new incarnation which the soul itself is unable to select as it otherwise *might* with the help of its good actions.'

"This does not mean that Lévi believed in the so-called Spiritualism. He derided both the Spiritualistic and the Spiritist theory of the return of the disembodied souls or spirits in an objective or materialized form on earth.

"It has been truly said that words mightily perplex the wisdom of the wisest, and like a Tartar's bow shoot backwards into the minds of those that follow them. So it is when we discuss the great subjects now under consideration. It is possible to twist and rend *any* sentence or pronouncement in such a way that the very reverse is proved of what was the original intention of the speaker. You will discover that when you tell the world of what I have been showing you—if ever you do this, and I think that you will—that a horde of unbelievers will fall upon you and will endeavour to prove that all the truths I have been telling you are lies. You must be prepared for scoffers and calumniators, but let this not deter you, my children, for you will be doing a great service to mankind—or to those who are ready for these revelations of the ancient wisdom; the rest do not matter for the time being; they will learn their lessons in the distant future. When Dante produced his masterly 'Inferno,' and placed in it several of his enemies, although they were then still alive on earth, he had some glimpse of the Astral Light, like every great Poet; but the malign influence of the then prevalent superstition of the conditions of Hell utterly distorted his vision.

These enemies of his had attached to them some of the elementaries described to you, and the secret knowledge of the ancient mysteries, which has always been in the possession of the Roman Church, may have been in the Poet's mind also. The question as to where the disembodied spirit dwells in between his earthly incarnations is not a matter of Judgment; of Salvation or Damnation; or of Heaven or Hell; but solely the operation of the Universal Law of Affinity and Attraction; in other words of Attunement. According to this Law we find ourselves in that part of the Astral World with which our actions and spiritual tendencies have put us in tune. There it stays until the next rebirth, and it *cannot*—even if it would—span the abyss that separates its state from the earthly conditions.

"You will hear of spiritualists who are certain that they have received elevating messages from—say—their father, and they continue to tell you that he was a kindly and spiritually-minded man who can never be classified amongst the 'devils,' which the Orthodox Church calls the entities that appear at séances. The truth of the matter is that such a person may have reached out to the spirit of his father, and not the reverse, as he thinks, by assuming that his father has descended into the earthly atmosphere. There is also the possibility of the highly intelligent but grossly material man whose shell dwells amongst the Elementaries, and who succeeds in dominating the weak mind of a medium, through which he sends intelligent messages instead of the usual gibberish. There is a further possibility of obtaining elevating and marvellous messages in the cases of fraudulent mediums. So long ago as the year 1881, Madame Blavatsky wrote: 'There are notorious trance mediums, especially women, who steadily work for their so-called trance orations, and these being really clever and working at good books, deliver essays of a respectable and at times almost first-class character. There is no spiritual influence at work here, the only apparently abnormal feature in these cases is that persons possessing such fair abilities should be willing to prostitute them, and that people who can talk so well and touchingly of truth and purity, should yet live such lives of falsehood and immorality. In the second place, in the case of pure and genuine mediums, who in a trance pass entirely under the influence of their own seventh principle [the spirit—an emanation from the *absolute*, uncreated, eternal, a state rather than a being] the Augoeides of the Greeks, the whole teachings come from the medium's own soul, and it is very rare to obtain thus anything higher than the medium's own intellect, when in a state of spiritual excitement, could produce.'

"This statement is absolutely true, and it is hoped that it will have the effect of a clarifying flame upon the subject.

"It is also possible, as in the case of those rare, high, because especially pure, mediums, whose Ego and Spirit or Soul and Higher Mind can soar together into the Astral Light when the rest of the combination is in a trance, that those can read there all highest thoughts that man has ever thought. But this can only be achieved when there is present the High Adept, under whose guidance this takes place.

"Remember to distinguish between the true *Ego*, or Soul and Higher Mind, or Divine Principle, which cannot penetrate into the earth's atmosphere after bodily death, and the human astral remnants with which the medium *can* get *en rapport*; or who control the medium. This is important, for otherwise a seeming contradiction will arise and confuse the mind.

"With regard to the production of so-called inspirational 'spirit-pictures' often produced by the medium in total darkness without this medium—who may be conscious or in a trance at the time of painting or drawing—ever having produced such quite subservient to, the will of the Mind via the physical brain. It acts automatically and according to the currents of thought-energy set up in the brain by the mind. And so—when sudden death takes place—these thought-currents involuntarily flow forth as lower mind sensations, and may reach a séance room, and, by means of the sensitive medium, find expression and result in a sort of message; often disconnected, as are the words heard or spoken, in a dream. Or, these thoughts may reach a loved one, who possibly will hear the Astral echo of the deceased's voice; or see a living picture of the same. In the latter case it would be an Astral reflection of the atmospheric waves. There is the well-known case of a patient who spent nine years in a room of a mental institution. Eventually he was cured and sent home. Shortly afterwards his 'ghost' began to appear in that room and wild cries were heard in the same voice as that of the previous tenant.

"Doctors and nurses heard these cries and all came to the conclusion that the man must have died and that his 'spirit' haunted its old abode. The news of these hauntings spread and eventually reached the ears of the old patient himself, who was quietly living with his family in another part of the country. He at once decided to put a stop to all these rumours by returning to the mental home and investigating the matter. His family doctor accompanied him, and when they arrived, the two—after much opposition from the resident doctor—were permitted to spend a night together in the old room. No sooner were they installed than the 'ghost' appeared and the cries were louder than ever. When, at dawn, the room was entered by the resident physician, the old patient was once more a raving lunatic, and his friend lay in a deadly swoon—completely overcome by the terrible and inexplicable happenings during the night. This is a true illustration of the mechanism of astral echoes and astral reflections upon the atmosphere, and in similar ways the machinery operating in all sorts of 'haunted' places may be understood."

"What is the difference between Spiritism and Spiritualism, dear Messenger?" asked Ma-uti.

"Spiritism differs from Spiritualism mainly because Spiritism includes among its tenets the doctrine of re-incarnation, to which Spiritualism is opposed. The word

'Spiritist' is sometimes applied to one who seeks only the physical phenomena and neglects the religious and philosophic aspect of Spiritualism."

"Under what names are the Elementals known who appear at the séance or in other places?" asked Ma-u.

"Their names are legion, my son. They may be peris, devs, djins, sylvans, satyrs, fauns, elves, dwarves, trolls, noms, nisses, kobolds, brownies, necks, stromkarls, pixies, piskies, moss people, good people, good neighbours, wild women, men of peace, white ladies, sylphs, undines, salamanders, and very many more. In the "*London Spiritualist*" of June 29th, 1877, for instance, is the account of a seeress, who, on the approach of a thunder-storm, saw 'a bright spirit emerge from a dark cloud and pass with lightning speed across the sky, and, a few minutes after, a diagonal line of dark spirits in the clouds.' These beings are called *Maruts* in the *Vedas*, as you may read in Max Muller's 'Rig-Veda Sanhita.' There are thousands and untold thousands of such descriptions of spirits who are very real indeed, and not the results of diseased imaginations. It needs clairvoyant faculties to see these beings, but then there are and always have been a great number of persons who possess such faculties. When a medium, or seer, describes happenings beyond the ordinary range of vision, this can be ascribed to an extension of consciousness, to projection of the Astral Body, together with the Higher Mind, or to transmural vision; in the latter case, for instance, when a person enclosed in a room without windows having access to the street, describes something that happens in that street without leaving the room. The seer, or seeress, seems to be looking through a chink into the astral, or the terrestrial world, and it depends on the acuteness of the clairvoyant's spiritual sight to see more or less through that chink. The gates are partially ajar, but only at death do they fly wide open and permit the soul and mind to behold the wonders of reality or imagination in the higher realms or in the astral worlds. Clairvoyant vision can also be made use of under hypnosis, and the French Academy of Medicine published a long report of well-attested therapeutical phenomena as early as the year 1831, in which such phenomena are classified under thirty-four different paragraphs. The organs of sight, smell, taste, touch, and hearing, are proved to become far acuter in a hypnotized subject than in the normal state, and the mind, disburdened of the shackles of the body, acquires a strength of perception impossible in the strongest and healthiest body when awake. This proves that consciousness is a quality of the mind (and of the soul) and that it can display activity independently of the body. In the 'History of Miracles' by Dr. Figuier, you can read that an epidemic of 'possession' broke out in Germany in the middle of the 19th Century, and that people possessed in this way would hang suspended in mid-air without visible means of support; stood on their heads for hours; correctly described distant events—verified later; and that old women climbed perpendicular walls, thirty feet high, with the agility of cats. The medical faculty ascribed all such happenings to 'hysteria'; a very useful word when the learned gentlemen are at a loss for a more correct description or diagnosis. Perhaps an explanation can be found when we consider the feats of the Eastern mercenary sorcerer who can hold his hands in a furnace of live coals until the coals have been reduced to cold cinders. In this case the sorcerer invokes the assistance of what he calls a 'little demon'; in reality a gnome, whom he knows how to invoke and control. Missionaries watching these performances generally say that the sorcerer has sold his soul to the devil, and that Satan enables the man to perform his juggling tricks!

"This is *real* superstition on the part of these worthy brethren, and there is something here that neither science nor the exponents of the Christian religion can understand.

"As St. Paul has said: 'We speak Wisdom among the perfect or initiated, not the wisdom of this world, nor of the archons of this world, but Divine Wisdom in a Mystery, secret—which none of the archons of this world know.' He referred here to the *Basileus* of the *Elensinian* initiation, who belonged to the staff of the great Hierophant and was an archon of Athens, and as such one of the *chief* Mystæ belonging to the *interior* Mysteries, to which only a very select few obtained entrance. These were the archons *not* of this world who *did* know. These Initiates had reached that Divine state of clairvoyance when everything pertaining to this earth disappears and the earthly sight is paralysed, and the soul and mind are united, free and pure, and One with the Spirit of God. *It sees itself* as a perfect whole, unblemished, united with the Divine Essence; thus it knows all. This is the *true* clairvoyance before which the paltry tricks and experiments of Spiritualism pale into dire insignificance and become as useless as the efforts of a blind man searching for light in a dark cellar. The true clairvoyance is that state which such seers as Plotinus and Apollonius termed the 'Union to the Deity'; which the ancient Yogins called 'Isvara'; and the modern ones call 'Samadhi.' This state is as far above spiritualistic clairvoyance as the stars are above fire-flies.

"It is the Initiate alone, rich with the Wisdom collected for him by untold generations of his predecessors, who can direct the inner eye, the 'Eye of Dangma,' toward the essence of all things material and spiritual; and who can know, the Divine Truth and the secrets of all conditions and actualities without being trapped in the snares of Illusion. He knows the extensions of matter and of the senses; and of motion, colour, taste and smell. By means of the permeability of sight, he enters clairvoyantly into that so-called fourth dimension for which so many thinkers have sought, and beholds eventually the permeability of all things in their extensions beyond the three dimensions of length, breadth and thickness. This means that he is able to liberate himself from the bonds of matter and the shackles of illusion by means of clairvoyance and psychometry of a high order of perfection. He reads the records with which all matter is impregnated, and a million years dissolve in a flash. He knows the true from the false and does not need to grope in ignorance; to him the whole of the Universe and all the inner and outer worlds are as an open book—full of marvels. He has the power of the mirific ineffable name which is the crown of the Shakti. He has conquered the Kingdom of Darkness and bathes in the Eternal Light, and, like Jesus, he has 'beheld Satan as lightning fall from Heaven.' His heart is lifted up because of the beauty and Wisdom which is his lot. He walks in the Garden of God, the anointed cherub, perfect in his ways—omnificent—glorified by purification; merciful and just. He hears the voices of the pure spirits, and they sound like silver bells; or like the tremulous munriur of an iEolian Harp, caressed by Zephyr on a summer's night. These sounds are full of sacred Wisdom and Love, and, once heard, can never be forgotten. Their voices are not articulated but consist of sweet sounds that kiss the soul with celestial and tender enchantment. Swedenborg compares their voices to a 'deep suspiration'; a heavenly sigh, communicating God's Divine Essence; supreme ecstasy.

"Spiritual phenomena should not be expected from the action of departed human beings, as the Spiritualists believe; it were better and wiser to look first into the powers of the human spirit still embodied in the flesh. Once it is realized how this spirit acts, how far it reaches, and what underlies it; then part of the veil will be lifted and there will be Light. It will then be known how the luminiferous ether of the scientists; the psychode, or spirit—or ectenic—or psychic force; the astral or sidereal light; or whatever else we care to term these forces, act and re-act one upon another. The Akasa, or life-principle, the all-pervading force known as such to the gymnosophists, magicians, and adepts of all countries for thousands of years, and used today by the Tibetan Lamas and the thaumaturgists of all nations, will yield to manipulations as it has always done, and become an instrument of power once again to those who have been found worthy of being trusted with such secrets.

"But the Light will never issue forth from dark cabinets or semi-dark séance rooms; and Spiritualists can never assure themselves of the genuineness of mediumistic manifestations such as materializations, levitations, the moving of objects, and so on, unless they occur in full light and under such test conditions that all possibility of fraud is ruled out. The feeble excuse that darkness, or at least semi-darkness is necessary for such demonstrations is an utter fallacy, as all true Occultists know. How the *pure* higher powers can use the spiritual and other forces present within the human frame is described by the anonymous adept, the author of *Art-Magic*. In that work you may read how an innocent little child-medium sits on the ground, lays her head on a tripod covered with blank writing-paper, embracing its support with her arms, and goes to sleep for an hour. During her sleep the sheets are filled up with exquisitely formed characters in ancient Sanscrit. The result of the psychographic medium-ship is a set of volumes of MSS., written without pencils, pen or ink. These volumes contain some of the highest teachings of Hermetic Philosophy and they bear the unmistakeable stamp of truth. But compare the conditions under which these volumes were produced with the conditions generally rife at modem spiritualistic séances!!

"The Infinite cannot be known by experiment and reason, but by divine wisdom and inspiration alone. The Adept, the Initiate, and the pure person will be surrounded by an aura or nimbus in which is clearly shown the grade of spiritual unfoldment of such a being; it will be pure, crystalline, limpid and opalescent as the morning dew. Men with such an aura can be approached by holy and pure influences; whilst evil spirits flee before their atmosphere of divine beneficence.

"On the other hand a negative person, or an evil one, will be surrounded by a dense, noisome, mephitic, or nauseating cloudy substance which repels the pure spirits and attracts the foul ones, who delight in it as the eel does in turbid waters. Mediums who pride themselves on being the faithful slaves of their 'guides,' give proof of a weakness that yields to strange beings, whose low intelligences control their actions and their thinking to the detriment of both medium and sitters.

"Side by side with these passive mediums appears the trained Occulist, who is not a medium but a mediator between the spirits and the terrestrial world. Only he can receive divine messages and remain consciously in full control. Amongst them we find such Adepts as Apollonius, Iamblichus, Plotinus, Jesus, and Buddha. Moreover, a medium cannot have his 'powers' developed, for a passive medium has no power. He only has certain conditions, moral and physical, which induce emanations or an aura, in which his controlling elementals or elementaries can live, and by which they can manifest themselves. He is the vehicle for *their* power! His state of perfection as a medium is in direct ratio to his passivity, and the dangers he incurs are in equal degree. The less power, the better the medium, and the less possibility of safe-guarding or defending himself.

"No spirit can control a positive person or a pure and moral one if they do not wish to be controlled. The dangers of passive mediumship are illustrated in the example of Socrates, who was refused admittance to the initiations or teachings of the Mysteries, for there was a law against the admission of such natural mediums. Being passive they were apt to be controlled, and when under control they might unconsciously betray the great Secrets of the Visions and Wonders of the Epoptai, of the Inner Temple.

"Mediumship is therefore the opposite of Adeptship, and to be discouraged whenever possible. A medium needs a foreign intelligence to overpower his physical and mental parts in order to get into a trance; an Adept requires only a few minutes of self-contemplation; his *will-power* is sufficient. He has complete control not only of the spiritual beings with whom he makes contact, but of all his own attributes also. He can So manipulate the astral body that it shrinks down to a pin-point to which everything is pervious; or he can enlarge it to a gigantic body which can touch the stars, or sink into the deeps of the earth. He can produce a luminous nebula from which will gradually develop a spirit-hand which can pick up a pencil and write intelligent messages, and dissolve it again a few minutes later.

"Do not be misled into comparing such phenomena with the faked spirit-hands you can see at some séances. Some of the more powerful elementals can produce similar phenomena by using the astral body of the passive medium for that purpose. In such cases the messages consist mainly of drivel."

"Is it possible that the Soul of a great teacher, like Jesus, remains in touch with humanity, dear Neteru-Hem?" asked Ma-uti.

"Certainly, my child. This is just what does happeft, for as it is possible for the human Adept on the earth-plane to project to distant places, or to extend his consciousness beyond his bodily dwelling-place, so can *the Adept* project His Soul to the earth from the Astral World. Remember that Soul and Mind are One in the Higher Realms in the case of an Adept. Having acquired the technique of projection on earth—when he has learned to send his *Mind* to distant places whilst the Soul remains on guard over the sleeping body—so can He separate the Mind from the Soul in the Celestial Realms, although they are one in Consciousness and Individuality or Personality. In this way can inspirational messages be received on earth from heaven. But such messages are only sent from the pure to the pure, as in the case of the child I have just mentioned; and such cases are comparatively rare. In this way a Jesus, or a Buddha, can be said to animate the minds of several persons at once. There axe many instances in which this has happened, such as the case of Shankara, who was overshadowed by the Buddha x and not a re-incamation of Buddha as has been averred about this great Brahmâ Adept."

"Who were the Epoptai you mentioned a short time ago?" asked Ma-u.

"The Epoptai were the Initiates or Seers of the Greater Mysteries, those who see all things unveiled. The Mystai, or veiled ones, belonged to the lesser Mysteries; and they were allowed to perceive things only through a mist."

"What is the principal colour of the Astral World?" Ma-uti wanted to know.

"The principal colour of the Astral World is Violet. When in meditation you will see other colours, such as green, indigo, and yellow. These are all good colours, but the principal colours to aim at are green-bronze, yellow-bronze, and indigo-bronze. When the yellow-bronze merges into the indigo you are on the right plane called the Mânasic Plane; from this Plane Manas stretches upward to Mahat, as it is termed. Reject all other colours, for they are not good and represent conditions you must try to avoid, as it is not possible to reach a state of pure spiritual consciousness when these colours are present to you."

And now the weird light that had been surrounding the Messenger, and Ma-u and Ma-uti, began to change and stretch out like a huge aura, surrounding the whole region. It was shot with opalescent and shifting colours such as are seen on a soap-bubble; but here the colours were not only on the surface, but drifted everywhere in great clouds of splendour and magnificent brilliance. These clouds were peopled with hosts of phantasmagorical beings, and strange landscapes, where all natural tints were reversed, became visible. There were red skies, and yellow trees, and blue grass, and violet stars in the sky and a pink moon. Weird animals and fearsome monsters roamed everywhere, and the trees waved and weaved about and stretched out gruesome tentacles with which they sought to capture any creature that came within their reach; insane imaginations of those who are possessed by elemental demons. A little Javanese girl with streaming hair and terrified eyes came running towards the Messenger, whilst showers, of stones which suddenly appeared within a few feet above fell all round her though never touching the child. Some of the stones were of huge size and fell with heavy thuds upon the soil. Neteru-Hem made a sign with his hand and both child and stone shower melted away, whilst reddish vapours in the form of impish-looking demons became visible for a moment and dissolved into nothingness.

"These are 'polter-geists' or Pichachas, or Bhûts, as the Hindus call them. They are responsible for all sorts of phenomena in the séance room, and use certain forces clustering about the mediums to play all sorts of tricks. They love to torment human beings, and persons who have these forces about them experience such manifestations as the throwing about of crockery or even furniture. Sometimes there are localities where such forces are available to the elementals, and whenever human beings visit such spots there is every likelihood of demonstrations of this sort taking place."

In the distance magnificent cities became visible, with golden palaces and houses of shining crystal; the walls garnished with precious stones.

Troops of horsemen came galloping along on ghostly steeds, manes and tails stretched out in the rushing air, chasing phantom game on soundless hoofs.

Shades of the ancient Turanians, Huns, and Tukui worshipped the spirits of the earth and sky; and Chinese spirits in the form of celestial, terrestrial, and wandering phantoms of their great Emperors, Philosophers and Sages, made a glittering pageant that passed in a blaze of splendour.

Beautiful girls threw handfuls of flowers high up in the clouds, and, as they ascended, these fragrant missiles melted in mid-air.

Now Neteru-Hem beckoned Ma-u and Ma-uti, who had been fascinated spectators of all the strange phantasies around them, and led them to a suburban-looking villa, which they entered. Passing right through the walls they came to a room which, but for the faint red light from a tiny lamp was in almost total darkness. A number of people were just discernable in the gloom, and silently they sat in front of a woman who, breathing heavily, sat in a cabinet, hands and feet bound with strong cords. Myriads of elementals were also present in that room, some very grim and malicious, others howling with mad joy and prodding that gasping and unconscious figure in the cabinet; whilst others bathed themselves in the auras of the sitters and absorbed the living forces of these people, who were totally unaware of what took place around them in the dark. A swirling group of elementals were crowding around one particular member of that audience, a rather vacant-looking young girl; and they tried to enter the body of that poor soul in order to obtain a vicarious existence on earth at the expense of their victim. Suddenly a heavy shudder ran across the girl's frame and with a frightened sob she collapsed. At that moment one of the elementals succeeded in entering her body, the rest screeching with rage at being foiled. Two of the sitters carried her outside the room and revived her, but, on opening her eyes, the vacant look was gone and replaced by one of malicious cunning. The pupils were contracted to pin-points and the eye-lids half closed, so that instead of the open-eyed creature who entered the séance room there was now a girl with a face full of craftiness; astute, sly and subtle; her destiny the mad-house, after the elemental form had used up the vital forces of his victim and destroyed the feeble brain.

Another group of elementals had in the meantime released the medium from her bonds and lifted her up to the ceiling, still unconscious, but with eyes wide open and staring.

"A levitation," murmured the sitters. "What a wonderful séance!"

The room faded away and changed into the interior of a great lamasery in Tibet. A droning chant of the multitudes of lamas present rises up in the temple. 'Ah-oum ma-ni pad-me houm,' repeated over and over again; and from the dancing beams of sunlight that enter the temple-windows the luminous form of a great Tibetan Saint separates itself in the form of a fiery cloud and holds converse with the congregation in a voice like the whisper of a breeze through the foliage of a forest.

"Here you have witnessed some of the dreams of the inhabitants of the Astral Worlds; something that really happened at a séance; and finally, in the Tibetan scene, a true demonstration of how the Adept residing in the sublime realms can contact the Adepts on earth."

"How would you describe to us the principles of the body, the Astral body, the spirit, and other attributes of man, dear Neteru-Hem?" asked Ma-u.

"In this talk about Spiritualism, my Son, I have made use of the customary terminology of the average man investigating the occult mysteries in an untrained manner; without understanding the true meanings of the terms he uses. A mail's body is so marvellously interwoven with his spiritual parts, that it is very difficult to give an explanation of how the material and spiritual act in conjunction.

"When we talk of the *Body* we refer to the Temple the *Mind* dwells in during its *earthly* existence.

"The Astral Body is that etheric or astral vehicle in which the *Mind* dwells in the finer, or Astral Spheres, after the *earthly* body expires. It is built up at the same time as the *material* body, and during earthly life it is the body's constant companion; except when it is used by the Adept for the purpose of astral projection; when the *Mind* can travel in it to near or distant places.

"There is a great difference between such *projections*, and what is called *extension of consciousness*; when the *Mind* fixes itself, as it were, on distant localities and can be aware Of what happens there without travelling in the astral or etheric body to these spots. The astral body can be seen clairvoyantly as a misty white shape, lbosely attached to the material, earthly body. The great Adept, however, can make his Astral Body so apparently solid that it becomes visible to all, and seems just as real as his own material body from which the projection was made, and which either lies entranced elsewhere, or even pursues its usual functions, guided by the *Soul*, although the *Mind* is elsewhere in his astral shape.

"The *Astral Body* gradually dissolves after bodily death, or it evaporates, or becomes rarefied, and when it has finally disappeared the *Mind* is sent into another *material body* on earth for the next incarnation.

"The Astral Body is of a *material* nature, though much more ethereal than the earthly body; and the *partly* material *Mind* uses this Astral vehicle in between the earthly incarnations.

"When the Alchemical Marriage has taken place, the *Soul Mind* does not need an astral body at all. It rapidly dissolves, being but an *empty* shell, whilst the soul-Mind — a pure and formless Essence — passes through the Astral planes, or planes of consciousness as they are sometimes called, and returns to the First Great and Divine Principle from which it originally emerged or separated for the purpose of commencing its cycles of incarnations on earth. Or it dwells in some of the finer celestial worlds in a spiritual *form* which cannot be described.

"In some of the ancient teachings the Soul, Mind, and Astral Body are split up, or divided, into various sub-sections, in order to make clear the gradual unfoldment and progress of these principles; but as it would require too much time I cannot enter into these details now, and if you should wish to study these doctrines more fully you should acquire or borrow the books in which all this is explained. The sacred books of the Buddhists contain these teachings, and they can also be found in the works of the ancient Greek Philosophers.

"The *Mind* is that spiritual part of man which uses the brain as its directing instrument when in earthly body, in order to make this body act as it wishes. Remember again the difference between the higher and the lower Minds — the higher mind being the negative counterpart of the

Soul, and the lower mind being that principle which animates and regulates the body. The Higher Mind is that part of the entity which enters the body at birth with the first breath for the purpose of learning its earthly lessons and experiences. Its main purpose is to transmute all material things and ideas into spiritual ones, in order to purify the material consciousness of itself in such a way that it reaches a state of perfection equal to the *Soul* itself. When this has been achieved it becomes an immortal and pure, divine Essence and joins the Soul, after which there is no further need for re-incamation.

"Both *Soul* and *Mind* have complete consciousness of their own status, and it does not matter if this status is called personality or individuality. Neither of these terms must be confused with the personal appearance of the human *body* in which the *Mind* dwells during each incarnation. Both *Soul* and *Mind* are the same in personality or individuality, though *seemingly* separated until the final union — which is that Alchemical Marriage to which I referred — so-called on account of the transmutation of the *partly* material Mind into an *absolutely* spiritual one when this Marriage has been consummated. This seeming separation and final union is the Great Mystery of *Life* in the spiritual sense, which cannot be understood by the material *Mind* and brain; or explained even *if* understood, for it is the ultimate Secret of God — the Immaculate Light.

"The *Soul* is the Divine Immortal Essence, a God-like Principle, without form or substance, and equal unto God — the Unknown. It overshadows and can inter-penetrate the living human being; and it is often called the Master Within — although it really is without. It has full awareness of itself and of all the incarnations of the Higher *Mind* in material human forms; and it is always connected with the *same* Mind when that is incarnated.

"Spirit is the Principle which issues forth from the Divine Source — via our Sun — and holds together all material things or beings by adhesion and cohesion; this 'Spirit' is the Æther.

"It keeps alive the *Spark* which feeds on it.

"This spirit-stream is entirely apart from the Great Spirits, the Sons of God, who created all things and plants, animals and men. The terms spirit-force and Spirit should never be confused.

"The *Spark* of God—is the vital principle which animates and lights up the material body. It is a part of the Astral Fire and may bum very brightly, as in the man of genius, or smoulder dimly in the lower evolved members of humanity, or in animals or plants. It is entirely individual to the body and its Astral Body as long as either has life, and it departs at re-incamation to return to the Eternal Fires of the Cosmic Worlds. It provides the heat which the material body requires, and radiates it in jgreater or lesser degrees, according to the amount of response it receives from the body and the materials the body is made of. It is the Fire of Prometheus, and was placed within the body by the Sons of God, who were sent to create men and all living beings and give them Life. Such are the parts which constitute all living beings, my children; and it may give you a greater understanding of some of life's mysteries, and the powers within all living creatures, both materially and spiritually."

During the final sentences of the Messenger the phantom beings of the Astral World had vanished, and the coloured clouds and atmosphere had turned into a bright yellow-golden hue.

A pleasant feeling of warmth spread all around, and Ma-u and Ma-uti began to sense a change, which brought with it a feeling of intense relief. Darkness had been cleared away completely, and, following the resplendent form of Neteru-Hem, they proceeded towards the regions of the Astral Fires, where further teachings and wonderful visions awaited them. They had done with the dark abodes for good now,and their further adventures would lead them to the glorious Light of the Supreme Being and the Celestial Hosts.

GOLD-STONE

The living Fires abound
In all the things
Thai lie or move around
Upon the shining Earth,
And in the hidden Worlds
Of Inner Being.

* * *

They smoulder in the smallest mote,
Or glow within the Poet's eye,
And blaze within the Heart of Love,
Or sparkle in the bright reflections
Which all good deeds irradiate
About them from Within,
And inwards from Without.

* * *

All brilliant Fires from God's own Breast,
To light and guide upon the winding Path
Along which ev'ry Soul or Thing must wend its way,
Back to the Source from which it fell
Within the dreaming voids of deep Illusion.

VISION 6
THE ASTRAL FIRE

Following Neteru-Hem, Ma-u and Ma-uti ascended a hill, and when they reached the top, a wonderful landscape lay spread before and around them.

Bathed in the golden radiance, several beautiful white marble Temples rose up in all directions and in the distance a circle of fairy-like castles was silhouetted on the horizon, floating, as it were, in golden transparent clouds of aureate haze.

Bright yellow flashes shone forth when a ray of light struck the golden ornaments with which the buildings were decorated in exquisite and choice designs, and green, blue and red flames leapt from the thousands of blazing jewels which covered the fabric of the wondrous structures; a carnival of pyrotechnical delight.

Terraces, and lovely gardens full of flowers bewitched the eyes; and softly splashing fountains murmured mystic songs and rose up golden in the air, to fall like sprays of shining gems within their basins.

Singing birds did chant their songs of jubilation and of joy; and peacocks, birds of paradise, and butterflies bedecked with shining greens and blues and reds deluged the senses with rapture.

"How lovely!" breathed Ma-uti, overcome by the felicity of all this glory.

"Where are we now?" asked Ma-u.

"This is the Prince-dom of the Rulers in the World of Astral Fire. Sacred and inviolable in its Purity it lies between the lower Astral Worlds and the Heavenly Realms. A Holy Barrier that hone but Holy Souls of Purity and Wisdom ever pass. It is cut off from earth and all the spheres below it and above, by walls of leaping flames that sear the Minds of those not qualified and blind their sight, so that, perforce, they must return to those abodes for which they are equipped by nature of their attributes of spiritual modulation. This is ordeal by Fire in the truest sense; for if a single speck; of earthly dross remains within their Minds, the fiery glow will seize upon that mote and bum it up. They shall not pass when so disqualified."

The advent of Neteru-Hem and his companions had evidently been noticed, for the golden doors of the main Temple swung open and a small group of venerable-looking priests in golden robes came out into the open and proceeded towards the hill where the Messenger and Ma-u and Ma-uti gazed upon the scene before them.

"Hail, Divine Messemger, and twice hail to his friends!" said the foremost of the priests, raising a hand in greeting.

Neteru-Hem bowed and introduced the pair, whereupon the whole party went towards a marble terrace in front of the main Temple and took seats, whence they could see all the surrounding gardens and the avenues that led from the Temple towards the other buildings and beyond.

A solemn bell struck seven chimes, and, when the last sound had died away, a procession of youths and maidens issued forth from the main entrance of the Temple. Dressed in white they were, carrying wreaths of roses and sprays of lovely flowers in their hands. Never before had Ma-u and Ma-uti seen beings so happy and so beautiful. An Essence of utter purity, love and goodness, seemed to stream out from them with an aura of golden rays, as if they were alight within. Proceeding towards the gardens the procession broke up, and they followed the paths towards the fountains, arbours, and flower-beds; filling the air with happy talk, and lighting up the atmosphere with their presence.

"These are the new arrivals who have just crossed the flames, after spending thousands of incarnations upon earth, learning their lessons of material experience. They rest here for a while before passing on to the higher Realms and the Mysteries of the Unknown."

Thus spoke the Chief Priest, and Ma-u and Ma-uti were surprised that he looked so young, although he had such a dignified bearing. When they had first seen him from the hill-top they thought that he was an elderly man, but upon closer acquaintance he and his companions had all the same look of youth as the beings who now filled the gardens with delight. As if he could read their thoughts, he continued: — " There is no such thing as age or time in these regions. Those who penetrate here have had millions of mortal and Astral years of experience and life. But time, such as we once knew it, is but an illusion, the same as light or darkness. There is no night here — but always bright and untroubled day, such as you now behold."

Heavenly singing sounded from within the Temple, voices of liquid gold rang forth, accompanied by an organ pouring forth harmonies such as never were heard on earth. The music raised the soul to highest ecstacy, and streams of soft colours rose up above the Temple, spreading out in drifting clouds of glory across the sky. The flowers responded to these celestial vibrations, for they too were of a nature entirely different from earthly vegetation, and a sweet redolence streamed out from their resplendent blooms and filled the air with an aroma of mystic incense.

"Oh," sighed Ma-uti, "I should like to stay in this marvellous place forever!"

"My child," replied Neteru-Hem, "this is but a foretaste of Heaven. These regions are still subject to form and structure, though not of an entirely material nature; all being subject to the Laws of Spiritual Vibrations, which are entirely different from material vibrations and hard to understand. Do not confuse these regions with those of the earthly and Astral worlds. For there all is subject to slower material vibrations, due to spirit-force flowing through the sun. There, also, the Minds of all the inhabitants are slaves to Illusion, whilst here all is actuality and not a dream within a dream. The only imagination here is the imagination of God, and not that of incarnated mortals, or mortals drifting between incarnations. Those who penetrate here have done with all material things, unless they wish to return to earth in order to lead, help, and serve humanity along its painful path. In such cases they can either return to earth and be born again, or they can use their spiritual body and either serve in the Astral Worlds and assist its temporary dwellers there, or they can direct and inspire such mortals as they wish to lead. In this way they act as a link between the spiritual and material states of existence, when they have reached a state of wisdom equal to that of the Sons of God who first came to earth to instruct mankind."

"But," said Ma-u, "I see no Fire here, except the golden sheen that seems to be everywhere. Yet, you said that this is the Prince-dom of the Rulers in the World of the Astral Fire; I cannot understand this, dear Messenger."

Neteru-Hem smiled and answered: "Although you do not seem to see the Astral Fire, my Son, you are actually within that great Ocean of Fire. The walls of Flame that surround this part of the Cosmic, and which also surround in a similar manner the whole of the material Universe and the Astral Regions, are but the outer manifestation of that which lies within this great Circle. Even if the impossible should happen, and an impure material Astral body or mind penetrate through the Flames, which are visible, the invisible Fire in which we are now would utterly destroy such a body or mind in a flash."

"But," said Ma-u and Ma-uti in one breath, "how is it that *we* are not destroyed in this manner, as we are both here with you?"

"Are you sure that you *are*, my dear children?" asked Neteru-Hem in return, while the Priests, who had smilingly listened to this conversation, regarded the pair with twinkling eyes.

"Are we not?" asked the two in amazed voices.

"Wait a little longer, my dear disciples," said the Messenger; "all will be made clear later."

"The Secret of the Fire lies hidden in the second letter of the Sacred Word, and the Guardians of it, the Devas of Fohatic heat, watch over it. When the Mighty One drew in His Breath and pronounced the Word, the Sacred Sparks went forth and gave all form Vitality that compelled expansion of consciousness and growth. When Matter and Water blended with Fire the inner Spark amalgamated all; and there was Life.

"As you can read in the Stanzas of Dzyan: 'When the great Wheel turned upon its own axis the seven lesser wheels came into being; and they revolved around, within, and forward; and all that has existence WAS. Although the Wheels are diverse, they are *one* in unification, and when the great Wheel was evolved the inner Fire burst forth. When it touched the first Wheel there was Life and in its circulation a million fires rose up. Then the Sons of God looked within the depth of the Flame and took from its heart the Sacred Stone of Fire and proceeded to the next Wheel. As each Wheel came into being new flames burst forth, and so seven Wheels evolved, and with each wheel a blue-white flame, which became a rosy light and the seven-fold eternal Principle. In the end the orange tint of the inner fire blended with yellow, rose, and blue, and mingled their subtle tones. And thus the Flame became the Fire and the Light shone forth. And Seven Rays came into being; from Logos they spread to man, and all manifestations, both spiritual and material, are subject to the influence and magnetism of these Rays.'

"The nature of Fire is threefold; but it is fivefold in manifestation, as represented by the five senses.

"There is the internal and vitalizing fire which animates the objective solar system and the bodies of all living beings in whatever state of evolution. There is also the mental fire which animates the mind of the Logos and vitalizes the mind of man; it links the mind of man by intelligent will to the Logos. And finally there is the Divine Flame; the dominant characteristic of the God of our Solar System; and this flame in man is equal to the highest thoughts of which he is capable. It leads him onward in his evolution, back to the Divine from the material.

"The vitalizing fire is responsible for the activity, the rotary motion, and the development of matter by means of friction. The mental fire controls the evolution of the mind and its vital energy, and also the mind's work in connection with its duty to' transform all things material with which it comes in contact into spiritual purification. The Divine Flame controls and aids the mind on its pathway back to the original divine source from which it first descended, and was thence projected into matter.

"The Seven Rays are connected with:—
1. Divine Will, Purpose and Power; also with the mineral kingdom.
2. Love and Wisdom; also the vegetable kingdom.
3. Active Intelligence and the animal kingdom.
4. Harmony, Art and Beauty, and Humanity as a whole.
5. Science and the Soul.
6. Devotion and Abstract Idealism; also the Planetary Lives.
7. Ceremonial Magic and the Solar Lives.

"The Fire of the lower, or animal, nature in the physical body is centralized at the base of the spine, from which it radiates in all directions by means of the spinal column, and works in close connection with the central ganglia; being especially associated with the spleen.

"In the astral, or etheric, body there is also the organ of active or radiatory fire, which is the exact counterpart of that of the physical body; in fact, these two fires are one.

"The spine and spleen are the most important parts necessary to health, and when the spleen is free from congestion and the spinal column duly adjusted, aligned and healthy, there will be very little illness of any sort.

"There are seven Lords of Fire, and they control numerous groups of entities, from the great Fire Devas right down to the little salamanders, who can be seen dancing in every flame, and in all the fires of the home and the factory. They belong to the same group as the Fire Elementals of the internal fires of the earth. In the heat of the animal or human body, as well as in the warmth of the terrestrial regions, dwell the Fire Spirits, who focus the essence of warmth within themselves. In volcanoes or in large conflagrations dwell the Agnichaitans, who are Fire Spirits, of a higher grade and more powerful. They are closely allied to the great Devas who form the Sun's fiery envelope.

"Then, there are the pranic elements of fire, which permeate the texture of the human or animal body, or of plants, and they blend with the fires of the Microcosm.

"Finally, there are some of the Devas who ensoul certain of the great Light Rays."

"May we see more of this realm, dear Messenger?" asked Ma-uti.

"Certainly you may, my child, follow me."

So saying, the Messenger took leave of the priests, and, descending from the terrace, followed a path that led towards a park-like stretch of Country. Ma-u and Ma-uti, following him, were amazed afresh at the beauty of their surroundings. Scene after scene of the most wonderful landscape unfolded on all sides as they proceeded. Georgeous copper-beeches spread their branches, filled with shining, warm foliage; chestnut trees were laden with their lovely and symmetrical white or pink candles; graceful silver birches raised their gleaming white boles, beplumed with drooping festoons of hanging slender branches laden with exquisite leaves, the most refined and chaste of all trees; and every tree, from the mysterious poplar to the mighty oak was represented; shining with the inward fires of vitality and joying in their splendour.

Everywhere there were huge May-trees and bushes in white, pink and deep red, cascading from their topmost branches right to the very soil with avalanches of blossoms, splendid emblems of innocence, purity and affection. The air was filled with their scent of vanilla, a heavenly aroma that creates visions of delight. Gorse and broom shone upon the open spaces, and lilac and laburnum in magnificent spates of glorious blooms, added glamour to the wondrous groves and thickets, from which prodigious bursts of melody of singing birds rang out; exhilarating, gay and pleasant. Deep pools and lakes upon which floated stately royal swans, and which were bedecked with lotus, water-lilies, and other plants with lovely flowers and leaves, reflected the golden sheen that hung within the atmosphere and filled the soul with bliss.

Eternal spring reigned everywhere; winsome, gentle, and irrepressible in its divine power and miraculous splendour; as if a soothing flow of nectar did slowly drip from rose-leaves upon eyelids worn with care.

Vernal spring; that makes the pulse§ leap with sense of healing and rebirth and fills with hope and gladness. Spring, that flings its garments wide, and laughingly spreads out upon the firmament above its rosy filmy clouds in misty sprays of lustrous brilliance; calls forth the opening buds and rising flowers with welcoming salute of joy.

As if in answer to their thoughts Neteru-Hem remarked: "Here it is always spring-time, and nothing ever decays or dies. The very air itself is filled with vibrant life, and every living thing retains eternal youth. This is a garden of Eden without a Serpent, for all temptation has been left behind."

Vista after lovely vista opened out wherever Ma-u and Ma-uti looked, dumb with wonder. A treasure of delightful gems besparkled all the emerald fields and plots of grass that gave relief and air and space, where multi-coloured flowers raised up their lovely petals to the golden light. Cradled in the Benediction of God's Love they lived for ever on.

At last the park-land ended, and, gasping with amazement, they now beheld the most wonderful scene of all.

They saw the widespread crescent of an enormous bay surrounding within its spacious horns such an ocean as no mortal eye has ever seen before.

The coast was made of deep-red golden rocks, that sent out streams of blazing light all round in lustrous scintillation.

The ocean's hue was a deep, hazy mauve, and sparkled with myriads of tiny fiery atoms which danced like motes in a sunbeam in eternal motion, passionately leaping and falling, swirling in every direction, eddying and gyrating in ecstasy of continuous oscillation.

Golden rocks and reefs rose up and stretched far out into the distant regions of that strange deep; whilst here and there great tracts within the main shone out in brilliant colours.

"This is that part of the ocean of Fire whence are sent the animating particles that vitalize all living organizations," said Neteru-Hem.

"Those pools of various colours you observe in different parts of the ocean are connected with the colours of the spectrum; also with twelve colours as yet unknown to man, and with the Seven Divine Rays, and the psychic centres in the body of man. An ocean of Inspiration this. And if but one such tiny spark you see descends into a Poet's Mind, Lo! an immortal work will be created. His pen drips honey and ambrosia, and with a careless gesture he scatters jewelled thoughts, like stars, upon the Universe of other minds. These sparks light up the minds of prophets with a Holy Knowledge of events to come! The psychic flower-centres within man correspond with some of the lovely colours you behold within this Ocean.

"That patch of orange fire you see is like the fiery flower of Kundalini; situated at the base of man's spine, it has four petals and vitalizes man's body. It is connected with the radiatory vitalizing fires between the shoulder-blades;

with the fires of the mind at the highest part of the spine, situated in the centre of the back of the throat; and with the fire of the Spirit, at the top of the head, from which issue forth the two united fires of matter, by means of the Higher Mind and Soul.

"All the fire-centres within man circulate, and, in the case of the fire of Kundalini, a threefold path of fire can be seen, extending the entire length of the spine, vivifying every centre in the body, when the higher man has succeeded in blending the three centres just mentioned with the ascending fire of Kundalini. This causes the elimination of all coarse and unsuitable matter in the body and takes within the sphere of its own influence all other matter that is keyed to its own vibration. It further cleanses the etheric or astral body from all impurities.

"The patch of rosy tint with an admixture of green you observe in the ocean there corresponds with the colours of the ten petals which form the solar plexus.

"That glowing golden pool over there is connected with the twelve golden petals of the heart centre in the human body. This silvery-blue lake has the same colour as the sixteen petals in the throat centre, in which blue dominates.

"The ninety-six petals which form one of the headcentres — between the eyebrows — have the same rose-and-yellow colour as that patch you see near those rocks; and the white-and-gold stretch of colour in that fjord is the colour of the twelve major petals, with their nine-hundred-and-sixty secondary petals arranged around them, which are situated in the centre at the very top of the head.

"In the aura of the highly developed man these colours, as well as numerous graduations and tints, are visible, just as you can observe them in this Ocean. These centres, together with many others, such as the pineal gland and the pituitary body, form a network of triangles within the human frame, just as you will see that the colour-patches in this ocean are also in the shape of interwoven triangles.

This is necessary; for unless these triangles are linked by the progression of the fire, the fire cannot perfectly vivify them in order to transmit the material into the spiritual. As soon as any of the fires has free passage along one of the triangles, that triangle remains in a continuous blaze; and when all the triangles are alight it will be seen that there is always one that burns with a brighter flame than the others. This will give the clue to that man's place in his evolution, and by it his attainments can be judged.

"When a man has reached the apex of his evolution, it will be seen that each of his seven principal psychic centres also has become a radiant fire; a wheel of living flame, rotating fiercely at terrific speed. Not only does it rotate in one specific direction, but it actually turns upon itself, having the appearance of a vivid flaming *iridescent* globe of pure fire. In the heart of each fire is contained a certain geometrical shape; yet the vibration of this shape is so rapid that it is difficult for the eye to realize it. At the top, and all around the head, a wonderful golden flame is seen mounting upwards and sideways in all directions. This golden flame attracts downward a sheet of electric-blue light, which descends from these astral planes of fire here to the man who has reached that necessary state of spiritual evolution which allows this holy blending. The development of each centre of psychic force takes place as follows: —

"At the first stage, it is but a shallow depression of dimly-glowing fire, diffused throughout the body, but of very little intensity. The wheel rotates so slowly that it can hardly be perceived. So it is in animals, and so it was in man of the early Lemurian Races; when man was no more than animal.

"At the second stage, a small point of glowing fire can be seen in the middle of the shallow depression, and the centre commences to rotate more rapidly. This shows the point when the Mind is beginning to be felt, and it corresponds to man's development in the later Lemurian period.

"At the third stage, the point of light in the centre of the rotating fire becomes more active, and the rotary motion causes, it to bum more brightly and to cast off rays of fire in two directions; seemingly splitting the vortex of fire in two parts. The motion is much accelerated, and the dividing flame shoots backwards and forwards, increasing and stimulating the glow of the centre until a much greater point of radiance is achieved. This is equal to the development of man in the days of Atlantis.

"Then comes the time when the centres are each divided into four parts. They have all become very active, and a cross has been formed within the periphery of each, rotating at the same time as the wheel itself; but independently. This causes an effect of great activity' and splendid beauty and shows that the man has reached a stage of high development mentally. He is sensing the activities of two principles within, symbolized by the rotating wheel and the inner rotating cross, and he is also sensing the spiritual part of himself; though he functions in the material.

"At the next stage, the centre becomes fourth-dimensional—if one may use this term—and the inner rotating cross commences to turn upon its axis, driving the flaming periphery to all sides; the centre really becoming a sphere of fire instead of a wheel. The centres are seen as globes of radiant fire in the end, sending out rays which merge with the purifying fires that bum up all material dross.

"The evolution of the centres is very slow and gradual and proceeds in definite cycles of incarnations, which vary according to the ray on which the man's mind functions. '

"As there are seven such rays, as you know already, the time needed for the full development of the human Mind runs into millions of years. To each Ray there is a great Master, a Heavenly Man, and they are identified with the seven centres in the body of the Logos, the Grand Man of the Heavens."

"What does a Heavenly Man look like?" asked Ma-uti, innocently.

"A very good description is found in Alice A. Bailey's 'Treatise on Cosmic Fire,' which you should study," replied Neteru-Hem smilingly.

"She says: — " 'A Heavenly Man is distinguished by:
1. His spheroidal shape. His ring-pass-not, during objectivity, is definite and seen.
2. His internal arrangement and His sphere of influence, or that activity animating the planetary chain.
3. His spiritual life control at any given period. It is the power whereby He animates His sevenfold nature.
4. His eventual ultimate synthesis from the seven into the three and from thence into one. This covers the obscuration of the globes, and the blending into unity of the seven principles which each globe is evolving.
5. His evolution under Law and consequent development.
6. His group relation.
7. His development of consciousness and of awareness.

'A solar Logos, the Grand Man of the Heavens, is equally spheroidal in shape. His ring-pass-not comprises the entire circumference of the solar system, and all that is included within the sphere or influence of the Sun.' "

"Dear Messenger," said Ma-u, "what happens when a man passes through the Wall of Flames on entering these regions?"

"When the Mind of a human being has been completely purified, so that the Alchemical Marriage-Rites of Mind and Soul have been consummated, the Soul-Mind faces the Flaming Wall once again—after many previous trials and failures at the end of preceding incarnations—but this time, being perfect in goodness and purity, he does not fail as before, but unflinchingly enters that dread conflagration. No sooner does he enter than a host of dreadful monsters assails him from all sides. They have no real existence, and are but figments and remnants of all the previous imperfections and shortcomings from which he suffered during his earthly sojourns; but they seem real enough and are very terrible to behold. This is the final test, and even more severe than the flames. It is but seldom that the pure Soul-Mind retreats before these foul images, for he has learned Wisdom and knows that these shapes have no reality; yet they are so fierce and awesome in appearance that even then the Soul-Mind may waver and retreat. In this case, the Soul-Mind must undergo another incarnation, in which he has to learn to have greater faith and courage, and a greater ability to distinguish between reality and actuality, or between illusion (which is that which the *senses* realize — realization of *reality*—), and TRUTH (which is *actuality*).

"When all these phantoms have been passed — and they retreat ever before the *fearless* spirit, just as all earthly terrors dissolve if faced with courage — then he reaches the other side of the fiery wall, and is received with loving care and warm welcome by the priests you beheld outside the Temple. Then there is rejoicing and gladness and bliss; for he meets with his equals who have entered here before, and unites with them in the spirit of Holiness and Saintliness for which they have all striven so long, along the different paths of experience and ordeal."

"How long do they stay here, dear Messenger?"

"In terms of earthly time conceptions, they may be here for thousands or millions of years; yet these periods are as nothing in Eternity and pass like a flash. There is still much to learn before they proceed to higher, or finer realms, and a time of rest in this felicitous abode is the reward for all that strife and sorrow which has gone before. And yet, as I said before, it is but a foretaste of the blessings which follow."

"Evil must be a great force if it can retard the progress of human beings for so many incarnations," said Ma-u.

"No, my son," replied Neteru-Hem, "evil is *not* a force. Goodness and evil are the two aspects which dominate the whole Cosmos of all thinking entities on earth under such appellations as Light and Darkness, White and Black, Love and Hatred. These are all realizations of the Mind and have no actual existence. There are, however, such things as positive and negative states of matter and mind; and we may divide them into positive *Forces* and negative *Conditions*. In this way we consider as positive *forces* such concepts as goodness, light and love, for instance; and under negative *conditions* we classify evil, darkness and hatred.

"The human mind cannot properly appreciate all the positive forces unless it has suffered from at least *some* of the negative conditions. This is one of the principal lessons the Mind has to learn, and when it has done so it will know that positive forces of good *always* overcome negative conditions of evil, under whatever form they manifest. The Mind will also know then that hatred cannot overcome hatred, for example; as a negative condition cannot master, rectify, modify, or change another negative condition; whereas the positive force of Love, *added* to Love, will double its potency.

"But all these aspects of positive and negative forces and conditions, considered from an earthly and intellectual standpoint, are but phantoms of the mind; which in itself is negative until it has become so pure that it can join with the positive Soul, and so make a complete *balance* of positive and negative. Then the *spiritual* manifestations of form and existence become possible; as you see in this world of Astral Fire. The pure and balanced Soul-Mind then needs no *material* aids in order to appear in a spiritual body in spiritual surroundings. Such bodies and surroundings may then be *changed,* but they can never be destroyed, dissolved, or broken down to their first material electrons—for they do not possess any that are subject to dissolution—as happens with material bodies or surroundings by means of death and decay."

"Then," remarked Ma-u, "these beings, and all those trees and plants and Temples have *real* and actual form and existence, without being illusions or realizations of the mind, such as we find on earth or in the Astral worlds, which are the 'Heavens,' 'Devachans,' or 'Summerlands' of the Spiritualists, the Religious Sects, and the average Occultist or Mystic?"

"That is true, my son," said the Messenger. "The Higher Mind of man, as well as the lower mind Of an animal, at plant, and all material things, resides in a latent state in the case of the latter. *Mind* needs a body to manifest itself on the material plane. This lasts as long as the *mind* of such a body is still entangled in material misconceptions and dreams. But as soon as the mind has full realization of its actual divine inheritance (such as it can reach in man), and releases itself from these illusions by meditation, service and purification and so becomes the equal of the Soul, then the false ideas are discarded; the Higher Mind joins the Soul and leaves the material worlds for ever, if it wishes to do so, and the true spiritual existence commences.

"It is extremely difficult to explain this progress; just as it is difficult to realize the misconceptions in man's mind about sin. If I say that Sin only has existence in a mind which has realization of sin, and if I add that sin does not exist when the mind has no such realization, no matter what the man in which that mind dwells does, then I state another. Truth that is almost impossible to understand. It is for this reason that I said just now that Love and Hatred, Light and Darkness, and so on, have no real existence on the material or astral planes. These concepts are not actualities, but only realizations. Ordinary language cannot make this clear; only in terms of spiritual and divine Wisdom can these Truths be explained or understood; not by means of the *material* intellect. The latter is of no use or value when we deal with Divine Teachings."

"What is the earthly counter-part, or correspondence of the Astral Fire?" asked Ma-uti.

"Apart from the Rays, and the fires in the bodily centres, there is internal and external heat in every atom," replied Neteru-Hem. "In other words: the Breath—or Spirit—of the Father, and the Breath—or Heat—of the Mother. In the ancient Teachings the 'Mother' referred to is *Matter*.

"It is the fire-in matter—matter vivified and held together by Spirit-force—that burns in the thoughts and passions of mankind. It causes the struggles, efforts and thoughts of the intellect; of progress; and the reaction of pleasure—which is pain. Where there is no fire there is the coldness of death, and an absence of action.

"To redeem mankind!, which at first was created god-like and perfect, and lead it back to the One Divine Source, the Celestial Beings offered themselves as voluntary victims; and they gave up their status, descending upon earth, where they took up their abode. These are the Fiery Angels of the exoteric theologies who were 'hurled' down from Heaven into the darkness of Hell—which is our Earth; the latter concept being a tremendous misconception of the true nature and work of these Fiery Beings."

"What are the actual colours of the Seven Rays, dear Messenger?" asked Ma-uti.

"The colour of the First Ray, the Ray of Will or Power, is a brilliant shining orange. This tint is quite distinct from the deep orange hue you may see in the aura of a prideful man; this is the exoteric interpretation of its colour; its esoteric colour is red. Orange light acts on the glands of humans or animals and makes them more active.

"The Second Ray, of Love and Wisdom, is also dual in its manifestation—as are all the others. One side presents lovely tints of crimson and rose; the colours of Love. The other side is ultra-marine, or cobalt-blue, and it sparkles with bright golden stars; these are the colours of Wisdom.

"The right side of man's body also radiates blue; this side emanates also negative magnetic rays. Blue is a very vitalizing colour, and, according to the ancient Indian teachings, it is the colour of air; just as the colour of fire is red, and the colour of earth yellow; this last colour is also vitalizing. Blue *light* is cold and increases the magnetism of the body, whilst blue *rays* have a calming effect and induce sleep; they also relieve neuralgia and rheumatism. The Chaldeans said that blue came from Jupiter and yellow from the Sun. There is a third aspect of this Ray, which exoterically shows indigo with a tinge of purple.

"The Third Ray, connected with active intelligence, has a brilliant lemon and primrose colour. This colour makes body and mind harmonious and strengthens the nerves. The left side of the body radiates positive magnetic streams of a yellowish-red hue; and the actual colour of the aura on the left side of the body is yellow. But exoterically it shows black too, and esoterically it is green.

"The Fourth Ray is the Ray of Harmony, Art and Beauty. Its colour is a shining light blue, or lilac blue. The exoteric colour is cream, and the esoteric is yellow.

"The Fifth Ray — that of Science — is emerald green. There are many shades of green, such as the pale luminous blue-green, which in the aura indicates sympathy or compassion; the bright apple-green of vitality; the grey-green of deceit or cunning; and the greenish brown of jealousy. Light green rays bring peace to the senses; they vitalize and stimulate the body harmoniously. Exoterically, it is a yellow ray, while the esoteric colour is indigo.

"The Sixth Ray is the Ray of Devotion and is coloured a brilliant red tinged with lilac; this is the exoteric aspect; the esoteric tint is a silvery rose.

"The Seventh Ray, connected with Ceremonial White Magic is of a dark clear blue, an indigo blue, or a deep rich violet blue, In black Ceremonial Magic these lovely tints are replaced by thick black clouds. The exoteric colour is white, and the esoteric is violet.

"And what denote the other tints and shades, dear Messenger?" asked Ma-uti.

"Every tint and shade influences the psychic centres of man in some way or another, but it is impossible to explain them all to you now. The colours in the aura tell you the disposition of a man, in the same way as they disclose his state of consciousness. If you see flashes of deep red on a dark ground in the aura it means that the person in question is violently angry. A lurid, sanguinary red denotes sensuality. Brilliant scarlet on the background of the aura shows noble indignation.

"Red excites the nervous centres and is detrimental to people who suffer from nervous complaints; but beneficial to those who are depressed, or suffer from melancholia. Red is also a tonic or stimulant in cases of physical or mental exhaustion, if ultra-violet rays are used afterwards in order to stabilize and increase the effects of the red rays.

"A dull, rusty-brown shade in the aura shows avarice; brown-grey, selfishness; leaden-grey, depression; livid grey, fear. Brown rays increase the blood formation.

"Violet rays stimulate the higher brain centres and are useful in the cure of epilepsy. Deep violet and mauve calm and steady the whole of the nervous system and the nerve centres; and ultra-violet in the aura denotes that the man has reached a high state of purity and spirituality.

"The seven Rays are further connected with the days of the week and the planets. The first with Sunday and the Sun; the second with Jupiter and Thursday; the third with Saturday and Saturn; the fourth with Wednesday and Mercury; the fifth with Friday and Venus; the sixth with Tuesday and Mars; and the seventh with Monday and the Moon.

"The relations of the Rays with the human psychic centres are as follows: the first ray with the top of the head; the second ray with the head-centre between the eyebrows; the third ray with the throat; the fourth ray with the heart; the fifth ray with the solar plexus; the sixth ray with the sacral centre; and the seventh ray with the base of the spine.

"There are two more important connections of the Rays with the human body:—

"The first ray's instrument of sensation is the light of Kundalini and its bodily location is in the vital airs of the brain. The second ray likewise in the ears, speech and the Word; its location is in the heart. The third uses the nervous system and is located in the centres of the spine. The fourth's instrument of sensation is sight; it is located in the eyes. The fifth—consciousness—is located in the brain. The sixth—the organs of speech; centred in the tongue and throat muscles. The seventh—the sense of smell; located in the nose.

"Finally, the first ray governs the Logoic or Divine Plane; the second the monadic plane; the third the Atmic, or Spiritual Worlds; the fourth the Buddhic, or intuitional; the fifth the lower mental; the sixth the Astral, or emotional desires.

"And now, my children, follow me," said the Messenger. Turning away from the fiery Ocean with regret the two followed Neteru-Hem, who turned presently into a marvellous avenue, with chestnut-trees laden with crimson blossoms on both sides of the roadway. As far as the eye could reach this avenue stretched away into the far distance. The path was covered thickly with glowing flowerets which had fallen from the upright candles with which the branches were laden in great profusion.

Ma-u and Ma-uti beheld this wonderful sight with admiration, but after a few moments the latter turned to Neteru-Hem and asked: "You told us that here nothing ever dies; if that is so, why is it that there is such a thick carpet of fallen petals, which surely must die or fade away in time?"

"These petals, my daughter, will never die. They have been here for untold thousands of years already, and each day more are added; whilst the clusters on the trees are continuously completed with fresh blossoms. This avenue itself continues in a huge circle all round these regions;

this circle is so large that it seems as if the double line of trees is placed along a perfectly straight road-way which never turns to form a circle; and it were impossible to say how many trillions of petals cover the path."

"But what is the reason for this?" asked Ma-u.

"Each petal you see here, my children, enshrines a loving thought, a beautiful verse, a great inspiration, an unselfish action, or a willing service performed by a human being who has no thought of reward. Every time such a thought or action occurs a petal falls and is added to this treasure-store; mute but everlasting testimonials of all that is good and kind and fine. Akâshic records such as no man has ever dreamed of — there they lie — riches stored up in Heaven, as it were.

"Proceed along this path, and have no fear of hurting the petals; for good deeds can never be destroyed."

They walked along that lane of glory, and on each side of the path were beautiful arbours and bowers, placed at short distances from each other between the trees; inviting to rest among their sweet arborescent beauties.

At last they entered one of these shady recesses wherein a huge shining white cypress overshadowed a well of rosy marble. Two beautiful maidens sat beside it and smiled a loving welcome to the Messenger and his guests. They looked like visions of celestial beings, with gold-blonde locks that shone around their heads like aureoles, and eyes like the velvet of blue violas, yet clear and translucent as the azure of heaven.

White ceremonial robes they wore, with golden threads, and embroidered with strange symbols; and when they spoke their voices rang like golden bells; clear and sweet.

"This is the Holy Well of Memory and Revelation, and these maidens are its guardians," said Neteru-Hem.

"The Sons of Earth and Starry Heaven come here to slake their thirst. Full it is of clear and sparkling living water, that shines and bubbles with life and looks as if it is made of liquid diamonds. Who drinks from this but once shall never thirst again in all Eternity, and all his longings shall be satisfied. The caves of Memory will open wide and all their treasures of lost love and beauty shall come forth and blaze in Royal Splendour. And all that has been hidden shall again be manifest in great refulgence; beaming bright in gorgeousness and grand magnificence; supernal and Divine."

So spake the Messenger, and, at his beck, the maidens took two silver vessels, in shape like unto Holy Grails, and filled them with the flashing, foaming liquid, glowing with deep golden hues within the cups, and handed them to Ma-u and Ma-uti.

"Drink, my children," commanded Neteru-Hem; and they quenched their thirst; and, looking upwards to the lustrous firmament they saw, shining against the orient sky, a gleaming golden Cross that reached into the Heavens and stretched its arms as if in welcome to the wanderer who longs for Home and Rest and Peace; which only God can grant.

RUBY

The glowing ardour of God's Love
Lights up the shining Rose upon the Cross
Of Man: — if he will hear the Message from the Christ
    within.

        *   *   *

And high above
In dark blue Southern skies
There glitters Blessed Cross of Holy Stars;
The Everlasting Emblem of the Wisdom
And the Law; which made the Universe
By Trigon and the Square, surrounded by the Circle.

        *   *   *

Red-blended, like the Ruby,
Did drops of Sacrifice descend
Upon the trembling Earth, and blend
And gleam within the tears
That lay in agony
Upon the Countenance
Of that great Son; and sear
Our Minds which hear —
Within — the Sigh of Anguish,
Torn from out His Holy Breast,
When, pierced by sword and spear
He breathed: —
"My God, my God, why hast Thou forsaken me?"

        *   *   *

Or later on, the Mind with Him rejoices;
When in a gust of jubilation
He speaks the Final Words: —
"Oh, Thou, my God: How I am Glorified!"

VISION 7
THE SYMBOL OF THE CROSS

Beneath the wonderful Symbol in the heavens, the Messenger and Ma-u and Ma-uti stood for a while in silence; heads bowed and eyes filled with tears.

Then Neteru-Hem took them by the hand, and, smiling farewell to the Guardians of the Well, proceeded towards the white marble buildings which glistened in the distance.

The air was fragrant with the scent of flowers and vibrant with their lovely colours, as slowly they walked amongst that glory; deep in thought.

"Would you like to attend a lecture on the symbolism of the Cross, my children?" asked the Messenger.

"Oh, please, Messenger, we should love it! " cried the two.

When the buildings were reached once more, the Messenger entered one of them, taking his guests with him.

In a large auditorium, on marble seats, a vast audience was listening to one of the priests, who, dressed in a flowing white garment, was in the middle of delivering a lecture. Neteru-Hem, and Ma-u and Ma-uti seated themselves silently and followed the priest's discourse with attention from the part he had reached when they entered.

... "and it therefore makes no difference how we interpret the cry from the Cross: 'My God, my God, why hast Thou forsaken me?' "or," continued the priest: " 'My God, my God, how Thou dost glorify me!' — for there is very great Truth m both these renderings."

"Both these things happen in the great Initiations, and the sufferings of Jesus in the Garden of Gethsemane, His Crucifixion and His Resurrection are indicative of a very high form of Initiation, namely, the Fourth, when the Candidate attunes with the nirvanic plane, after having been gradually prepared and developed in the buddhic consciousness during the stages following the first three Initiations.

"As you know, the Fourth Initiation is, as it were, a midway point on the path, and there may be seven more incarnations, or lives between the Fourth and the Fifth. These latter incarnations—if they do occur—follow each other rapidly, as the Initio ate no longer needs the interludes of rest in the Astral Worlds between these Incarnations. He is the Arhat; the worthy, capable, venerable or perfect man who has reached a very high level of evolution.

"The Fourth Initiation is always a crucifixion, for it seems as if all friends forsake the Initiate for a time, and he stands alone in his grief; but this part of the path is also his glorification—when in the midst of traitors, who twist his every word and distort his every act; when all good things are taken from him, and all his beloved ones desert him' when a shower of abuse descends upon him, and his holiness is despised and rejected; and when he even wavers in his own inner belief in the Love of his Father in Heaven, and seems to be cut off from all Divine Inspiration and comfort—when, in spite of all these tribulations, he still keeps his faith and turns to God, *then* comes the moment in which he is truly glorified, and the Father stretches out a loving hand which raises up the sufferer and translates him from the path of blindness and despair to that of Sight and Bliss. The agony of the Cross has then become the beatification of the Higher Mind and Soul, and a choir of jubilation resounds and echoes in all the Heavens, for the Initiate has learned to stand apart from all external things and conditions, and he knows triumphantly that he is *One* with the Logos and that all else is illusion and temptation. The Cross has been conquered and the shining Pathway stretches straight before him and continues for all Eternity, leading from Glory to Glory.

"In the Christian teachings the three first Initiations are symbolized by the Birth, the Baptism, and the Transfiguration; and the ancient Egyptian formula for the Fourth runs: 'Then shall the candidate be bound upon the wooden cross, he shall die, he shall be buried, and shall descend into the underworld; after the third day he shall be brought back from the dead.' As the old proverb says: 'No cross, no crown.'

"The sign of the cross as used in religious services and by individual members is a very powerful form of blessing and gives protection against the dark forces, especially if a strong sense of peace is held in the mind, together with a sincere wish that all the world may share in the benediction.

"The invocation of the Father, the Son, and the Holy Ghost, combined with this sign of power, adds to the potency of the sign, which has various aspects as a symbol.

"The active Logos is represented by the Greek cross — that with arms of equal length. The second aspect of the Logos, God the Son, the Second Person of the Blessed Trinity, is typified by the Latin cross; that with the longer stem. It is used in all benedictions and exorcisms to impress the will of the Priest upon the person or object with which he is dealing. Great power flows through this Sign; it may flow from one Priest to another; or from on High into the Priest himself at certain parts of the Service; or upon a man when he makes the sign upon himself. It helps him to remember that when the Name is invoked no evil shall befall us. In this way it becomes a kind of miniature creed, for as we touch in succession the forehead, the solar plexus, the left shoulder and finally the right shoulder, we remember that Christ came down from the Father to the earth-plane; that He descended from earth to the lower Astral World (the left-hand path), and proceeded from there to the right-hand of the Father in Heaven; there to dwell in glory for ever.

"It is well to use this sign often, for a man is sometimes forgetful of the protection he derives from dwelling upon the ideal worlds of God, which aids him to drive away all unwholesome thoughts and influences, especially when he is tempted to give way to irritation, or selfish and other undesirable thoughts. The man whose mind dwells always on the higher levels may not need these reminders; but there are very few such men, and the average person will receive much help from this small ceremonial action, which will drive away all unpleasant influences and retain all that is good.

"Man lives amongst a host and vast hordes of other beings; and although they are invisible to the average man, they are none the less powerful. Whenever a sign of power is made, or a word of power spoken, these beings gather around the actor or speaker, hoping that he will send out thoughts and vibrations that will be enjoyable to them. They need such vibrations; and the higher the thought, word, or sign, the better are the classes of elemental spirits it will attract. You will realize that this does not apply to the angelic beings, who, being perfect and pure, do not need the aid of any vibrations man can send out.

"Each time he feels that he has lost touch, for the time being, with the utter love, peace, understanding and unity of the Father, a man should make the Holy Sign of the Cross, and ask the Lord to turn to him again and give His protection and guidance. When reading the Gospels a man should make the sign of the Cross three times, and thus dedicate his mind, lips and heart to the work of spreading the Truth, and at the same time open up the three centres of the forehead, throat and breast to the holy influence which is about to be poured out. In this way the Holy Writings become centres of Force, surrounded by an aura of reverential and grateful thought, which will stimulate the mental and spiritual faculties. If before the opening of the Book he makes the sign of the Cross upon it, he will unlock the door of the treasure house from which the Holy Wisdom will flow and enter his being. It will bring the lower mind into harmony with the higher, and thus it aids the work of the Master within, in that he can now pour out the vials of Wisdom upon (the thirsting mind, seeking union with the Soul, which leads to God's Domains.

"After Prayer, or study of the Holy Writings, a final sign of the Cross should be made, which will produce a general intensification of the work done, and strengthen the link between Mind and Soul.

"The great power of this sign is illustrated in the rites of Consecration of a Bishop when the Consecrator makes the Sign of the Cross, first over the heart of the newly consecrated Bishop, then over his hands, and says: 'Mayest thou abound with the fullness of spiritual blessing,' making the sign of the cross again at the words 'spiritual blessing,' This opens fully the direct line of communication between intuition and emotion, so that if and when the intuition is developed, it may flash at once into what is intended to be its expression in physical life.

"There is also the pectoral cross of the Bishops. Upon this are mounted seven jewels corresponding with those embedded in the Altar-stone (as, for instance—in Liberal Catholic usage). When the Altar jewels glisten in response to the downpouring force, the jewels of the pectoral cross also flash. The Bishop's consecrated ring also plays a part by reacting upon the jewels in the altar and cross, resulting in an inter-weaving and intensification of these forces, which again is the means of an outpouring of force upon the congregation and upon the world in general.

"In the Roman Church this pectoral cross, or crozier, often contains a relic of some sort, possibly a fragment of the alleged wood of the True Cross.

"The seven jewels are connected with the seven Rays and when any person comes near the Cross, the jewel connected with the Ray on which this person manifests, flashes out, and if he is at all receptive that person may receive a great outpouring of strength and help.

"The Bishop wears this cross—in the Roman Church he wears it outside the mozetta, but inside the mantelletta—because, as a consecrated link with his Lord he becomes a highly charged battery, as it were, and the pectoral cross acts as a prism for the forces which should always be flowing through him. Its action during the various services of the Church is therefore very powerful. It acts upon the Bishop, it receives from him, and its rays pour out power upon the congregation. The clairvoyant can see these glowing rays, which are an expression of the triple Spirit in the Christ, and can be perceived only through the reflection of the same spirit in a highly developed man.

"The various forms of the cross, such as the ansated Egyptian cross, or Tau; the Jaina cross, or Swastika; and the Christian cross, are the symbols of generation. The *Taurus*, or Bull, was sacred in every Cosmogony; as with the Hindus, the Zoroastrians, the Chaldees, and the Egyptians. In the same sense the Serpent was the symbol for Wisdom.

"The cross in its Egyptian and Christian form is a combination of the triangle and the square, and it is the cube unfolded. The triangle and the square, being the universally accepted glyphs of male and female principles, Show the aspect of the evolving deity and can be seen shining in the heavens as the Southern Cross, which has the same significance as the Egyptian Crux Ansata.

"The numbers 3 and 4 counted on the cross show a form of the Hebrew golden candlestick in the Holy of Holies; and the numbers 3 and 4 combined give us the days in the circle of the week, as 7 lights of the Sun. This week of 7 lights, or days, of the Sun was the origin of the month and the year, and so it is the time-marker of birth. By the attachment of a man to the cross the symbol is completed, and this was made to coordinate with the idea of the *origin* of human life; hence its form, which is identical with the Tree of Life.

"The cross, as well as the circle, are universal symbols, and stand foremost on the list of the long series of signs which contain within themselves and express, great scientific truths. These two symbols are as old as humanity itself and have a direct bearing upon psychological as well as physiological mysteries.

"There always have been thinkers who have endeavoured to explain the mystery of the central point of the cross by making it the symbol of the Universal Presence. This is an erroneous conception; for the Boundless and the Infinite can never be limited and conditioned to one centre; nor can the presence of Christ upon the Cross be interpreted as the individualization of God in the central point of *that* Cross in the person of Jesus Christ.

"The four arms of the decussated cross, ✕ and of the Hermetic cross, pointing to the four cardinal points, which, by bending the ends of the cross turns it into the Swastika, presents one of the oldest symbols of the Ancient Races. The Swastika implies that the central point is not limited to one individual, however perfect. It further tells us that The Principle (God) is in Humanity and that Humanity is in IT, as well as all other beings and things which have existence; dwelling within God as drops within the ocean; the four ends, which point towards the four cardinal points, lose themselves in infinity, and the bending of these ends point to the cycles of reincarnation which the human mind must undergo before it can lose itself, or be projected into the mind's conception of infinity, Heaven, or God.

"The riddle of this cross is contained within these two sentences from the Smaragdine Tablet of Hermes: 'Separate the earth from the fire, the subtle from the gross . . . Ascend . . . from the earth to heaven and then descend again to earth.' Thus the Swastika cross becomes a circle, containing the cross, and we see at once that it has become the astronomical cross of Egypt, ⊕ the circle containing the Tau, ⊤ , in double aspect and joined together; one of the stems pointing down-ward, the other upward, ⊥/⊤ = ✛ . The separation of earth from fire, and the subtle from the gross, means the separation of the vital spark and the mind from the mortal, material body, after which they *'ascend'* from earth to 'heaven'; and descend back again after a while to earth into the next incarnation. The Tau in its perfect form shows the perpendicular descending male ray, $|$ and the horizontal line of matter, ——, the female principle; whilst the circle above the horizontal line completes the three attributes of Isis, ⚲, and is the glyph of the Sacred Egg.

"The so-called Christian Cross is of much more ancient origin, and we find Ezekiel stamping the foreheads of the men of Judah, who feared the Lord, with the *Signum Thau*, as it is translated in the Vulgate. The ancient Hebrews used the sign in this form: ✗ and in the Egyptian hieroglyphics it appears in the usual Christian form, ✝, and it is called *TAT*, the emblem of stability. It appears in Revelation where the Alpha and the Omega, or Spirit and Matter, $|$ and ——, the first and last — spirit being before matter — stamps the name of his Father on the foreheads of the *elect*.

"When Moses ordered his people to mark their doorposts with blood, in order to distinguish them from the doomed Egyptians, they used the mark of the Tau for that purpose, the identical Egyptian handled cross, with the half of which talisman Horus raised the dead, as can be seen on a sculptured ruin at Philae. The Swastika and the Tau are found everywhere; they can be seen on the statues of Easter Island, in Old Egypt, in Central Asia, in pre-Christian Scandinavia.

"In 'Numbers' you can read: 'Crucify them before the Lord against the Sun.'

"To crucify before (and not *against*) the Sun is a phrase used in the Initiations of Ancient Egypt and India, where the Initiated Adept, after he has successfully passed all the Trials in the Mysteries of Initiation, is attached, or bound, not *nailed*, on to a couch in the form of a Tau: — ┬ .

"There he remained in this state for three days and three nights, during which time his spiritual Self was said to 'confabulate' with the 'Gods,' descend into Hades, Amenti, or Pâtâla, all according to the country in which the Initiation took place, and serve and perform acts of charity to the invisible Beings in these Worlds, whilst his body remained on the Tau in a Temple crypt, or subterranean cave; or, as in Egypt, when it was placed in the Sarcophagus in the King's Chamber of the Great Pyramid, and carried during the night of the approaching third day to the entrance gallery. Here the beams of the rising Sun struck full on the face of the entranced Candidate at the appointed hour, when he awoke to be initiated by Osiris and Thoth, the God of Wisdom, by means of the sacramental words uttered by the Hierophant-Initiators; words spoken ostensibly to the Sun — Osiris, but in reality to the Spirit-Sun within, to enlighten the newly-born man.

"The Universal Soul, the material reflection of the material Ideal, is the source of life of all beings and life-principle of the three Kingdoms. This was 'septenary' with the Hermetic Philosophers and with all the ancient Sages; being represented as a sevenfold cross, the branches of which stand for light, heat, electricity, terrestrial magnetism, astral radiation, motion and intelligence, or consciousness of Self.

"The sign of the cross was used as a mark of recognition among Adepts and Neophytes long before Christianity adopted it, and the Neophytes were called 'Chrests.'

"The sign of the cross employed Kabalistically, represents the opposition and quaternary equilibrium of the elements.

"When the Initiate or Priest made the sign of the cross, he placed his hand against his forehead and said: *'To thee belong'* then he carried his hand to his breast and added: *'the kingdom,'* then to the left shoulder: *'Justice,'* then to the right shoulder: *'And Mercy.'* Then he joined the hands and said: '*Throughout the generating cycles — Tibi sunt Malchut et Geburah et Chesed per Monas*. The other version was given to the neophytes and the vulgar, who Were not aware of the first formula.

"The initiation in which the cross was used to lay the aspirant upon was known in South America by the early races living there. Carvings have been discovered there on the crest walls of the mountains, where in a series of drawings the form of a man springs from a cross and *vice versa*, so that the man can be either taken to be the cross, or the cross to be the man.

"There is also a form of initiation in Which a huge golden cross appears in a vision, which cross slowly turns around and reveals the upright form of a black elemental in the form of a man with arms spread wide. He bows to the initiate and silently awaits his commands. This is a test; for if he will, the initiate can command the elemental form to perform certain duties and obey his orders. If he does so, he is in great danger at once, but if he remains silent the form will fade away and the danger is past. The cross within the circle — ⊕ — is also called the mundane cross, and it is the sign of the origin of human and animal life. When the circle is taken away and only the ✝ is left, it means that the fall of man in matter is accomplished. The cross within the circle symbolizes pure Pantheism, and has the same meaning as the Tau within the circle, or the Jaina cross or Swastika. The Tau is the oldest form of the letter T and it was the glyph of the Third Root-Race until the day of its symbolic Fall; when the separation of the sexes by natural evolution took place and the figure became ⊖, or sexless life; modified or separated. Later on in the Fifth Race it changed again into the Egyptian emblem of Life, ☥, and still later into the sign of Venus, ♀.

"In the Western Kabala the sign ⊕ is called the 'Union of the Rose and Cross'; the symbol of pregenitic Kosmos; the great mystery of Occult Generation.

"The symbol of the Rose upon the Christian Cross represents the Soul of man (in reality the Mind) within the human body, according to the usual interpretation of this symbol. It really refers to the Mind, as I said, being crucified upon, or within the human frame, in order to grow an flourish there and become worthy of its ultimate union with the Divine Soul through accumulated experience and Wisdom gathered on the Path of Evolution.

" 'May the Rose bloom upon your Cross,' is an old Salutation; a kindly wish; and a brotherly Blessing.

"The ansated Egyptian Cross is the symbol of the *female-male*, Isis-Osiris, the germinal principle in all forms, based on the primal manifestation applicable in all directions and senses. In the kabalistic teachings the 'Tree of Life' is the ansated cross in its sexual aspect. The word Otz, meaning tree, composed of two letters in Hebrew, the value of which are 7 and 9, represents the holy feminine number 7, and the number 9 of male energy.

"With the Egyptians the number 7 was also the symbol for *life* eternal, and the Greek letter Z is but a double 7 and the initial letter of *Zab*, 'I live,' and of Zeus, the 'Father of all living.'

"Further meanings of the ansated cross ☥ are 'an oath,' 'a covenant,' and the circle on top of the Tau is the same as the hieroglyphic Ru, ⌒, set upright. This hieroglyphic sign means door, gate, mouth, place of outlet, and here it denotes the birthplace in the northern quarter of the heavens, from which the Sun is reborn. Therefore, the Ru of the ansated cross is the feminine symbol for birth-place in the North. It was in that quarter of the heavens that the 'Mother of the Revolutions,' the Goddess of the Seven Stars, gave birth to time in the earliest cycle of the year.

"The earliest shape of the ansated cross, or Ankh-cross, is the Ankh-tie, ⚲, a loop containing both the circle and the cross in one sign. It represented the circle made in the northern heaven by the Great Bear, which constituted the earliest year of time. The Ru of the Ankh-cross was continued in the Cypriote R, ⌒, and the Coptic Ro, ⲣ. The Ro again was carried into the Greek Cross, ⳨.

"The Ankh-tie is also found under the name of Pâsha, a chord which the four-armed Indian God Shiva holds in the hand of his right back arm, and the Ru sign is found as the third eye of a Mahâyogî, in the posture of an Indian ascetic.

"The Tau is the Alpha and the Omega of the Secret Divine Wisdom, and it is symbolized by the initial and final letters of Thoth (or Hermes), who was the inventor of the Egyptian alphabet. The Tau was also the final letter in the alphabets of the Jews and the Samaritans, who called this letter the 'end,' or 'perfection,' 'culmination,' and 'security.'

"When a cube is unfolded, ✛, its six faces will form a cross, and we find four squares for the upright part and three squares for the cross-bar, making *seven* in all. Four is the symbol of the Universe in its potential state, or Chaotic Matter; and it requires spirit to permeate it actively. In other words, the Triangle has to quit its one-dimensional quality and spread across that matter, thus forming a manifested basis on the three-dimensional space, so that the Universe shall manifest intelligently. This, the unfolding of the Cube achieves, and hence the ansated cross as the symbol of man, generation and life. In Egypt Ankh signified 'Soul,' 'Life,' and 'Blood'; or the *ensouled, living* man; the septenary.

"To return once again to the cross in the form of the Swastika, I would say that few symbols are more frought with real Occult meaning than that glyph. It is symbolized by the figure 6 and like that figure it points to the zenith and the nadir, to North, South, East and West. The Unit is found everywhere and is reflected in all and every unit. It is the emblem of the continual evolution of the 'Wheels,' and of the Four Elements, the Sacred Four, in their mystical as well as their cosmical meaning, and its four arms are intimately related to the Pythagorean and Hermetic Scales. On it the trained and initiated one can trace the evolution of the Kosmos with mathematical precision, and the relation of the Seen to the Unseen, as well as the first procreation of man and species. It is the most philosophically scientific of all symbols and the most comprehensible. It is the summary in a few lines of the whole work of creation and evolution, from Cosmotheogony down to Anthropogony, from the unknown God to the electron, whose genesis is as unknown to Science as is that of the All-Deity Itself. That the ancient Sages knew this is proved by the fact that the Swastika, is found heading the religious symbols of every old nation.

"In the Chaldean Book of Numbers it is the 'Worker's Hammer'; it is the 'Hammer' in the 'Book of Concealed Mystery,' which striketh sparks from the flint — or Space — and these Sparks become Worlds. It is Thor's hammer, a magic weapon forged by the Dwarfs against the Giants, or the Pre-Cosmic Titanic Forces of Nature.

It is at one and the same time an Alchemical, Cosmogonical, Anthropological, and Magical Sign; with seven keys to its meaning.

"Applied to the microcosm, Man, it shows him to be a link between Heaven and Earth, the right hand pointing to heaven, the left pointing to earth. It is the key to the cycle of science, divine and human; and he who comprehends its meaning fully is for ever liberated from the toils of the great Illusion, whilst the light that shines from under it is sufficient to dissipate the darkness of any human schemes and fictions.

"To the esoteric as well as the exoteric learned Oriental, it means the 'ten-thousand Truths,' which belong to the mysteries of the Unseen Universe and the Primordial Cosmogony and Theogony.

"In Tibet and Mongolia it is found on the heart of the images and statues of Buddha, and it is always placed on the breast of the defunct Mystics—as the ansated cross was so placed in ancient Egypt.

"There are two types of Swastika, and variations of same in design and position, etc. The one we are concerned with now is formed thus: ⊥⌐, with the upper arm pointing to the right. It is used in this form in all White Ceremonial Magic, Rites or Principles.

"But should it be reversed, with the upper arm pointing towards the left, the lower to the right, and so on, then it is an evil symbol. *Any* form of Swastika different from the 'White' type has to do with black and evil conditions and will bring disaster to the wearer or user.

"There are always two sides to all laws, as you know: good and bad; or positive and negative; and this applies to symbols as well as to everything else.

"In its perfect form the Swastika is used by the Occultists and Mystics of the 'Right-Hand Path.' It is the seal placed on the hearts of the living Initiates, and burnt into the flesh for ever with some, as a symbol and reminder that when they have learnt the secrets of the ten-thousands perfections they must never reveal them to the unworthy.

"The septary harmony of the cross in its so-called Christian form is analagous to the seven-piped flute of Pan, the emblem of the seven forces of Nature; to the seven planets; the seven rays that are reflected in the seven colours of the spectrum; the seven musical notes; in the golden Temple-Candlesticks of the Jews, with three sockets on one side and four on the other, making the number seven, the feminine number of generation; the six days of the week in Genesis, crowned by the seventh, which was used by itself as a base of circular measure.

"The circle, cross and seven are the first primordial symbols. Pythagoras and his followers regarded the number 7 as a compound of numbers 3 and 4, which they explained in a dual manner. To them the triangle was, as the first conception of the manifested Deity, its image: 'Father-Mother-Son'; and the square, the perfect number, was the ideal root of all numbers and things on the material plane. But the square was of secondary perfection; having to do with the physical worlds, whereas the triangle, the Greek letter Delta Δ was the vehicle of the unknown God. This was proved even in their spelling of God's name, Zeus, which was spelled Deus (Δεύς) by the Boeotians, thence the Deus of the Latins. This was the metaphysical conception of number 7 in relation to the meaning of the septenary in the phenomenal world; but for purposes of profane or exoteric interpretation the symbolism was changed. The triangle, or the number 3, became the symbol of the three material elements — Air, Water, Earth; and the square, or the number 4, became the principle of all incorporeal and unseen things and conditions.

"But for themselves the Pythagoreans regarded the number 7 as a compound of 6 and 1, the Senary and the Unity, and it became the invisible centre, the Spirit of everything, as there exists no hexagonal body without a *seventh* property being found as the central point in it. This number 7, of which the cross is the symbol, and the cross the symbol of the number 7, has all the perfection of the *unit* — the number of numbers. For, as, absolute *unity* is uncreated and impartite, hence number-less and no number can produce it, so is the *seven*; no digit contained within the Decad can beget or produce it.

"The Triangle with one of its points downwards, ▽, is the symbol of the Moist Principle and Water, the *first* Element, in which Fire was present in a latent state; as into

Water, or Chaos, the first seed of the Universe was thrown. The Triangle with one of its points upwards, △, is the symbol of Fire. When these two symbols are interlaced, ✡, they produce the so-called Solomon's Seal — which it is not, nor ever was, and this symbol produces all the ten numbers. With a point in its centre, ✡, it is a sevenfold sign, or septary; man, the cross, and so on. The two triangles show the presence of the Binary, or two; its triangles represent the number three; the two main triangles with the central point common to both yield the Quaternary, or four; the Quinary is traced by combination as a compound of two triangles and three sides to each triangle, making five; the six points represent the Senary, or number six; the complete sign itself is sevenfold, with its point in the centre, and therefore Septenary, which gives the number *seven*; this last number contains all others.

"When the Cube is unfolded and the Cross is formed it will be seen that the vertical stem, which is the male symbol, becomes a four-partitioned line; four being the *female* number, while the horizontal bar (the line of matter) becomes three-divisioned. This shows an apparent contradiction in terms, but, since the middle face of the unfolded cube is common to both the vertical stem and horizontal bar, it becomes neutral ground and belongs to neither, although both share it. The Male or Spirit stem therefore remains triadic, and the line of matter two-fold, and even number, and therefore female. The central point is the point of the union of male and female principles, or of Spirit and Matter: a symbol of *creation*. The numbers three and four, thus combined in the cross, give harmony to *both* and are the symbol of Nature's creative forces, and the central point is *Love Sublime*, Love in its highest aspect, equal to the Love of God Himself, when that Love is purified in Service, Sacrifice and Devotion. *Then* it will blossom forth on that central point like a Divine Rose, and its perfume will ascend to Heaven, immaculate in its aroma of Sanctity, Benevolence and Dedication.

"And all Nature will rejoice, and its melodious Voice will sound in union with the Music of the Seven Planets, swinging along their orbits, each blending its own ringing triumphant note with those of the rest, in perfect diapason.

"But although we may study every symbol, from the circle to the cross, from the Tau to the triangle and the square, and learn in this way the signs that point the way to evolution, we shall only see the effects, whilst the First Great Cause lies hidden still; a greater Mystery than ever.

"We may learn that from the Seed grows the genealogical Tree of Being, called the Universe, Three in One, the triple aspect of the seed, its form, colour and substance; but the force which directs its growth remains the ever unknown.

"What *is* this Vital Force, that makes the seed germinate, burst open and throw out shoots, then form the trunk and branches, which, in their turn, bend down and throw out *their* seed, which takes root and produces other trees? Yet there is an answer to the seeker who tries to fathom the mystery of that manifested Force, which lies latent within that same seeker too!

"You know that all physical and material phenomena are but illusions of the senses, aided by imagination. There is no such thing as a solid body on the material planes, for there is no substance there that cannot be made to become transparent by some 'ray'; so-called for lack of a better term.

"To those who possess clairvoyant sight these rays are not needed in order to pierce the veil of the material. When they switch on *their* 'ray' of clairvoyance, all things melt away and disappear; *actuality* is perceived instead of sensory scenes of illusion and imagination. The most solid seeming walls become like transparent glass; and they, and trees, plants, animals, and anything else material vanish, as if they never were — which they were NOT!'

"Please remember this when you follow the little demonstration I will now give; a small experiment which will show you how material life and being was first brought into existence. Let me add, before I commence, that you, and all human beings still on earth, can perform the same experiment: if you have the will and concentration to do so.

"Firstly, you must accept the fact that all that *is* on the material plane has *life*. There is no such thing as a dead substance there. Everything that can be felt and seen, or experienced in any way whatsoever has *life* — material life. If it had not you could not feel, or see, or sense it. The body of a 'dead' animal has *life*, a 'dead' tree trunk has *life*, a rock, a stone, a grain of sand, a snow-flake, a drop of rain — they all *live*. This applies to metals, minerals, chemicals and everything else you wish to mention. They *live*, and thrill and throb, and vibrate with LIFE!

"The four principal ingredients of this sort of life, or of physical nature, are: Hydrogen, Nitrogen, Oxygen and Carbon. They all have *life* of their own kind too!'

"Carbon is the *Basis* of all organic substances; Oxygen supports combustion, and is the *active* chemical agent of all organic life; Hydrogen bums in Oxygen and is the most *stable* of all compounds; it exists largely in all organisms; Nitrogen is an inert gas; it is the vehicle with which oxygen is mixed to adopt it for animal respiration; it enters largely in all organic substances. When these four principles are all together in any organic substance it needs only the addition of the vital spark, the living fire, to ignite the organism, and it can then develop and reproduce itself.

"I will show you this by *imaging* a simple cell; you can all do this if you try persistently."

So saying the lecturer stood silently in deep concentration, and in a few moments there floated in the air before him a small gelatinous ball, transparent and slightly phosphorescent.

"Here we have," he continued, "the first principle."

"Its symbol is the circle, ◯, the boundless circle, the No-Number, Zero; it is the symbol of darkness, unmanifested, and it only becomes a living number when another number precedes it. This is the germ—and to give it *life* it is necessary that the Ray of Light, the Divine Thought, flashes into it. Then the germ will become luminous with the Spark and its symbol becomes ⊙. Just as we can *image the* germ by means of thought power, so can we project our divine thought of Life into it."

He beckoned one of his listeners, who came forward.

"Now concentrate on this germ, if you will," he said, "and project from within yourself some of your own vital essence into it." The disciple did as he was told and presently a faint glow became visible, and a slow rotary movement began to revolve the little ball.

"Here you see a demonstration very similar to the action of the rotating psychic centres in an animal body," said the lecturer. "In order to show you how these germs evolve and reproduce themselves, I will speed up the process a little. Please watch carefully."

In a few moments there became visible a thin line which divided the cell into two parts, ⊖; each part retaining the glowing element within, and both, still connected, continuing their slow revolution. Then they slowly drew apart, both revolving round their own axis and also around each other; slowly filling out they grew into little balls, and now there were two; perfect in form and indistinguishable from each other. This process was repeated several times, until at last there was a number of these little germ-cells, all glowing with life and circulating like a universe in miniature.

"What you see here is a picture of the whirling atoms in the spiritual worlds. They are produced by Divine Thought, and the process of multiplication goes on for ever. To bring these creations into the material world the next step is the addition of an upright line, connecting the dividing line in the circular body with the lower half of the line of circumference; in other words, instead of a horizontal line we now find the Tau within the circle, ⊕. When this sign appears it means that, according to its path of evolution, the spiritual will now fall into material generation, or matter; for the upright line represents the male of the lower half, connected with the female part of the upper half; the two sexes being contained within one body.

"Then comes the next stage; that of the complete cross within the circle, ⊕.

"As in the psychic centres of the animal and human body the rate of revolution increases continually, the intensity of the glow becomes greater and greater until these little balls become whirling, flaming balls of power, and each cell contains a universe within itself. Thus the electrons of the material world are formed, and their combinations grow into bodies of plants, animals, and eventually the human race; according to the paths of evolution these electrons follow. The whole progress is summed up in the symbol of the circle containing the figure 1, ⊙. This refers to the ten celestial fruits, born out of the two male and female seeds, which at first are invisible to the material eye; being entirely spiritual before they take on the material body in which they manifest. This glyph is the symbol of the first Divine Manifestation, which contains every power of exact expression of proportion. The first circle is nought, the vertical diameter line is the First, or Primeval One; the Word of the Logos, from which spring the other digits up to nine—the limit of expansion. When the body

of man is complete in its animal form combined with the spiritual attributes we find the following principles. The four material principles of the human body are: —
1. The principle of animal desire, inseparable from animal existence; it is called Kama Rupa.
2. The vehicle of Life; which is an inert vehicle of form, which disappears soon after disintegration of the body; this is called Linga Sharîra.
3. The active power which produces all vital phenomena; this is called Life, or Prâna.
4. The gross matter of the body itself.

"Combined with these four human principles there is the triple aspect of the Deity. '
1. The unmanifested Logos, reflected from the Divine Cosmic Realms into the human spiritual Kingdom as Universal Spirit, or Divine Soul, completely conscious of its own Individuality in connection with each human being.
2. The Universal Cosmic Principle of Life, of which the human *Mind* is a small fraction, having complete Individuality or Personality, and consciousness of Self; that part of man's divine Spirit which comes into incarnation for the purpose of evolution until it has become worthy to join the Soul — its better half.
3. *Universal* active intelligence, reflected in *man's* intelligence, by which the Mind rises above the animal by evolution.

"These are the seven principles of man; the first four material, forming a square, the latter three spiritual, represented by the triangle; the sevenfold man, or septenary."

This was the end of the lecture, and Neteru-Hem and Ma-u and Ma-uti left the Temple, together with all the rest of the listeners, after thanking the lecturer for his discourse. When they arrived outside there was a magnificent display of golden clouds in majestic formations visible in the sky. Towards the horizon they shaded off in deep purples and mauves, and some were of a brilliant magenta and glowing deep cerise, whilst in between were patches of shining blue, like lakes and inlets, glittering between the vast assemblages of vaporous formations that hung aloft in splendid lustrous grandeur.

"How did you like that discourse, my children?" asked the Messenger.

"It has given us much to think about," replied Ma-u.

"But I should have thought that all these Souls who listened would have known all this already. Have they not spent many millions of years in their various incarnations on earth, and is it not true that they must have all knowledge before they can enter into these Divine Regions?"

The Messenger smiled and answered:—"Knowledge, which is so greatly esteemed upon earth, is no passport to the Heavenly Realms, my son. Nor is the ugliness of empty beauty, the shallowness of high ambition, the lowliness of a kingly throne, the poverty of great riches, or the sinfulness of prideful righteousness.

"Earthly intelligence is but stupid ignorance when compared with Heavenly Wisdom.

"To enter even into *these* Realms, which are not Heaven, but only the outer Courts of it, the Soul-Mind needs other attributes; such as the Wisdom of Simplicity; the Beauty of Love; the Elevation of Humility; the Riches acquired by unrewarded Service; the Purity of Trust and Faith in the Benevolence and the Protection of the All-Father-All-Mother.

"The shepherd who tends his flocks upon the hill-side; the peasant who this the patient soil; the mariner who sails the awesome deeps; they are much nearer to God than any man who prides himself upon his vast accumulations of wealth—often ill-gotten; or the man of might, who sits upon the chair of State and rules his subjects with the rod of iron and fear; or the intellectual, who only thinks in terms of material evidence and sneers at all that is of God and of the Spirit, because he cannot weigh or measure the extent of God's Divine Thoughts. All those latter men can never enter here; although they may explain and think they know all things on earth."

"But surely, those symbols which the lecturer used, being the tokens of Holy Wisdom, should be known before the Soul is worthy of entering here; is he not too ignorant to appreciate and understand his status in these spheres if he has not learned to use them?" asked Ma-u again.

"Symbols, my son, can be explained in a thousand ways; and they are only valuable in the hands of those who have acquired that state of Wisdom which enables them to use these symbols in the *right* manner; there is a great mystery behind these glyphs, but only the enlightened Soul can fully grasp their meanings. Once there were many wise men who had that Wisdom. They dedicated incarnation after incarnation for the sole purpose of evolving their minds in such a way that at last they began to see the true significance of these signs. And they had wonderful teachers, who knew how to choose and develop the right pupils for that purpose. Many tried to gain admittance to the Mystery Schools of old; but very few were admitted to these colleges; whilst fewer still reached the inner circle of the Higher Mysteries.

"Today there are hardly any of these High Initiates; fewer than there have ever been in the whole history of the present world cycle. For this reason the colleges, of which you have just seen an example, are established here; so that the purified ones shall be able to learn that Wisdom which it is so hard to acquire on earth.*

"When a human being has so evolved that he has the Light of Purity within him, then he may be allowed to enter and enjoy the bright and everlasting Day of the World of Astral Fire and attend the lectures; and the Angels will bless him.

---

* This was written about a year before the establishment of a truly great Occult School in Great Britain in 1940. The Author has since been privileged to study its wonderful Teachings.

"When the flower of Love Divine has opened its bud, and blooms within his heart without a thought of Self, he may enter here; and his loving Masters will embrace him and anoint him with the Emblem of God: a crimson rose upon his breast.

"When he has cherished his brothers and served without a hope of reward, then he can enter here and be the equal of those that served before; and they will kiss his brow in recognition of his noble Prince-hood.

"Such, my children, are the requisites for entering; and none that have them shall be turned away, for they shall be in Harmony with God, and the fruit of their virtues shall be Peace Profound."

"Then there is hope for all those who thus have ennobled themselves," said Ma-uti; "and how simple it really is to qualify for the sojourn in this happy clime."

"What is being taught in the other Temples?" asked Ma-u.

"Every subject the purified Soul-Mind needs in order to take his place in the Higher Realms," replied Nete-ru-Hem. "Would you like to attend some further lectures, my children?"

"Oh, *please*," they cried; and the Divine Messenger led them to the next building, where further instruction awaited them.

SAPPHIRE

Within the deep blue Dome of Night
The jewel Planets glitter —
Red and green and silver;
Reflections from the hidden Sun.
* * *

A mystic Symbol this of Life's Illusion,
Where real and unreal blend
With Actuality — Unseen.
* * *

We dwell within the Temples of the Spirit,
Erected by the Master Builders
Of the Bright Universe of God.
* * *

And Wonder upon Wonder is around;
Created deep within the Rhythm
Of the spinning Wheels Above,
Below, Without, Within the Realms
Of their Imagination:
Inspired with Love Divine.
* * *

Reflections of Reflections;
Essences of Essences;
Holy Thought; descending low
And rising up again in mighty Arcs,
Be-rayed with blazing colours of the Life and Light
Brought forth by Shatt'ring WORD;
Which caused the Fire to leap:
Exalted, whirling, spinning, weaving
In Eternity of Time, and Space, and POWER.

VISION 8
THE KOSMOS

When Neteru-Hem and Ma-u and Ma-uti had taken their seats in the next lecture hall, which was crowded, the Messenger said: " The Teacher who will speak presently produces generally the actual scenes on which he is discoursing before his audience; or else he takes you to strange regions in Time and Space. Be not afraid, therefore, if some very weird things seem to happen during his lecture. He is a great master of his subject and has tremendous powers; you can, therefore, absolutely trust him and have no reason for alarm at whatever you may behold."

After these somewhat disquieting words, Ma-u and Ma-uti looked with no little apprehension at the Priest as he entered. He was a majestic-looking individual, with a very magnetic personality and an aura that was visible to everyone. It floated in great rings around him from a white light close to the body, which light gradually deepened into a beautiful blue; this again became surrounded by a ring of orange; then a ring of mauve; then lavender; and then a deep crimson ring from which radiated every colour imaginable in living streams of brilliant fire. Stricken with a sense of deepest reverence and awe, Ma-u and Ma-uti stared speechlessly at him; amazed by the stateliness of this marvellous Being.

The shining rays streamed out from him unceasingly and filled the whole hall with a bright effulgence. It drew out from all those present a glittering response in soft beams of colour emanations, and the whole effect was so astonishing and stupendous that no words can describe it.

The only one present who did not respond in this way was the Messenger. Cold and immaculate in his pure white presence, he sat beside Ma-u and Ma-uti; utter Master of Himself and the functions of his auric radiations. Yet, it was a divine snowy whiteness; so spotless and unblemished that it outshone the warm colourings of all the irradiance in that audience of vital, sentient forms.

Ma-u and Ma-uti felt that in the frosted crystal immaculateness of the Divine Messenger was concentrated all the light and the warm colourings of the Teacher and the others; protective, safe, and holy.

And now the lecturer commenced:

"Our subject is the formation of the Kosmos,* and although it is only possible to give an outline of its building from the first formative Thought of the Supreme Being onwards, we venture to presume that there may be some interesting and even awe-inspiring moments, when we consider some of the Divine Wonders of the Inspiration of the Unknown God-Head: the Supreme Deity.

"This Highest of all Gods, whose dwelling-place is on a level so far removed from all that can even be guessed by the Logoi, the Creators, themselves, that nothing can be known about Him, the Mahat, the Highest Entity in the Universe. There is no diviner Entity beyond Him, and He will never be absorbed, as the Logoi are absorbed, at the end of a Mahâmanvantara, to emerge again in the next Cycle of active Creation. We can be *conscious* of that subtlest of all matters of which His Being consists, however, and this Consciousness is the Kosmic Seed of Superkosmic Omniscience; which has the potentiality of budding into the Divine Consciousness, which can raise Man up into the highest Realms of Celestial existence and Wisdom.

"The whole of a Kosmos, or Solar System, and the whole of a Universe as well, is contained within the Auric Envelope, which contains the whole scheme of the evolution of a manifesting Universe and all the Beings and conditions therein.

" 'What lies beyond this Auric Envelope?' you may ask.

"Beyond that Envelope there are other Universes without end, so unimaginably many, and so vast, that it is impossible to conceive their existence or their nature. There is no end to Eternity or to Boundless Space.

---

* 'In our terminology a Kosmos is a Solar System; a Universe, a group of Solar Systems. Deity is the Supreme God of the Universe; a Supreme Hidden Logos is the Lord of a Kosmos.

"But these wonders need not be considered by us in this discourse; nor can we consider the final dissolution of the Kosmos.

"What then is the first step in the acts of Creation and evolution? It is the division of the Vault above from the Abyss below, and the formation of seven circles, each containing a creative God within; the Heavenly Mansions, or Seven Zones. In this way a Kosmic or Solar System is prepared, seemingly complete in itself, arising from a single Supreme and Concealed Logos, and sustained by His Life through the medium of the Seven Creators; one in each Zone.

"An example of this is our own Solar System, of which the Sun is the lowest manifestation of the Logos as it acts as the centre of His Kosmos. It is the life-giving, controlling, regulative, co-ordinative, all-pervading central power. It reflects visibly the highest state of the *Universal Presence*, the Supreme Deity, and exhibits the first, or lowest, state of the seventh.

"All central Suns in every Kosmos are in their physical or objective substance the lowest state of the first Principle of the Breath, or the Word; or may be called the lowest state of the physical body of the Logos. They pour forth the Life of the Lord to His Kosmos, and all the physical forces and energies are but transmutations of the vital fluid of the Supreme Deity passing through, or reflected by, the Sun.

"We may term the Sun the Heart of the physical Kosmos, which again is reflected in its spiritual counterpart by the light of the Moon. The Sun is thus the material, male representative and principal part of the physical Kosmos, and the Moon the symbol of the spiritual and female part. The latter is also the dwelling-place of the spirits of men.

"For these reasons the Sun has stood as the symbol of the Creator in many of the ancient religions; this referring to the physical creation of the Kosmos in general, and, with man, to the earth and all that is in it, in particular.

"The Moon, on the other hand, has always been the symbol of the Divine Lady, the Mother of the Gods, the Holy Spouse of God the Supreme.

"When the Logos appears, this appearance heralds the birth-hour of a Kosmos, and the One manifested Life of the Kosmos *is* God, the manifested Lord.

"The Auric Envelope which contains the Kosmos within its shell, is exactly similar to an atom, which contains within its glowing outer covering a central sun, around which whirl a number of minute planets called electrons. Both Auric Envelope and atom are ovoid, or egg-shaped in form. For this reason the Kosmos is often referred to as the Auric Egg.

"As the huge planets of the Kosmic System within the Auric Envelope are each ruled by a Planetary Logos—God's own Viceroys—so are the minute planets within the atom also ruled by planetary Lords.

"Understand well that the terms 'huge' and 'minute' are only concepts of the mortal mind and have an entirely different meaning to God; just as Time and Space cannot be properly understood by the finite understanding of the human ego.

"The first requisite in the building of a Kosmos, therefore is the creation of the Auric Envelope. This is a material projection from God's spiritual mind; an image, a thought-form; obtaining material shape and substance by means of God's Will, which dwells in the Divine Light, from the radiance of which—it being in perpetual motion—comes the Breath, whence emanates the primordial Light in which is manifested Eternal Thought concealed in darkness; and this becomes the WORD of Creation. From this Word, or Mantram, not only the Auric Envelope, but the whole Kosmos comes into manifestation. For within the Envelope the Concealed Logos radiates a Ray which fructifies the germs of Sun and Planets in formation; and the Essence of this Ray expands, giving birth to Planetary Logoi, from whose Minds all things are born.

"Before the Planets are made there is Chaos; all the Essences of the future material worlds being in a state of flux; unformed. These are the 'Waters over which brooded the Spirit of God,' and all is darkness, needing the Breath of God to become Light. As the Auric Shell is lit up by that Light, the Word rings forth and comes into manifestation by the act of generation or production. What seems chaos to the human intellect is the eternal Root of Spiritual Wisdom. In this — the Waters of Life — are created, or re-awakened the primordial germs by means of the primordial Light. Thus, the Divine Spirit moves on the Waters of Space within the Auric Envelope and fructifies and infuses the Breath of Life into that germ, which becomes the centre in which the male planetary Logos is created; and from this the first Lord of Beings emerges and becomes the progenitor of mankind.

"This latter Lord is *not* the Absolute and Unknown Deity who contains the Universe within Himself, but a Logos who is connected with the procreation of species of a Planet or Globe. He becomes the Father of All, and between Him and the Infinite Deity stretches an Abyss; the Great Deep; the Great Mystery. And between Him and the Supreme Deity, there is the Hidden Logos; the Lord of that Kosmos.

"The seven Kosmic Planes are formed in the following manner: — First and highest is the 7th Plane, represented by the Auric Envelope; then is made the 6th Plane, called the Alayic-Prakritic, the Heart of the Spirit of the World, Anima-Mundi, which is an aspect of God the Unknown. Primordial Substance is still in a latent pre-cosmic state of undifferentiated subjectivity. At a certain moment it receives the impress of Divine Thought and becomes receptive of the male aspect of the Hidden Logos, and its Heart opens. The Primordial Substance becomes separated and differentiated, the Ray enters — an immaculate conception — and the Trinity of Father, Mother and Son is born and transformed into the Quaternary — Father, Mother,

Son, as a Unity, and the *Life* which radiates from the summits of the unreachable, concealed God. Thus the three principles needed for every body to become objective are Privation (which is the host of prototypes impressed in the Astral Light), Form, and Matter. The Ray is the Life Principle, producing the Living Manifestation. Thus Alaya, as it is called, is the original base, and an eternal ever-becoming, and it *is* before all else.

"The next Plane is the 5th, or Mâhatic Plane. This is the Plane of the creation of the senses and has to do with the *nascent* Centres of Force, intellectual and physical; the rudimentary Principles of nerve force; and the nascent Apperception of the lower Kingdoms, such as the third order of Elementals, who are succeeded by the objective Kingdom of minerals in which this apperception is entirely latent, to re-develop only in the plants. It is the middle point between the two lower and two higher Planes of the *esoteric* Kosmos.*

"The 4th, or Fohatic Plane, is the Plane of conscious Force, of constructive force; it contains all force. The cosmic atoms are set in motion by Fohat, and cosmic consciousness acts on it. Fohat is the Light which emanates from the One Source of energy. Fohat is called the Builder of the Builders, the Force that He personifies having formed our Septenary Chain. On the Cosmic Plane He is behind all such manifestations as light, heat, sound, adhesion, and so on, and is the 'spirit' of electricity which is the Life of the Universe. Fohat is the guiding Spirit of intelligent Law and Sentient Life. He is no personal god, but the emanation of the powers behind him, and he is the Messenger of the primordial Sons of Life and Light.

"The 3rd Plane is the Jaivic. This is the Plane of Jiva, also called Prâna, the Life-Principle. Jiva pervades everything and is present wherever there is an atom it can act upon. If there were not a particle of matter it could act

---

* Therefore Planes One and Two must *both* be considered as exoteric, and this is correct.

upon, it would be quiescent—dead. The action of Fohat upon a compound, or even upon a simple, produces life. When the action of Fohat is withdrawn from a living body, the Life-Principle—Jiva—is withdrawn also; but it retains its grip on the atoms and molecules which form the previously living, sentient body.

"The 2nd Plane is the Astral Plane, and the 1st, or lowest Plane is the objective material Plane.

"Here, in these Planes within the Auric Envelope, we have all the necessary ingredients of spiritual and material natures to give Life and Existence to a complete Kosmos.

"From the outside, the oval sphere of the Auric Egg shows a greater or lesser amount of radiance, according to its individual potency; and it is this glow which is perceived by the Higher Beings from other Planes; just as man might behold an atom. The future oceans lie asleep in the Waters that fill it; and also the continents, seas, mountains, planets, Gods, elementals and mankind.

"Thus lies the incipient chick concealed within the egg just laid; with all its potentialities in a latent state.

"Each of the seven Planes within the Auric Envelope contains, and corresponds with, an antetype, one on each Plane; which in their turn correspond to the seven states of matter and all other forces in Nature. It contains the spiritual aroma of every personality to come, and in it is the material from which the Adepts form their Astral Bodies and the Gods build theirs; from the highest to the lowest. After the physical death of the Adept, he remains within the purer Astral Regions and there he lives and moves, in possession of all his principles except the Astral and physical vehicles, which he no longer needs, having acquired a spiritual instrument of manifestation of a much higher and finer nature. But always he still exists within the Worlds contained within the Auric Egg; just as the man who has not yet reached Adeptship dwells in the lower spheres surrounding the earthly planet between his incarnations.

"And Prâna, or Jiva, pervades all the space within the Egg. As the life-principle it has no number, although it emanates from the Fourth Plane, but each number of the seven Planes might be applied to it. Moreover, Kosmos is not produced by number or through number, but by following the proportions of numbers, or geometrically.

"The seven Planes are also mirrored in the seven colours of the prism; each colour having a definite number or rate of vibration, similar to the seven Planes.

"The outer shape of the Auric Envelope is the same as the faintly pale violet aura around an atom or a man; a transitory emanation, preceding the formation of all living bodies in the same manner as the Auric Egg precedes the formation of a Universe within it.

"Within the Auric Egg of a Kosmos are reflected all the thoughts, words, and deeds of man, and it is the storehouse of all his positive and negative powers received and given out at his will; and also of every thought and every potentiality, 'which then immediately becomes a potency.

"The Auric Fluid within the Egg is a combination of the Life and Will principles, and it is contained in all things and beings from which it flows and emanates, visible in the Auric Light which surrounds all bodies. It can be directed at will by the Adept and its flow restrained or intensified.

"The Auric Egg also receives the impression of all the higher Gods as well as of the Devas and other Angelic Beings. Its Essence is in perpetual motion during the constant correlations and transformations which take place within it.

"Outside the Auric Egg is the Spiritual Sun, or Universal Spirit, which ensouls the boundless Universe, whether within or beyond Space and Time. The Essence of that Divine Ego is pure flame, to which nothing can be added and from which nothing can be taken. Therefore, it is never diminished by its countless creations, detached from it like flames from a flame. The flames of that Spiritual Sim bum for ever, and are inexhaustible.

"The Auric Egg is present in every form, plant, or animal; they each contain a replica of it; and the Auric Egg is to Man as the Astral Light is to Earth; or the surrounding Ether is to the Astral Light, or Akâsha—the Universal Soul—is to the Ether, which it surrounds as a supersubstantial Essence. In short: Akâsha is. the substance which forms the Auric Egg—pure abstract substance. We have dwelled upon some of the principles of the Auric Egg and considered it from different angles on account of its enormous importance in the Kosmic Scheme. It cannot be studied too much, for all else in the Kosmos depends upon it.

"You will appreciate that vast as a cosmic system with its Sun and Planets seems to us, it is nothing but a drop in the Ocean of the Great Universe. Nevertheless, and in spite of our inevitably vague and shadowy conceptions of its origin and constitution, we all show the God-like natures within us, by our ability to assign to it its proper place in the Universe, and grasp a broad idea of the relative magnitude of the whole system, of which our Planetary Chain in which we are functioning at present is but a small fragment. We manifest this also when we acquire some conception of the respective periods of its evolution and the evolution of all things and beings upon these planets and in the Astral and other Regions.

"When the Supreme Logos Manifests Himself in the first Construction of the Auric Envelope, he brings with him the fruits of a past Kosmos; namely, the mighty Spiritual Intelligences who are to be his co-workers and Agents in the Kosmos now to be built. The highest of these are the 'Seven,' who are called the Logoi; each in His place is the Centre of a definite part within the Kosmos, just as the Supreme Logos is the Centre of the whole. These Seven Beings, who are in the Sun, are self-born from the inherent power in the matrix of Mother-substance, and the energy from which they spring into conscious existence is the Breath of Absoluteness This spontaneous coming into conscious existence proceeds from the One manifested Life — which in itself is a reflection from the Absolute — and the One manifested Life is the Supreme Logos Himself.

"It is from this primary sevenfold division that our Kosmos takes on its sevenfold character, and all the subsequent divisions in their descending order reproduce this seven-keyed scale. Below each of the seven Logoi come the lower Hierarchies of Intelligences who form the governing Body of God's Kingdom. They are known by many names, and there are also the vast hosts of the builders, who shape and fashion all forms after the Ideas that dwell within the treasure-house of the mind of the Hidden Logos. These ideas pass from Him to the Seven, each of whom plans out His own Realm, under the Supreme direction of that God; but who give to each of their various own and separate Realms their Own individual colouring. These Seven Realms are called the Laya centres, and are the seven Zero points, which indicate starting points at which the scales of reckoning of differentiations begin. From the Laya centres, beyond which we may perceive a dim metaphysical outline of the 'Seven Sons' of Life and the Seven Logoi of the Hermetic and all other Philosophies, begins the differentiation of the elements which enter into the constitution of our Solar System.

"Whatsoever quits the Laya State becomes active Life; it is drawn into the vortex of Motion, but before evolution begins, nature is in a condition of Laya; or of absolute homogeneity. No World, and no Heavenly body could be constructed on the objective plane, had not the Elements been already sufficiently differentiated from their primeval Ilus, the Mother resting in Laya, which is a synonym for Nirvâna. It is, in fact, the Nirvânic dissociation of all substances, merged after a Life-Cycle into the latency of their primary conditions. It is the luminous but bodiless shadow of Matter that *was*; the realm of negativeness — wherein lie latent during their period of rest the active Forces of the Kosmos that is *to be*!

"But, you must also understand that the Worlds are built neither upon, nor over, nor in the Laya Centres; the Zero-point of a Laya Centre being a condition, not a mathematical point. A Kosmos is the realm of planetary evolution of a stupendous character, the field in which are lived out the stages of a life of which a physical planet, such as Venus or Mars, is but a transient embodiment; the same can be said of each Laya Centre.

"In each Laya Centre there is an Evolver, or Ruler, whom we may think of as a Planetary Logos. He draws from the matter of the Solar System, which is poured out from the Central Hidden Logos Himself, the crude materials He requires, and elaborates them by His own Life-energies; each Planetary Logos thus manipulating the matter of His own Realm in His own special manner and drawing it from the common stock, as it were. As the atomic state in each of the seven planes of His Kingdom is identical with the matter of each sub-plane of the whole Solar Kosmos, continuity is established throughout the whole. Atoms, change their combining equivalents on every planet, although they themselves are identical. Each atom has also seven planes of being, the same as our Kosmos.

"But when we compare an atom to a Kosmos, we should also remember that the Solar System is as much the Microcosm of the One Macrocosm, as man is the former when compared with his own Solar Kosmos. As each atom has seven planes of being, or existence, so each of these planes is governed by its specific laws of evolution and absorption. In each atom there is internal as well as external heat; remember this when presently we discuss Fohat.

"Before we proceed with our discussion of the Kosmos, let us consider the atom a little more closely; it will be useful to arrive at a better understanding of the Kosmos later on.

"You know that each atom has a central sun around which whirl a greater or lesser number of planets, called electrons. To man, the electron is so small that it is as yet beyond the domain of any visual detection; for no light-waves are small enough to be used in forming an image. Even if lenses for y-rays were available, these would be 100 times too long in wave-length to be used in viewing the electron. In spite of this, modern science on earth has succeeded in establishing the charge and mass of the electron; this 'new' constituent, as it is called! At the same time science thinks that the electron has not any of the properties of 'ordinary' material. One is tempted to ask: 'when does matter — as such, become extra-ordinary?' Science has two modes of approach to the problem of *size*. One is the study of collision processes; but here science is at once confronted with a difficulty; for first of all the electron is the lightest particle of matter known, and furthermore it is charged with electricity. Therefore, the only way to study it would be by comparison with other electrons. But the charges of electricity make this very difficult, for there are no laws known which' are infallible when applied to the collision processes between electrons. Some guesses can be made as to their dimensions, however, from collision processes between the more massive atomic constituents; and it is assumed that an electron must have a radius, defined by the change of inverse square law of repulsive force to one of a higher order, within certain limits of the centre. Since ordinary inertial matter is made up of nuclei, and electrons are separated by distances, large compared to the dimensions of electrons and nuclei, it is futile to attempt to describe the space dimensions of these particles in terms of the criteria applied to ordinary objects. Therefore, another line of attack is sought in order to find the size of an electron. It is assumed that the electron is not a piece of matter with ordinary gravitational inertia or mass . . . whatever that may be.

"But since the electron *has* inertia, or mass, it is believed that the whole mass or inertia lies in its electro-magnetic field. This field, comprising its hypothetical lines of force, extends through all Space.

"Here again, we have a subconscious allusion to Fohat.

"If the electron is to be set in motion it must be accelerated. Such acceleration means that an electro-magnetic disturbance, readjusting the force fields about an electron, must be propagated throughout all Space with the Velocity of light. This leads to the concept that the inertia of the electron may lie in its opposition to the readjustment of its status in nature. This inertia can be calculated from laws derived from Maxwell's laws of electro-dynamics. The resulting equations then give the radius of a sphere within which all the electrical charge of an electron must reside to possess the observed inertia, or mass, which has been measured.

"In other words, assuming that all the inertia of an electron lies in its electro-magnetic field, one can calculate the radius of a sphere in which its charge must be concentrated to give the observed mass.

"In like manner it has been discovered that the electron has a magnetic momentum of its own, and that it rotates in an orbit. A tendency for two electrons to pair has also been manifested, as in the case of two with a parallel and anti-parallel spin.

"Thus, science is beginning to discover the Occult Laws which have been known for thousands of years, and it now comes to the conclusions of the Ancients, though using different methods and technical terms, when it seeks to penetrate into the mysteries of nature.

"As above, so below; and as below, so above.

"The phenomena observed in the study of electrons are similar to the phenomena in the creation of a Kosmos.

"But Science does not realize that Matter is not an independent reality, and neither is Spirit. Both are symbols or aspects of the Absolute; which constitute the basis of conditioned Being, whether subjective or objective.

"This applies also to the Elements mentioned by Plato and Aristotle. They are the same as *the incorporeal principles* attached to the four great divisions of our Kosmic World; and in the ancient times they used a species of Magism, a psychic paganism, and a deification of potencies: a spiritualization which placed the believers in a close community with these potencies. So close, indeed, that the Hierarchies of these Potencies, or Forces, have been classified on a graduated scale of seven; from the ponderable to the imponderable. This is a Cosmic graduation in the true sense; from the chemical, or physical, to the spiritual.

"Every atom in the Universe has the potentiality of self-consciousness in it, and is a Universe in itself and for itself. It is an atom and an angel. Each atom, and each entity must win for itself the right of becoming divine through self-experience; and Hegel, the Philosopher, sensed this when he said that the Unconscious evolves in the Universe only in the hope of attaining clear self-consciousness.

"This is why the Kabalah teaches that:—'The Breath becomes a stone; the stone, a plant; the plant, an animal; the animal, a man; the man, a spirit; and the spirit, a God.

"Now we have to consider what happens when the Concealed Logos has constructed the Auric Egg; the groundwork of the coming Kosmos. First of all He sends a Ray from Himself into the primordial Kosmic Matter; this is the first manifestation. At the second stage the dual male and female abstract Forces are personified. From this Male-Female Personification of Matter is separated the Son, or third Principle, which consists of seven Forces, called the Creative Powers.

"These Seven Powers, or Sons, born from the Mother, or Darkness, are represented by the seven Planets. The Sun is not amongst these Seven as He came before the others.

"The Father—or Space—is the Eternal Cause of all, the Incomprehensible Deity whose invisible Robes are the mystic Root of all Matter, and of the Universe; the Robes consisting of undifferentiated Matter. It is this pre-Kosmic Root-substance which is that aspect of the Absolute which underlies all the subjective planes of Nature.

"The Universe is worked from within outwards. Every external motion, act or gesture, whether voluntary or mechanical, organic or mental, is produced and preceded by internal feeling or emotion, will or volition, and thought or mind. So also is the whole Kosmos guided and controlled, and animated by an almost endless series of Hierarchies of sentient Beings, each having a mission to perform as agents of the Cosmic Laws.

"The Universe, as well as a Kosmos, is in reality but a huge aggregation of various states of consciousness entirely compounded of septenary groups; for the capacity of perception exists in seven different aspects, corresponding to the seven conditions of matter, or the seven properties or states of it. Therefore, the series from one to seven begins in the Esoteric Calculations with the first manifested principle, which is number one if we commence from above, and number seven when reckoning from below, or from the lowest principle.

"The genesis of Gods and men takes rise from one and the same Point; which is the One Universal, Eternal and Absolute Unity. In the sphere of objectivity and Physics it becomes Primordial Substance and Force; male and female. In Metaphysics it becomes the Spirit of the Universe, or Cosmic Ideation; sometimes called the Logos; who is the apex of the Pythagorean Triangle.

"To each of the seven chief planets there is a Regent, who supervises the creative work of the Terrestrial Spirits. These Regents are the self-born Seven Sons of God, the Dhyân Chohans, or Pitris, who are the Fathers of the Chhâyâs, born from the brilliant bodies of the seven Lords. The Chhâyâs are called the Shadows, as you know.

"Of the seven Lords three were Holy and good, but four less Heavenly, and full of passion; and the Chhâyâs, the Phantoms, were of the same natures as their Fathers. Thus we account for the same differences in human nature, which is also divided in seven gradations of good and evil.

"Out of Space the Regents are born, and Space is called the Mother, before its cosmic activity, and *Father-Mother* at the first stage of awakening; after which it becomes Father-Mother-Son.

"And so all the planets are ruled by forces, originating in the first Seven Lords; which forces operate for good or evil, and imprint their likeness on our minds, nerves, marrow, veins, arteries, and our very brain-substance at the moment of drawing the first breath. We remain in their charge for as long as we live; and as the planets whirl in space, so change our conditions of mind, which can lead us on to overthrow states or individuals, according to the manner in which these potencies direct and influence us, *and we react- to them*!

"When we speak of Divine Thought, that does not imply the idea of a Divine Thinker, but of Absolute Being; with the past and future crystallized in an eternal Present.

"God is not Ego, or Non-Ego, nor is it consciousness; but though not itself an object of knowledge, it is capable of supporting and giving rise to every kind of object and existence which become objects of knowledge. It is the One Essence from which starts into existence a centre of energy. And so there is only one religion: the Worship of God's Spirit.

"The first condensation of Kosmic Matter took place about a central nucleus, its parent Sun; but *our* Sun (as well as all the other planets later on) detached itself from the rotating mass of that parent Sun as it contracted, and he is therefore the elder brother of the planets — being the first-born — and *not* their Father.

"After the Ray drops into the great Kosmic Depths at the first thrill of the new Dawn, it re-emerges as the New Life to be until the end of that Kosmic Cycle; the Germ of all things and Beings; the generator of Light and Life; the Blazing Dragon of Wisdom; the Word, the Thought Divine. He who bathes in this Light but once will never again be deceived by the Veil of Illusion. The Germ of all things—'the World Germ—is that matter which consists of spiritual particles, or supersensuous matter, existing in a state of primeval differentiation. In Theogony every seed is an eternal organism, from which evolves later on a Celestial Being—a God.

"The Globes to be, appear first as a long trail of Cosmic dust, or fire-mist, which moves and writhes like a serpent in Space. This Truth became the symbol of the ancient Nations, where it was taught that the Spirit of God, moving on Chaos, did so in the shape of a fiery serpent, breathing fire and light upon the primordial waters, until it had incubated cosmic matter and made it assume the annular shape of a serpent with its tail in its mouth; a glyph which symbolizes not only eternity and infinitude, but also the globular shape of all the planetary bodies formed within the Universe from that fiery mist.

"Chaos, Logos, and Kosmos are but the three symbols of their synthesis—which is Space.

"Matter is only Primordial at the beginning of every new reconstruction of a Universe; but as it is indestructible it is also eternal—without beginning or end; and it is the Root of all material phenomena; the Divine Essence, or Substance.

"The radiations of Matter are periodically aggregated into graduated forms; from pure spirit to gross matter, and in its abstract presence is the Deity Itself; the Ineffable and unknown ONE Cause. The 'Darkness' which 'was upon the face of the earth,' is the absolute Light, and the Root of the seven fundamental Kosmic Principles. In this sense it is the Deity Itself, as we stated before. Chaos is a shapeless liquid principle without form, sense or perception.

"Spirit is the all-vivifying intellectual principle.

"From the union of the two sprang into existence the Kosmos; chaotic Matter becoming its body. From this union with Spirit, matter obtained sense and 'shone with pleasure,' and thus came into being the first-born Light; the triangle of Spirit, Intellect and Matter; or Soul, Mind and Body.

"This triangle can be applied to all inner and outer manifestations within and without the Kosmos.

"Thus the Sun itself is three in one; namely, the *Central Sun*—hidden from all but the Initiate—being the universal cause of all, Sovereign Good and Perfection, the emblem and inner being of the Concealed Deity.

"The second part of the Sun is paramount Intelligence or Wisdom, and it has dominion over all thinking beings. The third part is our Sun, visible to mankind and manifesting in the material Kosmos.

"In other words, the *inner* Sun is the Grand Logos of the Universe, from whom the pure energy of Solar Intelligence proceeds; which is the Spirit Force which produces all through the visible Sun, and never operates *through* any other medium.

"For this reason the divinely inspired Philolaus, the Pythagorean said that: 'The sun is the mirror of Fire, the splendour of whose flames by their reflection in that mirror is poured upon us, and that splendour we call image.' Thus he referred in a hidden, or occult manner to the central, spiritual Sun, whose beams and effulgence are only mirrored by the central star of the Kosmos—our visible Sun.

"The triangle with one point upwards also represents the three higher planes of the septenary Kosmos, and the Divine and formless Worlds of Spirit. Whereas the triangle with one point downwards represents the Archetypal World, the Intellectual creative world, and the substantial or formative World. The rays from these three latter worlds descend upon the seventh plane—our Earth—the physical or material world.

"The two interlaced triangles ✡ with a dot in the centre could therefore be a symbol of the earth, surrounded by the six higher planes, from which all inspiration and all energy is poured down upon the seventh.

"The three higher planes being the abodes of divine and formless spirit cannot be known or understood by the beings on the physical plane; and the Archetypal World is not the world as it existed in the *Mind* of the Deity, in the sense that the Platonists gave to it, but in that it is the first model of the World to be, which will be followed and improved upon by the Worlds which succeed it physically. But these latter Worlds, being projected in the material, lose in purity to the same extent that they gain in material solidity.

"The seven fundamental transformations of the Planets, or of their constituent particles of matter are: —
1. Homogeneous.
2. Aëriform and radiant, or gaseous.
3. Nebulous.
4. Atomic, ethereal — beginning of motion, hence of differentiation.
5. Germinal, fiery, differentiated, but composed of the germs only of the Elements in their earliest states; they having seven states when completely developed on our earth.
6. Four-fold, vapoury; the future Earth.
7. Cold — and depending on the Sun for Life and Light.

"The first seven Lords are referred to in the Phoenician mythology as the seven Sons of Sydik, or Melchizedek; identical with the seven Elohim, the seven Kabiri, or the seven Sons of Ptah of the Egyptians, and the seven spirits of Ra in the Book of the Dead. In Assyria they were the seven Lumazi, or the seven Hi; always they are seven in number; the first-born — parentless — of the Mother in Space, or of Chaos.

"Space and Time are the sources of all that IS.

"From being powers of the air the Gods were promoted to become time-keepers for man, and seven constellations were assigned to them. These first seven Stars are not Planetary, for they are the leading Stars of seven constellations which turned round in the Great Bear in describing the circle of the year. There are two such constellations, the second being the Lesser Bear, whose stars were called the seven heads of the Polar Dragon; or the Beast with the Seven Heads of Revelation and the Akkadian Hymns.

"Plato has said that: 'Ideas are objects of pure conception for the human reason, and they are attributes of the Divine Reason.'

" 'God formed things as they first arose according to forms and numbers.'

"All the laws of nature assume the form of quantitive statement; this affirms the Pythagorean doctrine; for numbers are the best representations of the laws of harmony which pervade the Kosmos and the Universe.

"It has been said that the World is, through all its departments, a living arithmetic in its development, a realized geometry of unity in multiplicity; the one evolving the many and pervading the many. St. Paul confirms this when he says that: 'Out of Him and through Him and in Him all things are.'

"The mystic Decad $1+2+3+4 = 10$ is a way of expressing this idea. One being God, or Spirit; two, matter; three, combining Spirit and Matter and partaking of the nature of both, and four, being the phenomenal World. Therefore, the Decad—or Ten—is the sum of all and involves the entire Kosmos.

"The Seven Principles are reflected in man and they are the seven powers in nature, physically; and the seven Hierarchies are reflected ethereally and spiritually within the Mind of man.

"The combination of powers and the attunement of the Microcosm will give the geometrical equivalent of the invocation: '*A-UM MA-NI PAD-ME HUM:*

"The seven cycles of evolution in sevenfold Nature are:—

1. The spiritual, or divine.
2. The psychic, or semi-divine.
3. The intellectual.
4. The passional.

5. The instinctual, or cognitional.
6. The semi-corporeal, or astral.
7. The purely material, or physical.

"Thus we see creation proceeding in seven steps, and the first creation is the primordial self-evolution of that which has to become the Divine Mind, conscious and intelligent; esoterically the Spirit of the Universal Soul. It proceeds from the One who is neither first nor last, but All. Exoterically, it is the work of the Supreme One; a natural effect of an Eternal Cause.

"The second Creation is the period of the first Breath of Differentiation of the Pre-Cosmic Elements, or Matter. At this stage the second Hierarchy appears; the Dhyân Chohans, or Devas, who are the origin of form; the Rishis who become the informing Souls of the Seven Stars. This is during the Fire-Mist Period, the first stage of Cosmic Life after its Chaotic state, when Atoms issue from Laya.

"The third step is the Organic Creation, or the creation of the Senses. It abounds with the quality of goodness and is the creation of the first Immortals.

"The fourth Creation is the organic evolution of the Vegetable Kingdom from the latent Kingdom of Minerals. It is the middle point between the three higher and the three lower Kingdoms, which represent the seven esoteric Kingdoms of Kosmos, and of Earth.

"The fifth Creation is that of the germ of awakening consciousness and apperception, already faintly traceable in some sensitive plants on Earth. It is the creation of the animals. It is at this period of evolution that the absolutely eternal universal motion, or vibration, that which is called in *Esoteric*, language the 'Great Breath,' differentiates into the primordial, first manifested Atom.

"The sixth Creation is that of the Divinities who are the Prototypes of the First Race of Man. They are the Fathers of the coming Race in the — at that period — far distant future.

"The seventh Step is the creation of Man, complete in every way, and fully responsible for all his thoughts and actions.

"Let it be well understood that in Occult Metaphysics there are two Gods. The One, Unknown, unreachable Plane of Absoluteness and Infinity about whom nothing *can* be known; and the second God on the Plane of Emanations. This cannot be emphasized too often. The former God—the Supreme Deity—can neither emanate nor be divided, as He is eternal, absolute and immutable; but the second, being the reflection of the First One, *can* do so, for He is the Supreme Logos in the Universe of Illusion.

"From the ONE Essence comes into existence a centre of energy—who is called the Word and is also the Divine Christos, who is eternal in the bosom of His Father.

"And again: the Word, or Verbum, is the female Logos, and is represented by the Noumenal aspects of Light, Sound and Ether.

"As the Logos reflects *all* in the Universe of Plerdma, so man reflects in himself all that he sees in *his* Universe, the Earth.

"After the Breath, or the Word, has rung forth, Kosmic Matter scatters and forms itself into Elements, for the Great Breath is the perpetual Motion of the Universe in the limitless, ever-present Space.

"The Breath of Heaven—or the Breath of Life—is also in every animal, in every animated speck, and in every atom. But none of those have—like man—*consciousness of* the Highest Being. The Breath is the OEAOHOO, the whirlwind of ceaseless Cosmic Motion, the Force that moves it. Therefore, there is a regular contraction and expansion of the infinite and shoreless ocean of Matter; a pulsatory movement, which causes the universal vibration of all atoms. There is no rest or cessation of movement in Nature. But the Planets move by their *own* internal motion, for there is a plurality of forces proceeding from the Deity which possess inherent powers of their own.

"During the great mystery and drama of Life, the real Kosmos is like the figures thrown upon a white screen in the form of shadows. The actual figures and things remain invisible, and in this manner men and things are but the reflections on the white screen of the realities, or rather, the *actualities*, which lie behind the Great Illusion.

"Nothing is created; it is only transformed. Nothing can manifest *itself* in this universe, from the greatest planet or star down to a rapid thought, that was not in the Universe already. On the subjective plane there exists an eternal *is*, an eternal *being*, in spite of many spiritual transformations; and on the objective plane there is an ever-becoming, because all is transitory. At the same time, Nature, taken in its abstract sense, cannot be 'unconscious,' as it is an emanation from the Absolute Consciousness, and thus an aspect of it on the manifested plane.

"*Actuality* is hidden behind the Cosmic Veil, which is the mighty expanse of Cosmic Matter. It is an organ in Kosmic Creation through which radiate the Energy and Wisdom of the Unknown first Creator; who is as unknown to the Logoi of the Kosmos as He is to ourselves, and as the Logoi are unknown to mankind.

"Only in the light of Consciousness, and of mental arid physical perception can practical Occultism throw the Logoi into visibility by means of geometrical figures, which, when closely studied, will yield not only a scientific explanation of the real and actual existence of the Seven Sons of Divine Wisdom—which proceed from the Unknown First God and the Light of the Kosmos—but it will show that these Seven Sons, and their numberless emanations, centres of personified energy, are an absolute necessity, without whom there could be no Kosmos at all. This, in spite of the fact that esoterically all the forces, such as light, heat, electricity, etc., are called the Gods.

"There are three Chief Groups of Builders in the Kosmos, and three Chief Groups of Planetary Spirits; each Group again being divided into seven sub-groups.

"The Builders, or Creators, are the representatives of the first Mind-born Entities, the first Seven Sons. The first group rebuild every Kosmic System after each Night of Brahmâ, or period of 4,300,000,000 years; the second group is known as the Architects of our Planetary Chain; and the third group consists of the Progenitors of our humanity.

"The Planetary Spirits rule the destiny of men who are bora under one or other of their constellations.

"When we speak of Æther and Primordial Substance, we touch upon the Alpha and the Omega of Being; yet they are but two facts of the One Absolute Existence. Æther is the Astral Light, Primordial Substance is Matter. At the same time Æther is one of the lower principles of Primordial Substance.

"In Cosmic Substance we can spiritually *sense* Divine Thought by the numberless manifestations of Matter; the meaning of Divine Thought can never be explained nor defined in any other way — and there are but few who can sense it thus.

"That which we here discuss, however, relates only to our own visible Kosmos; the secrets of the *Universal* Kosmos are so deep that even the Highest Angels of our Kosmos could not know them, as they have never penetrated the mysteries beyond our boundaries that separate the millions of Solar Systems, each a Kosmos in itself, from the great Central Sun. We can only say here that each Universal Kosmos, or galactic system, has a central Sun, and with the 100-inch telescope there can be found evidence of between 50 and 100 millions of extra-galactic nebulae which are outside our own system in an area of approximately one-thousand million light years in extent. The great central Suns in these galactic systems cause Fohat to collect primordial dust, clouds of which can be observed in the Milky Way, in the form of the so-called dark nebulae; and this dust is concentrated in the form of balls, which are impelled by Fohat to move in converging lines, and finally to approach each other and aggregate.

"Being scattered in Space, without order or system, the World-Germs come into frequent collision until their final aggregation, after which they become comets. Then the battles and struggles begin. The older bodies attract the younger, while others repel them. Many perish, devoured by their stronger companions. Those that escape become Worlds. These are the 'battles of the Flames,' the 'wars in heaven,' the 'wars of the Titans,' and the struggles between Osiris and Typhon, of which you can read in the various mythologies.

"Fohat, the constructive Force of Kosmic Electricity, is said, metaphorically, to have sprung from the Brain of the Father and the Bosom of the Mother, and then to have metamorphosed himself into a male and a female; in other words polarized himself into positive and negative electricity.

"As the Father-Mother is identical with the Primordial Æther, or Astral Light, so is Kosmic Electricity cosmically Fohat — the Son — homogene with the Astral Light before the Sun was evolved from it. Fohat hardens and scatters the Seven Brothers; which means that Electricity forces into life and separates primordial substances, or pregenetic matter, into atoms, which are the source of all life and consciousness.

"It is through Fohat that the ideas of the Universal Mind are impressed upon Matter, and it is electricity *plus* intelligence. You should know that Fohat is seen in the Aurora Borealis and Australis, both of which manifest at the very centres of terrestrial and magnetic forces. The two poles are the storehouses, the receptacles and liberators of cosmic and terrestrial Vitality, which is Electricity, from the surplus of which the Earth, had it not been for these two natural safety-valves, would have been rent to pieces long ago. The phenomenon of the Polar lights is accompanied by, and productive of strong sounds, like whistling hissing and cracking.

"Thrilling through the bosom of inert Substance, Fohat impels it to activity and guides its primary differentiations over all the seven Planes of Cosmic Consciousness; the seven Protyles, or seven Prakritis of Aryan antiquity; or Natures serving severally as the relatively homogeneous bases; which in the course of the increasing heterogeneity, in the evolution of the Universe, differentiate into the marvellous complexity presented by the phenomena on the planes of perception.

"Fohat is the Fiery Whirlwind, the Messenger of the Will of the Primordial Seven Sons of God.

"Fohat is also the bridge by which the Ideas existing in the Divine Thought are impressed on Kosmic Substance as the Laws of Nature. It is the dynamic Energy of Kosmic Ideation, and also the intelligent medium, the Thought Divine, transmitted and made manifest through the Dhyân Chohans, the Architects of the visible World. It is also the mysterious link between Mind and Matter, the animating principle, electrifying every atom into life. In the unmanifested Universe Fohat has nought to do with Kosmos yet, for the latter is not born and still sleeps in the bosom of the Father-Mother. He is but an abstract philosophical conception or idea, for the time has not arrived when he produces anything by himself. He is simply a potential creative Power. When the time of awakening arrives, Fohat is said to produce seven Laya Centres. This means that for formative or creative purposes the Great Law stays, or modifies, its perpetual motion on seven invisible points within the era of the manifested Universe. Laya is the Zero-point or line, the realm of absolute negativeness, or the one real absolute Force, the neutral axis; not one of many aspects, but its centre. A neutral centre; the dream of those who would discover perpetual motion.

"Invisible intra-cosmic motion is eternal and ceaseless; cosmic motion, subject to perception, is finite and periodical. Only the intra-cosmic Soul, the ideal Kosmos in the immutable Divine Thought, never had a beginning; nor will it have an end.

"Fohat being everywhere, it is also in the Astral World, where it is used by the Minds which dwell there between incarnations in order to vivify their Astral Bodies during their time of existence there, just as human bodies are vivified by it in the shape of the Fiery Spark. Fohat there acts as a sort of protective and life-giving cloak, or aura, to the Astral Body as well.

"Fohat is closely related to the One Life, or the Supreme Deity. The Powers of Fohat are placed in the Circles of the Equator, the ecliptic, and the two parallels of declination, or the tropics, to preside over the climate.

"In the ancient Scriptures you can read that Fohat and His Sons were Radiant as the noon-tide Sun and the Moon combined; and that the Four Sons on the *middle* Four-fold Circle, 'Saw their Father's Songs, and *heard* his solar-selinic Radiance.'

"This means that the agitation of the Fohatic Forces at the North and South Poles of the Earth, which result in a multicoloured radiance at night, has in it several of the properties of Æther, Colour and Sound. Sound is the characteristic of Æther; it generates Air, the property of which is Touch; which by friction becomes productive of light and colour.

"Fohat, then, is the personified electric power, the transcendental binding unity of all cosmic energies, on the unseen as on the manifested planes; the action of which resembles—-on an inverse scale—that of a living Force created by Will, in those phenomena where the seemingly subjective acts on the seemingly objective, and propels it to action.

"Fohat is not only the living Symbol and Container of the Force, but is looked upon by the Occultists as an Entity; the forces it acts upon being Kosmic, human and terrestrial, and exercising their influence on all those planes respectively. On the earthly plane its influence is felt in the magnetic and active force generated by the strong desire of the magnetizer.

"On the Kosmic Plane, it is present in the constructive power that in the formation of things — from the planetary System down to the glow-worm and the lovely daisy — carries out the plan in the Mind of Nature, or in the Divine Thought, with regard to the development and growth of a particular thing or Being. It is, metaphysically, the objectivized Thought of the Gods, the 'Word made flesh' on a lower scale, and the Messenger of Kosmic and human Ideation; the active Force in Universal Life.

"In its secondary aspect, Fohat is the Solar Energy, the electric vital fluid, and the preserving Fourth Principle, the Animal Soul of Nature as it were, or — Electricity. We will go further than this and assert that Electricity is not only Substance, but that it is an emanation from an Entity which is neither God nor Devil, but one of the numberless Entities that rule and guide our World, according to the Eternal Laws.

"Science has also come to the conclusion that electricity is a tangible thing, with some of the properties of ordinary matter, and among them the ability to move; and in this manner it is also catching up with the ancient Occult Teachings.

"It knows that electricity may exist as separate electrons, protons, or positrons, or in collected charges of these entities, and that electric currents, for instance, present a variety of aspects.

"It knows of progressive motions of electrons in a conductor, which is called electric conduction, and of the two-way traffic of charged ions, called electrolytic conduction. The current may consist of a flight of electrons or other charged particles through a vacuum, or it may be a bodily movement of an electric charge, like that on one of the carriers of a static machine. It talks of displacement currents which are assumed to take place in a dielectric, or even in a vacuum, which accounts perhaps for the behaviour of electro-magnetic fields and radiation; but science has as yet no definite conception of the true nature of electricity, or Fohat in our terms.

"It is as great a mystery as that of gravitation, but in this instance there is *no* such thing as gravitation. Instead of it there is attraction and repulsion in the Kosmos, and this produces *balance*.

"The Sun is a huge magnet, and it has a tremendous magnetic field around it, in the same manner as all other heavenly bodies in our Kosmos have such magnetic fields, or the atom and all living and inanimate beings and things possess them.

"You will remember that I mentioned the attraction exercised when two electrons in an atom have an anti-parallel spin, when there is a tendency within these electrons to join. This applies also to the heavenly balls of incandescent matter, thrown off from the first central Sun during the beginning of the creation of the Kosmos. Some balls, in parallel spin, rapidly develop a magnetic field which protects them from any future collisions with other balls when shot off into Space at a tangent, and this repulses the rest and keeps them at their proper distance in Kosmic Space. These balls leave the Kosmos and become 'Comets'. The magnetic fields will seemingly bend light-rays, but actually nothing of the sort happens. This seeming disturbance of the straight path of a light-ray has led to many wrong conceptions and calculations on the part of some modem scientists, and it will be found later that the ancient teachings in regard to the nature of such and other phenomena are absolutely correct and that so-called 'modem' science is wrong.

"Kepler discovered, over 300 years ago, that the Sun was a magnet, although he had not discovered the laws of attraction and repulsion in Kosmos, which laws were called 'love' and 'hate' by Empedocles; having the same meaning as attraction and repulsion. These are no 'blind' laws, as Laplace thought; ignoring the presence of creative Forces, endowed with intelligence.

"The circle with a dot in the centre ⊙ could be the symbol of a planet with an aura, or magnetic field, around it; or an atom, or even the whole of our Kosmos, which itself possesses such a magnetic field in the form of the Auric Egg; or of the Earth with its surrounding magnetic field which reflects wireless waves and returns them to earth at a tangent; in other words the Ionosphere, or the Kennelly-Heaviside layer, from 100 to 400 miles above the Earth.

"This aura, in the case of human beings, can be opened at will, and then it can allow entrance to any forces or conditions with which the mind within the human body wishes to come *en rapport*. When the aura is kept in a closed condition by an effort of the *Will*, it can keep at bay all thought-forms, mental images from outside sources, or spiritual inspirations, whether good or bad. By opening the aura we can let in light or darkness, good or bad influences.

"When by constant concentration and meditation we produce around us such a strong spiritual field of protection, even material things, or other living beings, can be prevented from making material contact with us. This has often been proved in various ways, such as the cases when certain people are absolutely bullet-proof when a hail of shells rains around them during a battle-—they have what are termed 'charmed lives.' It is also demonstrated in the case of powerful magicians when they stand in the enchanted or magic circle, whilst a host of elementals vainly tries to reach them. It is also proved in the instances where even a loving thought will cast a protecting shell around a beloved one when in danger.

"In contrast to this we can, from within outwardly, project a strong thought-form through this aura or magnetic field, just as a sufficiently strong wave or current of electric matter or force could penetrate the Earth's Aura and soar into the Kosmic Spaces beyond and reach one of the planets of our Kosmic Chain. The luminous envelope around the Sun is called the photosphere or chromosphere; it is the very magnetic field, or aura, under consideration. It looks like mother-of-pearl and has been likened to the ocean on a tranquil summer-day, when its surface is slightly crisped by a gentle breeze. Within this ocean can be seen remarkable patterns, just as in the human aura. 'Sometimes they are lens-shaped, like willow leaves, crossing each other in all directions with an irregular motion, and assuming new shapes continually. These shapes are no less than 1,000 miles in length, and from 200 to 300 miles in breadth. These forms live, and produce heat, light and electricity, or Fohat, which is communicated to the ethereal medium in stellar space which conducts it to the planets. It is Vital Force, — Life and Energy. These Sun-fluids, or emanations, impart all motion and awaken all life within the Solar System, in harmony with the law of cyclic motion, designed from the beginning of the building of the Kosmos. These are immutable laws, but the motion is diverse and alters with every new cycle, and is regulated by the Intelligences within the Kosmic Soul. The creation of life by the Sun is as continuous as his light; nothing arrests or limits it. Actually these emanations are reflections.

"We may liken the Sun to the Kosmic Atom, which becomes seven Atoms on the plane of Matter, and each is transformed into a centre of energy. Each Atom becomes Seven Rays on the plane of Spirit; and the seven creative Forces of Nature, radiating from the Root-Essence, follow.

"The Atoms, emanated from the central point, produce within themselves two new centres of energy, which under the potential breath of Fohat, begin their work and multiply other minor centres.

These, in turn of evolution, form new roots; from men-bearing globes down to genera, species, and the classes of all the Kingdoms.

"The formless radiations, existing in the harmony of the Universal Will, and being what we term the collective, or the aggregate, of Kosmic Will on the plane of the subjective Universe, unite together an infinitude of Monads — each the mirror of its own Universe — and thus individualize for the time being an independent Mind, omniscient and universal. By the same process of magnetic aggregation they create for themselves objective, visible bodies, out of the interstellar Atoms. Thus, to the eye of the Seer, the Higher Planetary Powers appear under two aspects, the subjective—as *influences*, and the objective—as mystic *forms*, which become Presences; Spirit and Matter being *One!* For Spirit is Matter on the seventh Plane; Matter is Spirit at the lowest point of its cyclic activity; and both are *Illusion*.

"It is from the Sea of Fire, which is the Super-Astral Light, the first radiation from the Root, or the undifferentiated Kosmic Substance, that we derive *Astral* Matter; which is sometimes called the Fiery Serpent.

"Roughly viewed, the Monads may be divided into three distinct Hosts. The first, counting from the highest Plane are Gods, or Kosmic Spiritual Egos, the Architects of the Universe.

"The second are the Elementals, or the Monads, who form unconsciously the grand Universal Mirrors of everything connected with their respective Realms.

"Lastly come the 'Atoms' and material molecules, 'which are informed in their turn by their 'perceptive' Monads, just as every cell in a human body is so informed. There are shoals of such informed Atoms, which, in their turn, inform the molecules; an infinitude of Monads, or Elementals proper, and Countless Spiritual Forces—Monadless, for they are pure incorporealities, except under certain laws, when they *do* assume a form—not *necessarily* human. Only earth and water can bring forth a living being, for they form the *prima materia* and the creative female principle on the earth-plane. But they must first be impregnated by the Fiery Principle of the Sun, and the Spirit of the Sun, combined with the elements of matter, are the symbols of physical generation. Thus, the simple material cell, impregnated by the spirit will divide itself into two cells, and another being has been born in the mysterious way for which intellectual science cannot account. Within the cell germinates that consciousness which is the earliest manifestation of the causal consciousness of God. Minerals live, suffer from communicable diseases and reproduce their kind. Crystals move and exhibit generative processes similar to those of plants and they can be poisoned. These facts of nature have become known to the earthly scientists too of late.

"And all these beginnings of life occur on planets so infinitely minute that they become as awesome as the largest star in space. And whilst the proud pavane of time glides by, there are born the minute specks that will foregather and combine, and in the blood of animals there swarm multitudes of living entities. Four-and-a-half millions of tiny red cells, with lots of room to spare are afloat in the fluid of a cubic millimetre of blood! On a square millimetre, a million bacteria, measuring about one micron in diameter, such as for instance cocci, can be laid without much overlapping in a single layer of a thousand rows, having a thousand in each row. These make one-thousand-million cubic microns in a cubic millimetre.

"Two thousand millions of bacteria are normally present in a saltspoonful of soil, occupying one quarter of one per cent of the volume of the soil.

"And amœba by the trillion abound. Of no known shape of their own, they are like specks of living jelly; crawling about in their own peculiar amorphous manner, and extending any part of their bodies to enwrap particles of food. When in a resting condition in fluids they are spherical in form.

"Some kinds of bacteria develop flagella, by means of which they become *motile*, or can swim.

"Every human being or other mammal starts life as a single cell, the mammalian single-celled embryo being formed by the fusion of a male sperm-cell with a female egg. This has one nucleus, and when the nucleus and the cell which contains it divide into two, the halves are nearly — but not quite — identical.

"Still smaller are the viruses, or sub-microbes, or ultra-microbes. They may be defined as particulate bodies capable of causing infectious disease in animals or plants, and they are too small to be visible even with the best microscopes; nor is there any known filter through which they cannot pass.

"Whereas plants and animals die, microbes are potentially immortal. They only die by some violent death from a cause outside themselves. The reason is that microbes have nothing in common with the complex process of reproduction and recapitulation that is undergone by higher animals and plants. The microbes have nothing to recapitulate, being already at the lowest stage of evolution.

"The microbial cell is not only capable of independent existence, but can reproduce itself by division:—by dividing they multiply. Science does not yet know in detail what it is that induces a microbial cell to double itself by division. Science does not know either why some of the minute forms of life remain as they were in the Silurian epoch—such as the tabulate corals of that period, which are wonderfully like the millepore of our own seas—or the Foraminifera; Protozoa of the lowest type of life, which are the same today as they were so many millions of years ago, except for their now greater variety. Science is entirely ignorant of the Elemental Forces, under direct control of intelligent Entities, who build and mould, form and alter, and who have the secrets of all these wonders in their charge.

"Compare the human aspects or principles with the Kosmic aspects or principles, and the triple aspect of the Deity reflected from above to below. We find that the unmanifested Deity is reflected in the Universal Spirit; the Universal latent Ideation in the Spiritual Soul; and the Universal or Kosmic active intelligence in the human Soul. These are the three aspects of the Deity, reflected in man.

"We find that the Spirit of the Earth, Jehovah, Noah, or whatever other appellation you may choose, rules the Space containing Life, and His Kosmic or Chaotic Energy is reflected in the animal Soul; the Astral Ideation, reflecting terrestrial things is found in the Astral body; the Life-Essence of Jehovah is reflected in the Life-Essence of Man; and the Earth is reflected in the body.

"Everything that *is*, is double; mortal and immortal; material body and Astral body; Light and Darkness. Whatsoever is in the Mind of God is unalterable; all that is reflected upon Earth is subject to change. The earthly reflections can reflect back to Heaven by reaching out or going within.

"The things that are, exist first in the Spiritual Conception, and fall later on into generation on the material plane. In the Soul of God exists the Soul of the World to come; in the Minds of the Logoi exist the creative and intellectual faculties; in the Astral World is the formative or Astral world or body; from the physical body of the Gods come the reflected bodies of the material planets, things and beings.

"The seven globes of our Kosmos form a planetary ring or chain. This chain passes through seven distinct stages in its evolution, and they disintegrate and are reformed seven times during the planetary lives. Every such Chain of Worlds is the progeny and creation of another and lower chain, and its reincarnation, These seven incarnations make up the planetary evolution, the Realm of a Planetary Logos. As there are seven such Logoi, it will be seen that seven of these Planetary evolutions each distinct from the others, make up the Solar System. As it is described in one of the ancient teachings: —' From one Light Seven Lights; from each of the seven, seven times seven.'

"On each single globe evolve seven races of humanity, together with six other, non-human kingdoms, interdependent on each other. In the first round of the evolution of a globe, fire is the element, and the archetypal forms of minerals are brought down, to be completed in their densest form of the fourth round. In the second round air is the element and the vegetable kingdom is established, and in the fifth round it will reach perfection.

"In the third round there is the human archetypal form of man; ape-like and covered with hairy bristles. The archetypal forms of animals are brought down, and in the sixth round they will reach perfection. Water is the characteristic of this round. The fourth round is devoted to the archetypal forms of man as he is known today, to reach perfection in the seventh round. Earth is the element of this round; dense and in its most material form."

The speaker paused here, and, regarding his audience, stood still as if in deepest meditation. There was no sound or movement, but gradually the great hall seemed to darken, until only the shining and scintillating aura of the priest was visible and all other forms had faded away into nothingness. And presently even that radiant combination of glowing rings around him began to flicker and grow dim, until suddenly a deep and solid darkness and utter silence reigned.

In sudden fright, Ma-u and Ma-uti tried to take hold of each others hands, but to their great consternation they realized that not only could they not find each other, but that they had no material body left either, and to both it seemed as if they were afloat in a. vastness of inky blackness so immense that there were no boundaries to it anywhere.

Utterly alone they were in Space, shackled to the dark, unable to move or speak; two lost souls, petrified with terror.

And where was Neteru-Hem? Had he too forsaken them, or was he equally lost and helpless?

But after a while they remembered his warning before the lecture commenced, when he said:—' Be not afraid, he is a great Master and has tremendous powers; trust him, do not be alarmed.' And as soon as they remembered these words there shone in every direction a host of twinkling stars. They were above, below, and uncountable in their numberless millions; comforting with their friendly brilliant lustre; but there was no moon anywhere!

In the meantime, the silence was more dreadful than the loudest sound, though of unimaginable grandeur and power. Filled it was with awe and wonder, as if the Thought of God Himself was frozen, and His Whisper, which at times will reach the listening soul, was stilled for ever. It was the kind of silence in which mighty things are brooding; and thought builds up on thought with secret potency of unseen essence of the spirit of creative force, which raises mighty citadels and temples, bedecked with inspiration's glowing symmetry and grace, emblazoned with the glory of poetic exaltation. Yet it was lonely and remote, and filled with longing for that sweet companionship of sympathetic understanding which only kindred souls can give, one to another.

And still that dreadful vault of darkness spreading everywhere, no nearer bourn than those far stars, illimitable distances away; whilst in that silent void, immovable, Ma-uti and Ma-u awaited they knew not what; and once again a sense of dread foreboding rose up within their souls.

Without any warning an indescribable thrill is suddenly felt within the dark; a rippling wave of tremulous motion seems to agitate the mystic gloom, undulating through the black massed solitudes, and then a booming but melodious thunder shatters echoing through the wide expanse, but sonorous in its pealing; rousing . . . vast intensity of glory!

The WORD rings out in all the awful grandeur of the descant melody of Unknown Deity; Mighty Lord, beyond all comprehension, Holy beyond all Holiness, Sacred beyond all Sanctity; the Paraclete; the Highest Point of Blessed Trinity J beyond the consecrated depths of Wisdom of His Viceroys in the Kosmic Realms themselves.

Peal after peal, majestic thunder of the Word resounds within these catacombs of gloom. Impelling, awakening, until is felt a heavier tremor running through the seeming emptiness of Night; as if with mighty sweeps of monstrous pinions a million thousand-winged Giant Bats soar up from out the threat'ning caverns of the sullen mountain-chains of ebon death that seem to rise up from the deeps of Kosmic emptiness.

A hissing sound is heard; as if a regiment of savage horsemen, riding to assault, draw out in one concerted action curved scimitars from silver scabbards.

A swirling, undulating wave of unrest rolls in restless billows, rising from the boundless deeps, and heaving high towards the domes of stars so far away.

And still the Word Tings out; its seven times seven times seven syllables a-chant like tolling bells and Choirs of singing Angels, and throbbing of great drums, and from out the interstellar realms shoots forth a mighty beam of brilliant light, which penetrates the massed fortresses of darkness and of Chaos. Swift and sure it stabs the gloom, like gleam of ent'ring sword in quiv'ring body.

Within the core of that vast aggregation of thick pre-cosmic density a mighty Fire has been lit, which roars and leaps with Life. The blinding flames rise up and swirl and dance with joy and gladness, whilst clouds of Kosmic Dust descend into the flames from all directions, and ever higher leap the roaring tongues of fire, and vaster becomes the conflagration until a central Sun is formed within the Kosmic Deep, a glowing ball of incandescence, slowly turning round upon itself and lighting up the vast and hollow caves within the starry fields, till, one by one they disappear from sight, and Night gives way to glorious Light, which streams from that vast Lamp of God in answer to the ringing Word.

And there is Light and Life and Joy where darkness reigned before. The bats of night have gone away and will be seen no more as long as Bright Face, Son of Dark Space, rules supreme within that Auric Shell of God's Creation.

And now the great Wheel spins and turns upon its axis; vaster and vaster it spins and gains momentum. And ever brighter shines the Fire of Joy, and great infinitudes expand, and sweet they are and pleasant. And out of the Fire rise up the Fiery Spirits which rise above and join each other. One by one they rise up, and first of all there comes a Shining One — First-Born is He — who takes his central place within the Space, and there He stands, forever fixed, and smiling brilliantly upon the firmament and eke within the Circle. And seven more of these great Beings come out and form a mighty Chain; and soon they also turn upon themselves, and turn around the Central One in giant orbits, doing Homage to their Elder Brother as long as Time will last in Space and Light.

And ever bums the Central Fire, awakened first by that great Beam of Light from God—but now invisible. The Heavens do rejoice, and as the Shining Ones proceed along their fiery Paths there sings a Choir Celestial, made up from the resounding Voices of jubilant Seven Sons:— The Music of the Spheres.

MOONSTONE

ULEB ATTAO TIBISWI,
AAD AFESEF TOTI: —
ATAFIS DODIS.

Oh, Inscrutable Father-Mother God,
And Holy Soul of Hermes: —
Crown the Doer of Right.

* * *

Within the dreaming Wells of Consciousness
Lie hid the mighty Truths of unknown God.
Behind the Veils, material and dense,
Dwell many Holy Wonders
Of greatest Power, Beauty, Wisdom, Love:
Divinest Magic of a vibrant Life
In endless Bliss;
So full of Witchery and Deep Delight.

* * *

And when the Heart of Man awakes,
The Heavens open wide.
The Veil is torn, the Mind is raised
And sails away on fervid Wings . . .
Or swoons in Ecstacy.

* * *

The Music of the Spheres behind the Veil
Brings Visions too Divine to tell.
Its melodies ring out Within
With sounds of Minstrelsy and Rhapsody:
In descant of REMEMBRANCE.

The very Air perfumed with Glory
Of that great Song of Songs;
The like of which was never heard
In World of Phantoms down below.

* * *

A Symphony Celestial, so wonderful;
A benison so rare: that all the Soul
Does thrill with mystic glow.

* * *

And once that Sacred Song is heard:
The rest is nought but emptiness.
As if a Holy Shrine
Forsaken in the Desert lies;
Its lustrous consecrated Radiance
Seems lost for Aye.

* * *

And only Longing fills the Mind and Soul
For swift return to Realms Empyreal
So far away, and yet so near, that Kingdom;
Fragrant with Beatitudes, and Blessings.

VISION 9
COSMIC CONSCIOUSNESS

"And thus," said the Messenger, "are all Memories of the Splendours of Time and Space retained within the Soul; and we need only one sip from the Cup of Life—the *real* Life—in order to awaken the old Visions and Experiences, and give them form and shape once more."

His voice sounded to Ma-u and Ma-uti as if it came from a far distance, or as the voice we dimly hear in dreams at times. It seemed to them as if they were still suspended in Space without visible bodies, but the awesome spectacle they had seen was fading, and both felt as if they were in the half bemused state between sleeping and awakening...

Suddenly their normal sight came back to them and to their utter surprise they found they were still standing in front of the Holy Well, the cups—which apparently they had just drained—still in their hands, and the two Guardians of the Well and Neteru-Hem smilingly looking at them.

"How did we get back here again?" exclaimed Ma-uti.

"You two have never left this place," said the Messenger, as Ma-u and Ma-uti handed back the cups.

"You have just drunk from the Waters of Memory and Revelation, and this has brought back some of the recollections of the past—even before you first took human shape on earth."

"But what about the lectures we have attended, and the teachers there, especially the one with the marvellous aura?" asked Ma-u.

"These are memories of lectures you attended in the past, my children," said the Messenger.

"But it was all so real, and the Temples we went into with you were just the same as those we saw here when we first arrived," said Ma-uti.

"Have I not told you that there is no change, and that all things are here for ever, and that there is no decay or death in these regions?" asked Neteru-Hem.

The pair looked still so bewildered that the two Guardians and Neteru-Hem burst put in joyous laughter.

"It means that you both have perfect memories of all that happened in your previous lives, and also of the events in the Astral Regions where you lived in between these incarnations. Did I not tell you at the very beginning that your 'Shell' was wearing thin? Although your objective memory may not always be able to recall the happenings of past lives and rests, the Soul is fully conscious Of them. When the Mind has also acquired the ability of looking back into the far away past, then you have attained 'Cosmic Consciousness,' for these memories will, help you to raise the Veil which conceals Divine Truth. Until you can do so you are as blind as the rest of humanity who think that the shadow, or reflection, is the real and actual thing; the world and all that is in and around it being but shadows or reflections. But the actuality beyond the Veil is forever hidden from those who have not reached that Cosmic Consciousness."

"But," argued Ma-u," how *can* we have heard these lectures in the past? Some of the references to modem science in them were quite up-to-date, and according to the very latest discoveries!"

"There is no such thing as an 'up-to-date' Truth," replied Neteru-Hem. "Truth is eternal and always was, is, and will be Truth, whether human beings realize it as such or not. This applies also to 'modem' science and 'modem' discoveries!

"When I use the term 'Cosmic Consciousness,' I may refer to the Consciousness of the Kosmos Itself, which is God, or to the human consciousness of Cosmic Truth—which is also God. If a human has this Cosmic Consciousness he is aware of *all* things and conditions at the same time. He knows past, present, and future, and they are ONE! The lectures you both heard may have been a blend of all past, present and future lectures; given here or elsewhere. *All* is contained within the Consciousness of God, and therefore in the Soul of Man. If his Mind knows how to raise the Veil, or is helped to do so, he can attune with that Consciousness of God and Man. Once he has raised the Veil and beheld the interior of the Temple Within, he has established an everlasting connection between his outer and his inner Consciousness. At that divine moment he has contacted Truth, and he can never forget it nor deny its existence, nor obliterate it from his outer or inner memory.

"And it is of the utmost importance for Man to make this Holy contact, for as he realizes spiritual Truth when in the flesh, so he will take this realization with him when he dwells in the Astral Worlds, or beyond, between his earthly incarnations. This realization is all he can take with him when he leaves the shackles of the earthly body, for all the rest perishes or dissolves like shadows—being only Illusion, and false, and without actual existence.

"This realization of Truth he can attain by contemplation and meditation; withdrawing from the outer world and going within; by leaving—in spirit—the lower regions and ascending to the higher; by turning his back upon the shadows and focusing his inner sight upon the Light.

"There can be no Religion more true or just than to know the things that ARE; and to acknowledge thanks for all things to Him Who made them.

"True Piety and Religion are the best and highest Philosophy one can ever attain, and without these it is impossible to attain Cosmic Consciousness, which is a realization of the Intelligence existing beyond the mind of man. Only when Man knows the great Truths which lie concealed there will he be able to explain the immediate mysteries of his environment on earth. He will become 'immersed in God' and have a perception of the Universal Presence.

"This perception cannot be obtained by any process of thought; for mere thinking will bring at most a dim apprehension of the higher faculties of the Soul:—although this process is already a mode of perception which transcends the mere intellect.

"But Cosmic Consciousness can only be attained by clairvoyant perception, transcending all bodily limitations, and bringing the consciousness of the Higher Mind *en rapport* with conditions in the higher Worlds by means of attunement with the *Soul*; which in turn is in direct communication with all the Souls in the superior regions—which are ONE!

"Apuleius—an Initiate of the Isiac Mysteries—has said:—'I approached the confines of death, and having trod on the threshold of Proserpine, I returned therefrom, being borne through all the elements. At midnight I saw the Sim shining with its brilliant light, and I approached the presence of the Gods beneath and the Gods above, and stood near and worshipped them. Behold, I have related to you things of which, though heard by you, you must necessarily remain ignorant.'

"To attain Cosmic Consciousness, or even to strive after it, is the most profound homage that Man can render to God.

" 'To that God,' says Porphyry, 'who is above all things, neither external speech ought to be addressed, nor yet that which is inward, when it is defiled by the passion of the Soul [the Mind], but we should venerate Him in pure silence and through pure conceptions of His Nature.'

"But before Cosmic Consciousness can be attained, it is necessary to obtain full consciousness and knowledge of the illusion of self-hood in Man, for the Hermetic axiom tells us that 'who knows himself knows all things in himself.'

"And whilst a man devotes his attention to divine things, he must at the same time faithfully perform the duties of practical life; for he is placed within the Temple of the body in order to execute certain worldly duties, and to serve his fellows.

"And having done this: 'the mortal who approaches the Fire shall receive a Light from Divinity: for unto the persevering mortal the blessed Immortals are swift! '

"These truths are hard to understand by man who moves within the earthly spheres and therein finds his dim delights; imprisoned is he by the senses, which take their joy and gladness from the illusive pictures that make the web of tapestry of Nature and all its beauties. He beholds effects, but not the cause; to him the material reflection from the spiritual reflection of the One Actuality—a double dream this—is *reality*. That reality is not the *actuality*, but only a realization of the senses which image within the earthly mind a further reflection of that reality which has only objective existence that hides the Truth.

"How can he withdraw from these earthly illusions, how achieve extinction of desire, cessation of longing, leading to that Peace Profound which is the goal of all seekers in quest of the Divine Mysteries? Only by forsaking greed and hatred and by turning to love and service can the curtain be lifted and the Truth be revealed.

"Those of coarse minds, moving in the darkness of earthly preoccupations and dwelling in the world of forms, can *never* behold it. But those who once see the Light *must* spread the Message, for there are those who are ready and only await the kindly word in order to *hear*; they only need the cooling touch of a healing hand upon their aching eyes to *see* opened to them the Gates of Eternity.

"Tell them, my children; speak the word, and thy toil will bring forth abundant fruit.

"It will be heard by the dull and the brilliant, the pure and the impure, the stupid and the wise, and those in between such conditions of mind, who all need what they are qualified to take of the shining pearls of Holy Wisdom.

"Julian has said that—' The Oracles of the Gods declare that through purifying ceremonies, not the Soul only, [in other words, the Higher *Mind* in our terminology] but bodies themselves become worthy of receiving much assistance and health: 'for (say they) the mortal vestment of bitter matter will by these means be preserved.'

"Plato taught that:—' Purification is to be derived from the five mathematical disciplines, viz., from Arithmetic, Geometry, Stereometry—the Art of measuring solid bodies, and finding their solid contents—Music and Astronomy.'

"The parts of Initiation into the Sacred Mysteries were also five, and the first of these parts consisted of the purification. 'The fifth gradation is the most perfect felicity . . . and according to Plato an assimilation to divinity as far as it is possible to mankind,' says Theon of Smyrna in his *'Mathematica.'* In the Golden Verses of Pythagoras you can read:—'Thou shalt know also that men draw their misfortunes upon themselves of their own choice. Wretches! they neither see nor understand that their God is close at hand. Few know how to free themselves from their misfortunes. Such is the Fate that takes away the sense of men.

"But be of good heart, the race of men is divine. Holy Nature shews them all her mysteries. Take the Supreme Mind as thy guide (who must ever direct and restrain thy course).'

"And when, after having thrown aside the body, thou comest to the realms of the most pure ether, thou shalt be God, immortal, incorruptible.'

"This can only be done by attuning to the pure and divine realms of God's Love and Wisdom. Ordinary natural reasoning will never lead man to an understanding of transmundane knowledge, for the Essence of God is the domain of Light, and into that Celestial Region no speculations of the unfolded reason can penetrate. The Philosopher Kant taught this, but the real meaning of his wisdom is so hidden that but few can follow the trend of his elevated teachings. The principal cause of that inability is the fact that most students overlook, or cannot see, the difference between intellectual reasoning, which is of a material nature, and therefore corrupt, and the Light of Inspirational Wisdom, which is divine, and therefore eternal and pure. This is the 'pure' reason of Kant; a god-like attribute of the *Soul* of man, as compared with the earthly thinking of man's *mind*, which prevents a realization of transcendental Truth. This can only be revealed to those who have faith; for only by faith (not religion in this sense) can the inner perceptions unfold.

"Thus man acquires a sense of divine realities, opening up an entirely new world of the spirit which is hidden from the average 'thinker.' He then realizes the difference between the earthly dwelling-place of the mind (the human body in the material and temporary sphere), and the divine dwelling-places such as you have perceived in this region of the Astral Fire, which is real and everlasting and in accordance with the Divine Revelation Jesus made to St. Peter, and in which the Soul-Mind exists in an eternal vehicle if it wishes to do so. St. Paul says:—'For it is written, I will destroy the wisdom of the wise (by which he means the human *intellect*), and will bring to nothing the understanding of the prudent. Where *is* the wise? Where *is* the scribe? Where is the disputer of this world? Hath not God made foolish the wisdom of this world?

"For after that in the wisdom of God the world by wisdom (intellect) knew not God, it pleased God by the foolishness of preaching to save them that believe. For the Jews require a sign, and the Greeks seek after wisdom. But we preach Christ crucified; unto the Jews a stumbling-block, and unto the Greeks a foolishness. But unto them which are called, both Jews and Greeks, Christ the power of God, and the wisdom of God. Because the foolishness of God is wiser than men; and the weakness of God is stronger than men. But God hath chosen the foolish things of the world to confound the wise; and God hath chosen the weak things of the world to confound the things which are mighty. According as it is written, He that glorieth, let him glory in the Lord.' Thus spoke the wise Apostle; and it has always seemed foolish to the worldly-wise that some by faith have claimed to receive inspiration and revelation; neither of which can be measured or proven by material standards. They belong to the Soul, which has sent a message to the Mind; Only *that* Mind which receives such a Holy Ray of Light can realize the Truth in the Radiance and Splendour of this Illumination. To all other minds, who have not received it, that Light is darkness; and in darkness they dwell until *their* time arrives.

"How often does it happen that a Teacher gives forth a particle of Truth. As long as he is speaking his listeners will *Hear* and *Realize*, if they blend their Minds with the Mind of the Teacher whilst he speaks. During that time they are illuminated, and Mind mingles with Mind in perfect understanding. But the moment the Teacher ceases, or a few moments, or days, weeks or months afterwards, the other Minds begin to *reason*, as they imagine. They use their *intellect*, which ever deceives; and instead of the Light of Illumination, they draw unto themselves the Twilight of Doubt, or even retreat into the Darkness of Ignorance. The material always stretches out its greedy tentacles and endeavours to drag down again that principle of the human mind which, on perceiving a Ray from the Divine, unfolds its spiritual wings in order to rise upwards; away from the nether abodes of earth towards the Light. The wings of very few are strong enough to attempt the flight, and whilst they hesitate the powers of the lower regions take hold, and with a fluttering sigh the attempt is over. Thus many times must the mortal Mind receive that Ray before it can raise itself up and achieve release from the heavy shackles that drag it ever down.

"Ignorance; the dawn of reason; intellect; the dawn of real understanding, or initiation; and finally Wisdom; these are the five steps which raise the man from brute to spirit. There are many intermediate stages, such as fear, doubt, superstition, dogma, fanaticism; each and every one of which has to be fought and overcome before the Light is reached. But to those who succeed in the end the reward is great, and the struggle is worth while, for it gives experience and strength.

"Emmanuel Kant has said:—'I confess I am much disposed to assert the existence of immaterial natures in the world, and to place my own soul in the class of these beings. It will, hereafter,—I know not where, or when—yet be proved that the human Soul stands even in this life in indissoluble connection with all immaterial natures in the spirit world, that it reciprocally acts upon these and receives impressions from them.'

"Here again we must read 'mind' instead of 'soul.'

"Both Kant and Laplace had the idea that, at the origin of things, all that Matter which now enters into the composition of planetary bodies was spread over all the Space comprised in the Solar System—and even beyond.

"In your last vision you have seen how that matter was brought to sentient life.

"Plutarch taught that an Idea is a Being incorporeal, which has no subsistence by itself, but gives figure and form unto shapeless matter, and becomes the cause of the manifestation. We see a realization of this in Descarte's *Plenum* 'of matter differentiated into particles;' in Leibnitz's 'ethereal fluid'; in Kant's 'primitive fluid' dissolved into its elements, and in Kepler's 'solar vortex' and 'systemic vortices.'

"And Leibnitz shows a metaphysical intuition in the structure of his divisions—however incomplete they are and faulty from the standpoint of Occult Science—which no other scientist, not even Descartes or Kant, has equalled.

"Besides—although the sum of knowledge increases daily in mankind, intellectual capacity does not grow with it. We only need compare the intellect, if not the physical knowledge, of such men as Euclid, Plato, Socrates, Pythagoras, and other giants of the past with modem science, to know that this is true.

"Science itself has proved that the brain-volume of Polynesians is considerably greater than that of Europeans; even of the French, who rank highest in this respect. Not only that, but the average measurements of the men living in the stone age in the North, in England, and in Wales, are *larger* than the average European of today. Strangely enough, perhaps, the stone age men of France had a slightly smaller average than even the modem European, whilst the Hottentots' skulls measure still less. This shows two things: The size of the brain of the earliest human beings known is not such as to place them on a lower level than the present-day man. Secondly, it shows that it is not a question of brain-quantity, but quality that counts. Yet modem science states that neither matter, nor even the number of convolutions of the brain, make a definite difference in the mental capacity of a man. Nor does the breadth of the brain, as the index of breadth among Scandinavians is at 75; among the English at 76; among some of the German groups at 77 to 80; Schiller's skull showed an index of breadth of 82 — but, the Madurese tribe also show an index number of 82! Wherein, then, lies the basis of intellectual capacity? And what about the much vaunted modem progress of the intellect? In the presence of these facts the Occult Scientist can but smile when in our *learned* age Wisdom of the Ancients is ascribed to Fables!

"They did not rely on intellect, but knew that there is a higher rate of illumination, the revelations of which can *never* be attained or grasped by material thinking.

"There are men of these latter days, however, apart from such well known names as Kant, Herbert Spencer, du Bois-Reymond, and Tyndall — to quote a few at random — who do have this realization; and Tyndall has stated that: —' The passage from the Physics of the brain to the corresponding facts of consciousness is unthinkable. Were our minds and senses so ... illuminated as to enable us to see and feel the very molecules of the brain; were we capable of following all their motions, all their groupings ... electric discharges ... we should be as far as ever from the solution of the problem ... The chasm between the two classes of phenomena would still remain intellectually impassable!' It is the same with the realization which accompanies Cosmic Consciousness, as with the question of the possibility of life on other planets than the Earth. Those who know it can never be shaken in their acceptance of these two facts; the rest do not matter yet; their time will come later. That there *is* life on other planets is proved—if we must have proof of a material nature—by the fact that in some meteorites has been found graphite; a form of carbon known to be invariably associated with organic life on Earth. This presence of carbon was not due to any action occurring within the Earth's atmosphere, as it has been found in the very centre of the meteorites when analysed. And in 1357 at Argueil, in the South of France, there fell a meteorite, which, upon being split and analysed, was found to contain water and decomposed vegetable matter.

"Here are facts which even science can understand; yet the question as to the possibility of life on other planets is still doubted. But that which can be fully realized by our reason and senses is but the superficial; they can never reach the true inner substance of things. Thus spoke Kant, who must be admitted to be one of the greatest Philosophers of modem times.

"One must first be able to see one's Self—and this can only be done by means of Cosmic Consciousness; for once we see—or know—ourselves as we are, the secrets of the Kosmos are revealed also.

"In the Mysteries, the third part of the sacred rites was called *Epopteia*, or revelation, reception into the secrets. It means the highest state of clairvoyance—the divine. The word means overseer, inspector, and master-builder.

"When St. Paul states that:—'According to the Grace of God which is given unto me, as a wise *master-builder*, I have laid the foundation,' he refers to these rites. Incidentally, it is the only time that this term is used in the Bible.

"St. Paul belonged to this group of Initiates. For this reason Paul was hated by Peter, John and James, who looked upon him as a magician, a man polluted with the Gnosis, with the Wisdom of the Pagan Greek Mysteries. But they overlooked the fact that Jesus Himself was said to be such an Initiate, as were Plato and Euclid, and also Pythagoras; the latter one of the grandest of Scientists. Cosmic Consciousness is a reaching out beyond gross matter. We can do so only through one of our seven *spiritual* senses, either by training one or another, or if one is a born Seer. Cosmic Consciousness is further a 'togetherness' with all things and beings contained within the Kosmos.

"One must be able to identify himself with a stone, a flower, an animal, and feel with their feelings, latent or active, and so attune and become conscious of all they are within. One must become ONE with all Nature. When gazing at a planet we must sink our identities *in* that planet; attune with its rays and vibrations, become aware of what it consists, how it operates and is operated; what it feels as it swings along its majestic circuit through the heavens; how it is repulsed by and attracted to its brother-planets; know how it sings and rings with joy and adds its vibrant note to the rest of the songs of its celestial kin. It should be possible thus to hear these tones, just as science has discovered that the note A rings and hums in the light-rays of the Moon. Each Planet, Sun, or other Star within the sky has its own note, and the whole makes up a harmony so sublime that all the senses exult when they succeed in feeling, hearing, or seeing these Royal Chords.

"And so has all that *is* its own inner tone; even to the simplest atom (although it is a Kosmos in itself, in spite of its seeming simplicity), and the spiritual ear can hear, the eye of the spirit see, and the spiritual divine inner senses blend with all these wonders of God. We can draw forth their inner fires and increase our own vitality with these powers, provided that we return that which we have borrowed with interest and so restore the balance. We can send forth some of our own vital forces when one of the things, or beings, of earth needs them, and they will be returned to *us* in due course in a form more sublime and vibrant than they were when we sent them out. Always the balance must and will be restored, and if we help ourselves without repaying, *then* we err and have to suffer until we *do* once more correct the scales and restore the equilibrium. To do these things, you must go within your inner self and dig and burrow until the treasure comes to light. No one can help you to do this, except to point the way; but once you obtain the first glimmer of that wisdom — understanding will come with it.

"This knowledge is as ancient as the stars, but mankind has forgotten it, or wicked and selfish teachers have kept it to themselves. One can unite with all the forces of nature in this way. The elements will become your servants and lend you their powers, if you use these powers in the right manner and unselfishly. If you try to master them for your *own* use they will destroy you. This is an awful secret; and full of wonder, power and aspirations of the loftiest kind. All that is manifested *lives*, and the blending of our own consciousness with all the rest is *real* Cosmic Consciousness of the highest kind and draws their inner being within ourselves, bringing about a definite relationship within our own systems. So we can share the powers of nature with it and experience the *One-ness* of it all in the Temples of our hearts, and worship God together with all the manifested realms at one and the same time. Not. only that; but we shall be as Gods ourselves within the realms of our own personal Kosmos, the body in which we dwell; and have full power and understanding of all its potentialities, and so find a greater awareness of the One God Himself. There will be no more loneliness, no more fear, no more hatred, but only compassion and love, patience and good-will towards all other beings in the Universe.

"So the channels will be opened and cleared, and communication with nature become possible; feeling through and with all; at-one-ness in the highest sense; and the keys of the Sanctuary in your hands — to use as you will: for good or evil.

"The fact that Science has now discovered the note A in the rays of the Moon is an interesting modern point of contact with the most ancient teachings; inasmuch as the ancient Wisdom states that the Souls of Men dwell behind the Moon, and the note A is the equivalent of the colour Indigo, which is the highest spiritual colour known to Occultism. It is the colour which the Seer can only perceive when in the highest state of ecstacy and attunement with the most sublime spiritual realms, and this colour necessarily being within the light of the Moon before that note can sound forth, indicates the presence of great spiritual potencies there.

"Yet even a Seer—such as Swedenborg, for instance— may be led by the visions he sees in the Astral Light, to mistake for God or Angels the denizens of the *Astral* Spheres of which he may occasionally catch a glimpse.

"The seven spiritual senses of man correspond with every other septenate in nature—and in man.

"Physically, though invisibly, the human Auric Envelope has seven layers, the same as Cosmic Space. It is this Aura which, according to our mental and physical state of purity or impurity, either opens for us vistas into other worlds, or shuts us out altogether from anything but the three-dimensional world of Matter.

"The seven physical senses, and also the seven states of consciousness are:—
1. Waking.
2. Waking-dreaming.
3. Natural sleeping.
4. Induced or trance-sleep.
5. Psychic.
6. Super-psychic.
7. Purely Spiritual;

and each of them corresponds with one of the seven Cosmic Planes. Each uses and develops one of the seven super-senses, and is connected directly, in its use on the terrestro-spiritual plane, with the Cosmic and Divine Centre of a Force that gave it birth, and which is its direct Creator.

"By attunement with the higher planes of the Divine and Formless Spirit man can attain Spirit-Knowledge, or Âtmâ. Vidyâ.; what the Sufis call Rohanee.

"Thus, by this means he penetrates into the Substantial or Formative World, next to the Physical World.

"The next to the Formative is the Intellectual or Creative World; then comes the Archetypal World.

"These four divisions have all to do with the material, but the next three, the higher planes of the septenary Kosmos, are so far beyond the understanding of even the most developed mystic that it is almost, if not altogether, impossible for the average Mind to soar up to these Realms. Before it can do so it must be able to attune the three higher states in itself to those three highest Planes in the Kosmos.

"As Hermes says:—'Knowledge differs much from sense; for sense is of the things that surmount it, but Knowledge is the end of sense.' In other words: worldly intellect is the illusion of our physical mind and its understanding; a contrast between the laboriously acquired knowledge of the senses and the Divine Knowledge of the Soul.

"During the periods of rest, or the Nights of Brahmâ, there can be no manifestation of Consciousness, semi-consciousness, or even unconscious purposiveness, for these states of perception need the vehicle of Matter in order to manifest and behold manifestation. On the earthly plane, the human consciousness in its *normal* state cannot soar beyond transcendental metaphysics. It is only through some molecular aggregation that spirit wells up in a stream of individual or subconscious subjectivity. Matter existing apart from perception is a mere abstraction, for both these aspects of the Absolute—cosmic Substance and Cosmic Ideation—are mutually interdependent. The cooperation of Subject and Object results in the sense-object, or phenomenon. Without this cooperation matter and sense would be non-existent; for as sense needs matter to perceive, so matter not perceived has no existence; for there would be no one to perceive it. The phenomena of the *earth*-plane are the creations of the perceiving Ego—the modifications of its own subjectivity; and all states of matter representing the aggregate of perceived objects can have but a relative and purely phenomenal existence for the inhabitants of the earth.

"But this does not necessarily lead to the conclusion that it is the same on all other planes.

"From the standpoint of the highest metaphysics, the whole Universe, God included, is an Illusion. But the illusion to him who is in himself an illusion, several times removed, differs on every plane of consciousness; and no one has the right to dogmatize about the possible nature of perceptive faculties of an Ego, say, on the Second Higher Spiritual Plane, or the Sixth Plane of the Septenary Kosmos, any more than a human Ego can have a true perception of the state of consciousness of an ant, and its modes of perception.

"Actually there is but *One* Absolute Consciousness, whether it is called that or Cosmic Consciousness, or by any other name; it is the ONE REALITY, the ABSOLUTE, the ONE LIFE; it is that ESSENCE which is out of all relation to *conditioned* existence, and of which conscious existence is a conditioned symbol; conditioned existence being material, subject to change, error and illusion. The duality of consciousness and matter, subject and object, are to be regarded as the two symbols or aspects of the Absolute, and not as independent realities.

"Once these Truths are understood all sense of the I-ness of an individual falls away, never to return.

"The term 'I-am-I' is no more than a physical basis, necessary to focus a Ray of the Universal Consciousness at a certain stage of complexity in individual matter.

"The nearer a soul is to the Absolute, the more it approaches to the *true* Cosmic Consciousness, and the further it is removed from material illusion. On the way to absolute consciousness it passes through a number of stages.

The unevolved Mind will dwell in the Astral World after each of thousands of incarnations, until it grows in spiritual perception and may dwell for hundreds of intervals between its earthly lives on the next or higher plane. Then it may be ready for the next, which takes many millions of years. On each plane it will have different realizations of *physical* existence in different shapes. It will assume many bodily forms, extensions of the human shape, in more spiritualized or ethereal manifestations as it ascends. The last plane where this happens is the World of Astral Fire, the Fourth Plane, counting upwards from the Earth-Plane, which is the First.

"After this the consciousness expands still more and in the three Higher Planes the Soul-Mind enters into conditions of bliss and intelligence, blazing with life, extended and magnified to a high condition of such perfection that it cannot be spoken of but only realized; for no words could describe the nature of these planes or the sensations experienced there. Even if one were told of it, he would only hear but not understand: unless he himself knew from experience.

"A still greater mystery is that as man's Soul-Mind rises to the higher spheres he calls these regions into being, and gives them life and form by his perceptions and realizations, in the same manner as he brings to life the conditions on the lowest plane of the septenary Kosmos—the Earth.

"From the physical planes he rises to the intellectual, and thence to the spiritual planes, thus ascending the three *finite* aspects, or reflections on the fields of Cosmic Illusion, until the seventh plane of perception is reached; the Highest Reality possible in the *Spiritual* Realms *below* the Divine!"

"Can the Soul leave the body and Mind, departing to these higher planes whilst the body, with a very depraved Mind, for instance, remains alive on Earth?" asked Ma-u.

"This doctrine is taught in some of the Occult teachings, and especially in Chinese and Buddhist Philosophies," replied Neteru-Hem.

"But," he continued, "there is a misunderstanding in such doctrines; for the Soul is never *in* the body, but surrounds it, as it were; or accompanies it, would be a better term. As long as life lasts the Soul is *with* the body, and it can even penetrate and pervade it, thus increasing the radiance of the aura. It acts as a sort of Guardian Angel, ever ready to guide, lead and advise the higher Mind—if the latter will only listen to it.

"It is called 'The Master within' by some, and this is a very good description of it. When the Soul finally severs its connection with the body and its lower mind, the body, together *with* the lower mind, disintegrates, and the higher mind—dwelling within the Astral Body—departs from the lowest plane to inhabit one of the others for the time being.

"A human unit on the planes of illusion, when once freed from the three forms of egotism, or individualization, the I-making principle necessary in order that self-consciousness may be evolved, but transcended when its work is over—the principle acting in the physical, mental and Astral Worlds—this unit then merges in full consciousness with all the other previously arrived units which now dwell within the Eternal Mind of the One Life. They know all that is within that One Cause, having absolutely *merged* with the shining Intelligences which form that indescribable Unity and Fiery Glory: alert, alive, brilliantly wise and sagacious, profound and enlightened and quick. A whirlwind of Spiritual Wisdom and erudition, information and attainment, such as the human mind, no matter how full of learning and genius, could never contain; a supra-Divine Intelligence beyond human comprehension; all-powerful, merciful and loving. They have learned to know the things that are, how they are ordered and governed, and by whom and for what cause, or to what end, and they acknowledge thanks to the Workman as to a good Father, an excellent Nurse, and a faithful Steward; they know what the Truth is, and knowing this they worship and adore THAT which IS.

"So it was taught by the Divine Trismegistus, and so it is and will be for all Eternity.

"And this Truth can only be learned after much strife and dissention within the Mind, which must first overcome itself before that which is good can be set at liberty, and is no longer ensnared in the fields of Illusion. For whatsoever is in Heaven is unalterable, and all that is not is subject to change; whilst the middle region of Fire partakes of both.

"Hermes further teaches that in the highest Realms all is known, and in the lower nothing is known for certain, for the material things upon Earth and in the Astral Regions cannot communicate with Heaven.

"The Generation of Man is corruption and the corruption of the earthly and Astral man is the beginning of the generation of the Spirit.

"Heaven is the true receptacle of *everlasting bodies*, whilst all upon Earth is corruptible, for as God is the immutable and unalterable Good, so man is an unchangeable evil as man; and not until he frees his Mind from the bondage of the material and the ethereal in whatever form, can it become equal unto the Soul which *is* Good unalterable—and God.

These teachings are not for the multitude but for the few; and like always takes like unto itself, but the unlike never agrees with the unlike. The evil man who hears these words is led to sharpen and whet his maliciousness upon them; for it is the' whole Nature and Composition of those living things called men to be prone to maliciousness, which nourishes and delights them; and when they learn that all things are done according to Providence and Necessity, they will only despise all things because they are made, and lay the cause of their evil doings upon Fate and Destiny, so that they will never refrain from their evil works. But when they do *not* know of the hidden Laws they may be less evil, for fear of that which is secret.

"Being inharmonious within they are out of harmony with that which is from within outward, and of Truth they have none. Only harmony within the Mind can blend with the harmony of the Soul, when the Mind *Knows* Itself as part of the One Life, which must mingle and become One with the Light of the Soul.

"Life leading to Light results in the Greater Life *in* Light. When life leads to darkness, the final result is eternal death. But unless a man be holy and good, pure and merciful, the Light cannot come into his life; his Mind cannot hear the voice of his Soul. But once the Mind *hears*, the Soul's presence will manifest in many wonderful ways; for forthwith the Mind will know all things, and lovingly it will supplicate the Father, and, blessing Him, give thanks, being ordered and directed by filial Affection and natural Love. And before such enlightened ones give up their bodies they will *know* the senses that operate them for what they are—'Illusion. That condition may be reached in many ways, such as the doing of good deeds and abstaining from revenge when the recipient of your services turns and rends you. It cannot be attained by words and self-indulgence. The understanding of it will come gradually to those who are tolerant and strive unselfishly. Thus it is possible to return to the Father, and surrender to the powers, in order to become a power in God.

"The attainment of Cosmic Consciousness whilst still in the flesh gives a deep understanding of all mankind, so that you can become a guide and way-leader to those who are worthy, and lead them back to the One Reality.

"You will teach them that they can free themselves from death, as all have the power to partake of Immortality by departing from the ways of Error and the darkness of Ignorance.

"The Prayer of Hermes is:—

'Holy is God the Father of All Things.

'Holy is God Whose Will is Performed and Accomplished by His Own Powers.

'Holy is God, that Determineth to be Known, and is Known of His Own, or Those that are His.

'Holy are Thou, that by Thy Word hast established all Things.

'Holy art Thou of Whom all Nature is the Image.

'Holy art Thou Whom Nature hath not Formed.

'Holy art Thou that art Stronger than all Power.

'Holy art Thou, that art Greater than all Excellency.

'Holy art Thou, Who art Better than all Praise.

'Accept these Reasonable Sacrifices from a Pure Soul, and a Heart stretched out unto Thee.

'O Thou Unspeakable, Unutterable, to be Praised with Silence! I beseech Thee, that I may never Err from the Knowledge of Thee. Look Mercifully upon Me, and Enable Me, and Enlighten with this Grace, those that are in Ignorance, the Brothers of my Kind, but Thy Sons.

'Therefore I Believe Thee, and Bear Witness, and go into the Life and Light.

'Blessed art Thou, O Father, Thy Man would be Sanctified with Thee, as Thou hast given Him all Power.'

"The greatest Sin of which the Mind is capable is Ignorance; for the Mind that knows not the things that *art*, nor their natures) is blinded, and rushes and dashes against the bodily Passions; not ruling but ruled. This is the greatest mischief of the Mind of Man.

"But Knowledge is the Virtue of the Mind, for he that *knows* is good and worships the All-Being, and therefore he is already half Divine.

"And he will attend in Silence; for God is neither spoken nor heard.

"This knowledge is the gift of God; for all knowledge of the Divine is unbodily. It uses the Mind as an instrument, as the Mind uses the body.

"God is in the Soul, the Soul pervades the Mind, the Mind is in Matter; and all are Eternal.

"And there is but ONE Soul, ONE Life, and ONE Matter; and all are contained in ONE God alone.

"Life is the Union of the Soul with the Mind in Matter.

"But death is not the destruction of those three principles, but a dissolving of the Union.

"For the Image of God is Eternity, of Eternity the Kosmos, of the Kosmos the Sun, of the Sun, Man.

"Everything that moves is of the Spirit; all that *is* moved is a body, and spirit is moved into the bodies by the Soul. Motion, however, is Passion, and both Mind and body suffer through Passion; but once the Mind is freed from the body, it is freed likewise from Passion, and it moves without action or Passion — which are both the same.

"Generation is not a creation of Life, but a Production of Things to Sense, and making them manifest. Neither is change Death, but an Occultation or Hiding of that which was evident to the senses; and man can so expand his Consciousness that he sees and touches Heaven with his senses.

"Whether you speak of Matter, body, or of Spirit, these are all acts of God. The Act of Matter is materiality; of the body corporality; and of Spirit essentiality; and this is God the whole. And in the whole there is nothing that is not God. Wherefore, about God there is neither Greatness, Place, Quality, Figure, or Time; for He is All, and the All, through All, and about All. And the only service to God is not to be evil. But God is not — as it seems to some who blaspheme through ignorance — without sense and without Mind or Understanding; for the Sense and Understanding of God is to move all things always, and neither is there anything without Him, nor He without anything.

"These Teachings are one form of Cosmic Consciousness, just as the Teachings of the Master Jesus were, and those of Buddha, and some of the Divinely inspired messages of St. Paul and others. The attainment of Cosmic Consciousness brings to a man an elevation of all the senses, so that he becomes a shining beacon in the world of Error, giving forth a blaze of illumination. To him will gravitate all that are good and that is good. The Spirits of Darkness will first attack him and then dissolve into Nothingness, for they *are* not; being only reflections of the illusions which surround man on Earth, and therefore still more powerless than man himself—if he ignores them. He can dissolve these illusive shadows with soothing words, for those they cannot understand. Therefore they fear them as things mysterious and unknown, as a troop of wolves will not dare to approach the fleeing sleigh from which dangles an end of string upon the snow. For that mysterious, dancing twine or cord has all the terrors of the inscrutable, and in the same manner the utter calm of one who has received enlightenment will embarrass and perplex, abash and nonplus those whose Minds dwell in a state of agitation, of evil temper, or spiteful malevolence. They wilt against that serene and majestic barrier of placid tranquillity of the man who has mastered all his principles, and therefore mastered all the Wisdom of Nature and Beyond.

"In the Cosmic Consciousness which inspired Buddha, we learn that one so Blessed considers only the Truth, and, having utterly abandoned the thought of Self he is clear in perception, having slain Illusion and standing face to face with reality, as a man speaks with a friend. All doubt and fear, troubles and confusions have departed from such a one. He knows that none can save a man or hurt him but himself; neither on Earth nor in Heaven. By himself he must find the Path and walk along it. This cannot be done by outward forms of righteousness, for it is not possible to placate the Gods by rites and ceremonies. He must find that Love is the Path of Wisdom to true understanding and union with all that IS. As it is taught in the Beatitudes, Man should:—

'Shun the company of the foolish, pay homage to the learned, and worship that which is worship-worthy.'

"He should: 'Dwell among good men and guard well the actions; hear and see much in order to acquire knowledge; study all science that does not lead to sin; use the right language and study the right manners.'

"He should do no evil when tempted; give nobly and follow the precepts of law and virtue; walk in humility and dwell in content and gratitude. He should be patient and endure suffering; rejoice in good words and talk on high matters.

"He should be unmoved, of serene mind, exempt from passion, and fearless amid all earthly dangers.

"Whoever possesses these blessings shall never be overcome; shall in all things find joy and thus attain the Peace.

"Thus taught the enlightened one, and these precepts hold good for all time; and:—' Wisdom walked on his left hand and Love on his right, and Light as of the Sun surrounded him.' Here the Messenger paused.

"Does Cosmic Consciousness bring Power to those who acquire it?" asked Ma-u.

"My son; Power comes only to those who have given up striving after it. Then—when the realization of Power is felt—it increases continually, if the recipient does not make use of it. To have all Power, and all Wisdom, and to forego the use of these Divine Principles for selfish purposes, is the true Power and the true Wisdom. This is hard to understand, perhaps, but perfectly true. All methods for increasing the Will, in order to obtain what humans call Power and Success, must fail; for the Cosmic Powers can *never* be used in this way. All these methods aim at the glorification of the Ego—which is a double illusion; for both glory and Ego are but shadows; just as nonsuccess, non-power and all disasters are shadows which have no actual existence, but are mere realizations of the earthly Mind.

"The moment that Mind becomes spiritualized it ceases to be earthly and material, and therefore corrupt; it becomes conscious of the true meaning of Cosmic Power and Wisdom, in other words it attains Cosmic Consciousness, and it is then purified and selfless."

"But why do mystics all over the world intone affirmations, and practise concentration and meditation in order to obtain power, if it is only an illusion?" queried Ma-uti.

"These affirmations and so on are not for the purpose of obtaining power, my child; or if they are used for that reason they fail. Take, for instance, the Tibetan 'A-um Mani Padme Hum,' which is everlastingly intoned there and elsewhere. The real purpose of it is to attain a pure state of meditation by successively closing all the gates to the various worlds of illusion. A-um (or Om, as it is wrongly spelled and pronounced), is used to shut out the illusion of the Heavenly World; Ma—the World of Spirits; Ni—the earthly human world; Pad—the animal world; Me—the world of tantalized spectres or elementaries and elementals; Hum—the nether world, or Hell. The only trouble is, that the mere mumbling of this phrase is entirely useless, and the devotee should meditate on the purpose of each *syllable* for a considerable time, so that he actually succeeds in the closing of all those gates—and the way to Truth opens. Moreover, these words should be meditated upon—not *spoken*."

"This teaching will upset many students of the Occult," observed Ma-u.

"That will be very good indeed," replied Neteru-Hem.

"It is to be hoped that what I have shown and told you may reveal some of the many errors which hold Occult theories and doctrines in most parts of the world in almost unbreakable chains; preventing the student from making the progress he longs for, so that many give up in despair and drift helplessly along. The investigation of Occult lore, undertaken for the sole purpose of gaining power by learning a few magic tricks, has generally quite the opposite results from those aimed at. This is the reason why so many materially-minded persons, who study the Occult or Mysticism in any way, very often find themselves landed in a morass of unhappiness and failure. They endeavour to obtain *material* gain, or material happiness as they conceive it, in various ways, by studying *spiritual* laws, or natural or Cosmic laws if you like.

"These two principles oppose each other, and it would be just as practicable for a spiritually-minded person to become a rank materialist in order to gain entrance into Heaven! "It is possible to describe it in another way by saying that the moment a materialist seeks the Light of the non-material worlds, and tries to raise himself up from the dense material miasma in which he has dwelt hitherto, the other dwellers — his comrades — in those lower regions will try to drag him down again by withdrawing from him their previous cooperation, which may have given him a semblance of success amongst those shadows.

"Even if he is a poor person, and very unhappy in many ways, the dark community will still exert all its hideous wiles to prevent him from escaping to the higher realms.

"In both cases it will be seen that he fails in everything he tries to do materially. He stands alone, and flounders in an atmosphere of doubt, or fear, or illness or financial distress. It needs uncommon strength of mind, wise guidance', and a capacity for understanding the principles as they *are*, and not as one would *like* them to be, for the aspirant to stand fast; fearless, without any doubt at all, patient, enduring, in order to succeed in gaining entrance to the realms of pure spirit. This is not for weaklings or cowards, or selfish individuals — but only for heroes, full of courage, ardour, fire, zeal, without being *fanatics*. It needs at the same time a heart full of tenderness, patience and love; and a willingness to share even the last crust with those who are in a still worse condition — or *seem* to be. All earthly cleverness, distrust of other people's motives, suspicion of trickery, and other *worldly* 'wisdom,' is useless to the student who invokes the tolerance of the higher powers, who are only too well aware of his own many failings — but regard them with indulgence; knowing how weak the human Mind is, and how easily it is led astray.

"As long as he lives in an atmosphere of suspicion, unfriendliness towards others, and is unwilling to *give* and *lose* freely without afterthought, the aspirant *cannot* make any progress at all; for he judges others whilst he himself is full of blemishes.

"The road is long, and the stones are very hard and sharp to the weary traveller towards the distant Light.

"But if he is steadfast, there will anon shine out a ray of hope upon the far horizon.

"Then, gradually, and often speedily, the spiritual Sun will rise within his Heaven; a great awakening of the inner man takes place, and the moment comes when he can realize the majesty of *true* Cosmic Consciousness and Power, such as no materialist could ever dream; a consciousness of Cosmic Power that will place the weather-beaten warrior upon the Heights, where nothing of the shadow-land below can reach him.

"And there he stands: liberated, glorified, and full of Joy beyond all earthly comprehension.

"But the road to this delight is long—the stones are very hard and sharp—yet, O, Ye Lords of Mercy and of Wisdom-Power, how Glorious the Goal!"

CRYSTAL

HEFAS, AIO, AHI!
ATOSU TUO HIO.
HAIL, MIGHTY GOD!
I ADORE THEE.

Hail to the Light!
From which all Manifested Realms
Sprang into Being at God's Behest.
Its Crystal Clearness Blest
And mirrored in the shining
Glory Of all that lives on Earth,
And in the Upper Regions of the Spirit.
* * *

It ever rises in Effulgence Bright,
As step by step the Soul and Mind ascend
The Golden Stairway to the Source
Of Holiness and Wisdom;
Shedding the Shadows, one by one.
* * *

Until in limpid, lucid Purity,
Transparent silv'ry Dawn does break
Upon the Essence of the Inner Source
Of Being; and glowing Symphonies
Of Sound and Colour glamour
In a Blaze of vast Illumination . . .
Hail to the LIGHT!

VISION 10
THE GREAT LIGHT

Whence falls the Word, unspoken, within the slumb'ring Mind; and wakes with lightning Flash the Dreamer?

Whence comes the Holy Vision; when Heaven opens wide its Golden Gates and floods the trembling Soul with Radiance Sublime?

Whose is the Velvet Touch upon the glowing cheek, that calms the stormy Mind?

Whose are the flutt'ring, downy Wings that waft caress of Fragrant Benediction on the Thinker's Brow?

Why is the noon-sky's purest blue a mirror of the shining sun-webs spun on Angels' loom?

Whence come the thoughts, like rosy, fleecy clouds on summer's breeze, that float within the vaults of all our Meditations?

Whence comes the Inspiration that like a beauteous Rose unfolds upon the World of all our Dreams?

Till Thoughts and Dreams do blend with all the Spirits of Imagination — drifting by in evening sky like swarms of birds upon the wing; who, sailing swiftly in the glow of sunset's glory come swooping down in multitudes, till all the air is whirring with the pulsing beat of myriad wings a-joying; or rise up nimbly in great shoals towards the stars in vast velocity of exaltation.

Thus stood Ma-u and Ma-uti, lost in speculation by the Holy Well, when Neteru-Hem had ended his discourse. The Guardians had long since put away the sacred Drinking Cups and stood beside the White Cypress, their presence a silent blessing as it seemed, and in the Well the Living Waters swirled and sparkled and gleamed with life. They were surrounded by the glory of that beautiful region of the Astral Fire; so pure and clean and full of delight; a living beauty underneath the ethereal and golden canopy of Heaven, as if the whole of those Realms were placed within the heart of a spiritualized Sun which cleansed without burning, and was *Life* itself. A Paradise indeed; with many paths that wound their way through palmy fern and waving branch in every tint of fresh young green, or drowned in apple-bloom; exalted by the piety of Heaven's Hosts and Love Eternal. A boundless landscape full of Radiance; and treasures rich in colour everywhere. And as in silent awe they gazed about, a greater radiance began to fill the sky. A brighter effluence of that bright golden Essence spreading luminosity till all began to shine in keen electric bluish white; luciferous, pellucid, splendidly scintillant, so strong that both Ma-uti and Ma-u cried out and had to shade their eyes and cover them with both their hands. But still the glowing, blazing, argent flame increased in power and seared the brain with dazzling beams of fulgid silvery splendour.

"Oh, Messenger, it is too much," sobbed Ma-uti at last.

"Be calm, my children," answered he, and laid cool hands upon their brows.

Miraculously, the pain caused by that unbearable brightness ceased, and presently the two opened their eyes and found that all the Region of Astral Fire had vanished. There was nothing but LIGHT. They seemed to be standing upon it and leaning against it and even be part of it, for it went right through them as if they were made of crystal. The effect was indescribable and beautiful. Within the white radiance every shade and tint of colour imaginable could be seen; yet — all was White! And every colour had its being in a note of sweetest music; and all the notes did blend in softest harmony and seemed to *live* in super-consciousness of Being. On every vibration of the Cosmic Scale rang out a coloured sound which floated in that Great White Light, or dashed with lightning speed in every direction; as if a shining star with myriad points had burst and every point became a mile-long silver spear — thrown by the Gods themselves.

Sweet and clear the sounds rang out, like silver bells and golden; or mellow organ tones; or tinkling lyres with dulcet-sounding strings; or swift glissandos on vast harps, each with a million chords, all tuned in harmonies seraphic, diffused in vivid rays of animated splendour.

The Zaguan of Heaven! The true Portal!!

A Kaleidoscopaedia of Celestial Radiance; an exhibition of LIGHT as an organic whole in a range of splendid hues unknown to Man—who can only see reflections of this glory; a variety of diaphanous and beautiful colours and symmetrical forms: surging like the zalembius of a sea of living Fire.

"Behold the Light," said Netru-Hem, "the goal of every seeker. It is the same as Darkness, the two, being identical in themselves, are divisible only in the human Mind.

"It has been said that Darkness adopted Illumination in order to make itself visible. And Eastern Occultism teaches that Darkness is the one true Actuality, the basis and Root of Light, without which the latter could never manifest itself, nor even exist. Light is Matter, and Darkness true Spirit. Darkness, in its radial, metaphysical basis, is subjective and Absolute Light; while the latter in all its seeming effulgence and glory is really a mass of shadows, as it can never be eternal and is simply an illusion. But this teaching applies to the light of the Earth, and not to the Great Light you now behold.

"In *Genesis* light is created out of darkness—'and darkness was upon the face of the deep'—and not *vice versa*. 'In him [in darkness] was life; and the life was the light of men.'

"This may explain the verse in the Gospel of John that says:—'And the light shineth in darkness; and the darkness comprehendeth it not.' The word 'darkness' here does not apply to man's spiritual eyesight, but indeed to Darkness, the Absolute, that comprehendeth not transient Light, however transcendental to human eyes. But this is only *one* explanation.

"In the 'Beginning,' that which is called in mystic phraseology 'Cosmic Desire' evolves into Absolute Light.

Light without any shadow — such as you see here — is Absolute Light. When there is shadow it appears under the form of primordial matter, allegorized in the shape of the Spirit of Creative Fire, Heat, or Fohat. Science calls it the primordial 'fire-mist'; it is that which causes the Universe to move with circular motion.

"On the material plane Light, Flame, Cold Flame, Fire, Heat, Water, and Water of Life, are the progeny of electricity; the latter being the One Life at the upper Rung of Being, whilst at the lower rung it is the Astral Fluid, the Athanor of the Alchemists.

"Fire is the creator, preserver and the destroyer, generated by Electricity; which is also the creator of that Light which is the essence of our divine ancestors; and of Flame — the soul of things.

"Light is called the cold flame because the energy that actuates matter, after its first formation into atoms, is generated oh the material plane by Cosmic Heat; and before this happens Kosmos, in the sense of dissociated matter, did not exist.

"The first Primordial Matter, eternal and coëval with Space, which has neither beginning nor end, is neither hot nor cold, but is of its own special nature. Heat and Cold are relative qualities and pertain to the realms of manifested worlds, which all proceed from the manifested primordial substance, which, in its absolutely latent aspect, is referred to as the 'Cold Virgin,' and when awakened to life as the 'Mother.' Therefore, primordial matter, before it emerges from the plane of the never-manifesting, and awakens to the thrill of action under the impulse of Fohat, is but a cool radiance; colourless, formless, tasteless, and devoid of every quality and aspect.

"Of such nature are the first great Entities that develop later into the Cosmic Elements, and they are then successively Âkâshic — or primordial, super-etheric, beyond the ether known to Science, or even to Occultism — Ethereal, Watery and Fiery. This first-named

Element—Akâsha—is the cause of sound; a psychical and spiritual cause, not a material one. It is technically called Tattva, which is the manifestation of the Third Logos on the Âtmic Plane. From all this the lower or more outward manifestations proceed.

"The Four Elements, Air, Fire, Water and Earth, are all but lower manifestations of the primordial substance. These elements may be termed parahydrogenic; 'para' signifying the force beyond, or outside, paraoxygenic, oxyhydrogenic, and ozonic, or perhaps nitrozonic; the latter forces, or gases, being the most effective and active when energising on the plane of more grossly differentiated matter.

"These elements are both electro-positive and electro-negative. They are known by other names in Alchemy and to the Occultists who practise phenomenal powers. It is by combining and recombining, or dissociating the Elements in a certain way by means of Astral Fire that the greatest phenomena are produced.

"It is written:—'As a spider throws out and retracts its web, as herbs spring up in the ground . . . so is the Universe derived from the undecaying One; for the Germ of the Unknown Darkness is the material from which all evolves and develops. The Germ expands and becomes the Universe, woven out of his own substance.'

"It has been well said that light is inconceivable except as coming from some source which is the cause of it; and as, in the case of Primordial Light, that source is unknown, though so strongly demanded by reason and logic, therefore it is called Darkness, from an intellectual point of view. As to borrowed or secondary light, such as comes from the Sun, or whatever else its source, it can only be temporary in character. Darkness, therefore, is the eternal matrix in which the sources of light constantly appear and disappear. Nothing is added to Darkness to make of it light, or to light to make it darkness, on the earthly plane. They are interchangeable; and, scientifically, light is but a mode of darkness, and darkness a mode of light. Yet both are phenomena of the same object of pure reason, which is apprehended by the intuition or understanding alone, without the aid of the senses, and this object is the absolute darkness of the scientific mind, and but a grey twilight to the perception of the average mystic; although to the spiritual eye of the Initiate it is Absolute Light.

"When the light of our Kosmos is lit and shines forth, the Above is shut out and the Below is seen as the Great Illusion, which blinds the eyes of Man.

"In the Scandinavian poem of Wöluspa, the Song of the Prophetess, the Mundane Egg is again discovered in the Phantom-Germ of the Universe, which is represented as lying in the Cup of Illusion, the Boundless and Void Abyss. In this World's Matrix, formerly a region of Night and Desolation, the Mist-Place in the Astral Light, dropped a Ray of Cold Light which overflowed this Cup and froze in it. Then the Invisible blew a scorching Wind which dissolved the frozen Waters and cleared the Mist. (The Word, or Breath, awakening Chaos.)

"These Waters, distilling in vivifying drops, fell down and created the Earth and the Giant Ymir, who had only the semblance of a man (the Heavenly Man), and the Cow, Audumla (the Mother, Astral Light or Cosmic Soul), from whose udder flowed four streams of milk—the four Cardinal Points; the four heads of the four rivers of Eden, and so on, which four are symbolized by the Cube in all its various and mystical meanings.

In Eastern Esotericism and the Kabalah, in order to bring the Logos within the range of human conception, He has been resolved into the abstract synthesis of concrete images, such as Avalokiteshvara, Brahmâ, Ormazd, Osiris, Adam Kadmon, which are all aspects, or manvantaric emanations of the Dhyân Chohans, the Elohim, the Devas, etc. Metaphysicians explain the root and germ of the latter as the first manifestation of the Cosmic Logos, which is the highest trinity that man is capable of understanding, inasmuch as He is the Veil, God, and the conscious energy of God; or matter, ego, and force, the root of Self, of which every other kind of self is but a manifestation or a reflection. And the 'Seven Sons of Divine Wisdom' is the Light of the Logos, split up into numberless emanations and centres of energy personified.

"Milton's 'Light Ethereal, first of things, quintessence pure,' is both spirit and matter to the Occultist. It is the Spirit of Light, the first-born of the Eternal pure Element, whose energy, or emanation, is stored in the Sun, the great Life-Giver of the Physical World, as the hidden concealed Spiritual Sun is the Light and Life-Giver of the Spiritual and Psychic Realms. It is the Light in Darkness and the Darkness in Light: the 'Breath which is eternal.' It is that Darkness which radiates Light, and the Light is the source from which dropped that shining Ray into Chaos, producing another awakening of the Eternal but hidden Sun of our Kosmos, as you beheld it. The Root remains, the Light remains; an everlasting mystery of the One God. In one sense the rootless Root of all; in another sense the manifested One Life, the eternal Living Unity.

"It is the source of all Wisdom, which is *Light*, and the opposite to *Intellect*, which is a groping in the twilight, and even in darkness at times. All this groping leads nowhere, and although men, in their ignorance of intellectual pride, think that all Truth can be discovered by earthly reasoning, they but hide it by the use of meaningless phrases, theories, doctrines and dogmas, and quarrel one with another about the meaning of words; the letter killing the spirit time and again.

"This is especially manifest in modem philosophy, and such men as Spinoza, Malebranche, Descartes and Leibnitz, the so-called metaphysicians, have added nothing to Truth; although the last-named one had glimpses of it. When I say they have added nothing to Truth, I speak figuratively of course, for Truth is always the same, and nothing can be added to or taken away from it. But they have thickened the fog of materialism by using their erring sensual reasonings in order to describe that which is above all earthly reason and can be only discovered by the Spirit, and not by the senses. Therefore, they should not be called meta-physicians, for although they *think* to deal with that which is beyond physics, they are all the time ensnared by the web of physical thinking—which is *not*, and never can be, Spiritual Wisdom, or the *Light* of the Occultists.

"In the case of Descartes, his intellectual fame rests in the creation of analytical mathematics. His contributions to physics were of little value, as what was new in them was not true, and what was true in them was not new. Descartes himself refused the truths of religion, for, says he, they are *supernatural* revelations, and not the *natural* knowledge that he required. But his fundamental rules of simplicity, complexity and truth are neither illustrated nor defined in his writings. He takes no pains to discriminate judgments from concepts, and his new system, as manipulated by him, led to nothing else but hopeless fallacies.

"One of them was that he seemingly identified Being with Thought; and as *both* being and thought in the light of human perception are illusions, we have the key to his failures. But actually he meant that whatever else is not, he, the thinker, certainly *was*, for the act of thinking assured him of his existence, and therefore he was a substance the whole essence of which consisted in thought; independent of place and material objects. This would have been very good indeed if he had realized at the same time that these same senses which produce thought were *material* senses, and reflections of actuality, and not actualities themselves. He confused thoughts about *reality*—or realizations of the senses—with the Actualities of God's Mind in the Light of His Wisdom.

"That this was so is proved by Descartes' further argument, in which he states that as the certainty of his own existence has no other guarantee than the clearness with which it is inferred from the fact of his thinking, it must therefore be a safe rule to conclude that whatever things we conceive very clearly and distinctly are all true!!

"Although this great thinker affirmed the general conclusions of Greek Philosophy in the superiority of mind to matter, Soul to Body, and Spirit to Sense, he had not the advantage of the Greek Adepts, who learned the *real* meaning of these Truths in the ancient Mystery Schools; but only to a small extent.

"But he anticipated modem psychology in his doctrine of intellectual assent as an act of the will.

"It is the same with the speculations of Occasionalism as promulgated by Geulinx and Malebranche, although in the case of the latter we find the interesting statement that the divine archetypal ideas alone exist, and that we apprehend them by a mystical communion with the Divine Consciousness; which idea has misled other thinkers into believing that it leads to the Pantheism of Spinoza. Nothing is farther from the truth, for that statement of Malebranche is absolutely correct, and, following Plotinus, he calls it intelligible extension [of consciousness]. This consciousness is reflected in the material worlds and Man, and Man can extend his material consciousness back to God and the Archetypal Worlds and further regions.

"It must not be supposed that the Logos is but a single centre of energy, such as the Sun, for instance, who stands as the central Essence synthetically, and as a diffused essence of radiated Entities, different in substance, but not in essence. There are innumerable Logoi and their number is almost infinite. The Spirits of those who descend and ascend during the course of cyclic evolution shall cross the threshold of the spiritual world only on the day of their approach to the second field of manifestation of the Central Logos. In that Realm the Past, Present and even the Future humanities will be one and the same; everything will be merged in the Divine Unity. When they reach it the Unknown Darkness shall then become for all of them

Light during the whole period of the Great Night, namely, 311,040,000,000,000 years. This is the period of rest; the Day of 'Be with us.' The Darkness of ignorance has then been absorbed in its own Realm of Eternal Light, and as the Objective emanated from the Subjective, so it will have re-assumed its Spiritual Form and returned to its Divine Heritage in the eternal Absolute.

"The Logos has been compared to the Sun through which light and heat radiate, but whose energy, light and heat, exist in some unknown condition in Space and are diffused in Space only as visible light and heat, the Sun being only the Agent thereof. This is the first triadic hypostasis. The quaternary is made up by the energizing light shed by the Logos.

"We must seek for the ultimate causes of light and heat in Matter, existing in supersensuous states; which states are as fully objective, however, to the spiritual eye of man as an ordinary object is to the ordinary mortal. Light and heat are the shadow or ghost of Matter in motion. Such states can be perceived by the Seer or Adept during the hours of trance or illumination. In Leslie's 'Fluid Theory of Light and Heat' we can read that: 'There is no fundamental difference between light and heat . . . each is merely a metamorphosis of the other . . . Heat is Light in complete repose. Light is Heat in rapid motion. Directly light is combined with a body it becomes heat; but when it is thrown off from that body it again becomes light.'

"Science further teaches that the excitation of molecular motion produces heat, and that heat can be converted into mechanical motion. Therefore, the fluid theory of heat is disproved, or at any rate these facts are obstacles to its acceptance. But just as electricity is called a fluid, so science stated that heat was a fluid, until science decided that it was *not* a fluid but a mode of motion, as it was thought. But *Occult* Science knows that this is not so.

"Heat, light, electricity and magnetism are not causes, but effects. It is on the doctrine of the illusive nature of

Matter, and the infinite divisibility of the Atom, that the whole Science of Occultism is built. It opens limitless horizons to Substance, informed by the divine breath of its Soul in every possible state of tenuity; states still undreamed of by the most spiritually disposed Chemists and Physicists.

"Force is the passage of one state of motion into another state of the same; of electricity into heat and light, of heat into sound and some mechanical function, and so on. So it is on the plane of manifestation of illusionary matter; but Force is not the cause of motion but a result, while the cause of that Force, or Forces, is not the Substance of Matter, but Motion itself; and the cause of Motion is Spirit.

"Modem Physics, which borrowed its Atomic Theory from the Ancients, ignored the most important part of the doctrine by omitting the fact that from Anaxagoras to Epicurus, to the Roman Lucretius, and finally even to Galilee, all the Philosophers believed to a greater or lesser extent in animated atoms; not in invisible specks of 'brute' matter. They taught that rotary motion was generated by the more divine and pure Atoms forcing other atoms downwards; whilst the lighter ones were simultaneously thrust upward. This means esoterically that there is an eternal cyclic curve of differentiated Elements downward and upward through inter-cyclic phases of existence (as illustrated by the symbol of the Swastika), until each again reaches its point of emergence. This idea is physical as well as metaphysical, for the hidden interpretation embraces Gods or Souls, in the shape of Atoms, as the causes of all the effects produced on Earth by the secretions from the divine bodies, or turbulent Elements, as Plato terms them in Timaeus. No Ancient Philosopher, not even the Jewish Kabalists, ever dissociated Spirit from Matter, or Matter from Spirit. All that originates in the One Life returns to the One Life. 'Light becomes heat, and consolidates into fiery particles,' said Valentius. Pymander, the

Divine Logos, said:—'The Light is I, I am the Nous [the Mind, or God], I am the God, and I am far older than the human principle which escapes from the Shadow' [darkness or the divine principle]. 'Fire and Flame destroy the body of an Arhat, their essence makes him immortal' as it is written in *Bodthmur*.

"The Tibetan word Od, used by v. Reichenbach in the same sense, is the name for the first Light in Creation, the first Light of the primordial Elohim, the vital fluid, the 'sky' in an Occult sense, or scientifically, Electricity and Life; and in Hermetic Philosophy it means 'Life infused into Primordial Matter.'

"Ob is the nefarious evil fluid, the messenger of death used by sorcerers.

"Aour is the synthesis of the two: Astral Light.

"Hermes separates the subtle Light from the solid. This has several meanings, one of which is that he distinguished the pure, divine Light, which is darkness to man, from the light of this world, coming from the Sun, which is darkness to the dwellers in the Divine Light of the Celestial Realms.

"Man must learn to separate the two kinds of light and know them for what they are.

"Zeno taught that the Universe evolves, and that its primary substance is transformed from the state of Fire into that of Air, then into that of Water, and so on.

"Heraclitus of Ephesus said that fire is the principle that underlies all Nature, and the Universe is fire, and fire intelligence.

"Anaximenes said the same of air, and Thales of Miletus, of water, but Occult Science knows that the Great Light is the Divine Source of All.

"The teachings of all these Philosophers were right, but none complete. 'Without Him was not anything made that was made. In Him was life; and the Life was the Light of men.'

"Light is the one instrument with which the Logos works.

"The light of the Spirit is the eternal Sabbath of the Mystic or Occultist, and he pays little attention to that of mere sense.

"The allegorical sentence *'Fiat Lux'* let there be Light, is esoterically rendered: 'Let there be the Sons of Light.' They are called that because they emanate from, and are self-generated in, that infinite Ocean of Light, whose one pole is pure Spirit, lost in the absoluteness of Non-Being, and the other pole the Matter in which it condenses, *crystallizing* into a more and more gross type as it descends into manifestation. The hosts of these Sons of Light, the Mind-born Sons of the first manifested Ray of the Unknown Deity, are the very Root of Spiritual Man; these seven Sons are also called Stars.

"There are three kinds of Light in Occultism, as in the Kabalah. The first is the Abstract and Absolute Light, which is Darkness to humanity, and the most sublime manifestation of the Unknown first Lord.

"The second is the Light of the first and hidden Logos; that which lights up the Astral Regions.

"The third is the latter light reflected in the minor Logoi, who in their turn shed it upon the objective Universe. "The Kabalists of the thirteenth Century adjusted these three Lights in order to fit them in with the Christian tenets, and they describe them as the clear penetrating light of Jehovah; the reflected light; and the light in the abstract. This light, taken in the abstract sense, or in a metaphysical or symbolical sense is Elohim—God; while the clear penetrating light is Jehovah. The light of Elohim belongs to the world in general, in its allness and general fullness, but the light of Jehovah is that penetrating to the chief production man, whom this light penetrated and made.

"The Eastern Occultists call this Light Daiviprakriti, the light of the All-Logos, the direct reflection of the ever unknowable on the plane of universal manifestation.

"There is neither Light nor Darkness in the Realms of Truth, for both are twins, the progeny of Space and Time under the sway of Illusion. Neither can exist without the other, since each has been generated and created out of the other in order to come into being, and both must be known and appreciated before becoming objects of perception; hence, in mortal mind, they must be divided.

"The Zohar speaks of Black Fire, which is Absolute Light, or Wisdom. Were it solely Light, inactive and absolute, the human mind could not appreciate nor even realize it. Therefore, there is also Shadow, which is that which enables Light to manifest itself and gives it objective reality. For this reason Shadow is not evil, but is the necessary and indispensable corollary which completes Light, or Good; it is its creator on Earth. The Gnostics called it immutable Light and Shadow, or Good and Evil, which are virtually One; and, having existed through all Eternity, they will ever continue to exist so long as there are manifested worlds — which will be for ever!

"The German Philosopher Moleschott once said that without phosphorus there could be no thought; he referred here to the Astral Fire and Light, burning in the fierce flames of terrestrial passions, which must be overcome before the true light can be discerned.

"Before the ray of divine reason had enlightened the slumbering mind of man he lived in ignorance and was called mindless. Then the Sons of Wisdom lit up a Light within the sons of men and they SAW! They left the animal stage, and from that moment man's progress towards God commenced.

"It has been said that mental perception, to become physical perception, must have the Cosmic Principle of Light: — and, by this, our mental circle must become visible through light; or, for its complete, manifestation, the circle must be that of physical visibility or light itself; this applies to psychical perception in the same manner.

"Things visible are but the shadow and delineation of things that we cannot see. 'All that is on earth,' said the Lord, 'is the shadow of something that is in the superior spheres. Such luminous objects as light and fire are the shadows of that which is still more luminous than itself, and so on till it reaches me, who am the light of lights.'

"Not until man has become 'twice-born,' or initiated, shall he behold that great luminosity.

"When the Elohim are referred to as the Sons of Darkness, it is done to form a philosophical and logical contrast to the Light Immutable and Eternal. The earliest Zoroastrians did not believe that Darkness (or Evil) was coetemal with Light (or Good); and they give the same interpretation. Ahriman is the manifested *Shadow* of Ahura Mazda, who himself issued from the Boundless Circle of Time, or the Unknown Cause. They say that this Cause is the 'glory too exalted, its light too resplendent for either human intellect or mortal eye to grasp and see.'

"It is from that Light that the Forms of the 'Lords of Being' condense into existence; the first and highest being the Logos of the Greek Philosophers. From these downwards—formed from the ever-consolidating waves of that Light, which becomes gross matter on the objective plane—proceed the numerous Hierarchies of the Creative Forces; some formless, others having their own distinctive form; others again, the lowest Elementals, having no form of their own, but assuming every form according to the surrounding conditions. So they descend from the Light of every light that is in the boundless Lights.

"Jesus says, in the *Pistis Sophia*:—'Do ye seek after these mysteries? No mystery is more excellent than they: which shall bring your souls unto the Light of Lights, unto the place of Truth and Goodness, unto the place where is neither male nor female, neither form in that place but Light, everlasting, not to be uttered. And no Name is more excellent than all these, a Name wherein be contained all Names, and all Lights, and all the [forty-nine] Powers.'

"This Light and Name are the Light of Initiation and the name of the 'Fire-Self,' which is no name, no action, but a Spiritual, Ever-Living Power.

"According to the Ancient Teachings, the colours of Light were symbolic of life and death; white being the quintessence of Light. Towards its negative pole white is condensed in blue and fixed in black; towards its positive pole white is condensed in yellow and fixed in red. Blue invites to repose or slumber, whilst black is absolute rest, the sleep of death. Yellow is active, red is absolute motion, and white is the equilibrium of motion, or healthful activity.

"The progress in life—unfoldment—is from black to red; red is the Zenith of manhood's prime; in the decline of life the course is from red to black. In both unfoldment and decline white is traversed; in the healthful, elastic period of first maturity and in the medium stage of old age.

"White is the aggregation of light, and black its absence; the three colours of the Light-Scale—red, yellow and blue, with the four not noted herein, constitute the Syllipsis, or luminous synthesis. Positive, *plus* Light in its extreme polarity is Life at its prime; negative, *minus* Light in its extreme depolarity is Death.

"Light is saturated with Life. The red colour of the vital fluid, the blood, is a polarization of the most positive ray, polarized and fixed therein when the oxygen of the air drives out and replaces the carbonic acid introduced with the food and generated in the excrementory organs and glands.

"The actinic or chemical ray is not the sole or even the chief actor in producing molecular changes, for the actinic element simply dissolves old forms and prepares the molecules or atoms for the action of the calorific ray, or rather for its next neighbour, the red ray, which is the creator of new forms by imparting new affinitive attraction to the molecules or atoms prepared for it. These two principles form the two atomic forces, attraction and repulsion, the former being the red, and the latter the blue in action.

"And the whole of all these actions and reactions is but a series of reflections from 'Darkness,' which is the absolute Light, and the Root of the seven fundamental Cosmic Principles; that Darkness which, in a sense, is the Deity itself: Iao-Pater, he who was, who is, and who will be; the Eternal One, whose ineffable, unpronounceable Name is the Name *par excellence* of the Jews; the name of the oracle of Dodona, the fair nymph of the Ocean, beloved by Jupiter; the God whose name is the same as the Vaidic Indra and the Biblical Jehovah. As Pindarus says: 'Happy he who descends into the grave thus initiated, for he knows the end of his life and the kingdom given by Jupiter.'

"Above, LIGHT; below, LIFE. The former is ever immutable, the latter manifests under the aspects of countless differentiations. According to the Occult Law, all potentialities included in the higher become differentiated reflections in the lower; and according to the same law nothing which is differentiated can be blended with the homogeneous; nothing can endure of that which lives and breathes and has its being in the seething waves of the world, or plane of differentiation.

"The Hermetic 'Tres Matres,' and the 'Three Mothers' of the *Sepher Jetzirah* are the same; they are no Demon-Goddesses, but Light, Heat, and Electricity, the whole of the forces of agencies which have a place assigned to them in the modem system of the correlation of forces; and they are the same as the three powers of the three great Gods: Brahmâ, Vishnu and Shiva.

"At the periods of new generation, perpetual motion becomes Breath; from the Breath comes forth primordial Light, through whose radiance manifests the Eternal Thought concealed in Darkness, and this becomes the Word. From that Word all the Kosmos springs into being from the act of generation or production. You cannot invoke this Divine Light with impunity, for once you have asked that Sublime Radiance to shine and search through all the dark comers of your being, you have consciously invoked Divine Justice to take note of your *motives*, to scrutinize your actions, and to enter up all in your account. It is an irrevocable step and never again can you force yourself back into the matrix of illusion and irresponsibility, Though you flee to the uttermost corners of the earth, and hide yourself from the sight of men, or seek oblivion in the tumult of the social whirl, that radiant Light will find you out and light up your every thought, word or deed.

"But in spite of this warning: be brave; and if you fail — as all inevitably do — try again; for failures are not irremediable if you follow them up with ever renewed struggles upward. And always remember that although you may see no guiding Angel beside you, the Holy Power is ever there, and the Holy Light will shine in your hour of Spiritual need.

"In the Crata Nepoa, the priestly mysteries in Egypt, after a preliminary trial at Thebes, the neophyte had to pass through many probations, called 'The Twelve Tortures,' and in order that he might come out triumphant and never cease to govern his passions, he was commanded to concentrate all the time on the God-Power — or the Great Light — within himself. When he had conquered the terrors of his trials, after many wanderings in darkness in the secret labyrinths, ending in the hall called the 'Gates of Death,' he was conducted to the 'Hall of Spirits' and judged by them. Among the rules in which he was instructed he was ordered: Never to desire or seek revenge; to be always ready to help a brother in danger, even unto the risk of his own life and possessions; to bury every dead body; to honour his parents above all; to respect old age; and to protect those weaker than himself; and, finally, to ever bear in mind the hour of death, and that of resurrection in a new and' imperishable body. In this manner the neophyte was made into a Kristophoros, and the mystery-name of I AO was communicated to him, and henceforth he walked in the paths of LIGHT and Primeval Wisdom. In him was placed the seed which led to

Avatarism; the seed of which contains the potency and cause of all divine incarnations as World-Saviours, Bodhisattvas and Avatars.

"Those Adepts who thus sacrifice themselves to live upon earth, giving up their rightful places in the Heavenly Realms, become the Vehicles of a 'Son of Light' from still higher spheres, who, being a formless Entity on the highest planes, has no ^ Astral Body of his own fit for the lower or earthly levels, for he has become identified with the First, or Highest, Principle of the One God., This is real sacrifice, the explanation of which pertains to the highest Initiation of Occult Knowledge." Here the Messenger paused.

The music of the colours within the Light blazed forth like unto mighty conflagrations, tearing down and consuming the last shreds of earthly Illusion. This was a new existence, deep and rich and beautifully clear beyond telling, and far beyond anything they had ever conceived within themselves and others, or without. Here were riches surpassing all earthly dreams of wealth and splendour.

"If the Spirit of God is reflected within the hidden, central Sun, of which the visible Sun is a reflection, reflected in the earth and planets, man being a reflection of the earth, the higher mind a reflection of the Soul, as it were, and the lower mind a reflection of the higher; how then can the higher mind—being only a reflection, which has no more actual existence than body, earth and planets, Sun visible and Sun invisible—how can this mind achieve realization by itself of the true and only Actuality?" asked Ma-u.

"It can only do this by attuning with the Soul—which *is* God," replied Neteru-Hem.

"The Higher Mind is not quite the illusion you seem to think. It is that part of the Soul which descends into Man, whose lower mind has risen from the lowest forms of matter, and rises by successive stages until it finds itself within the human body, rich with material experience. Then comes the struggle of the Higher Mind, overcoming the material and attuning with the Spiritual. It must release itself from the delusive selves of consciousness, sensation, perception, and material predispositions even in the earthly life. When it has succeeded in doing this, it has reached illumination and knows that all these illusionary principles do not form the true Ego. Whilst the brain, body and all false perception perish with so-called death, the essential part of man escapes and dwells elsewhere for a time, or forever. The doctrine of total extinction of man's Soul and Mind, or spirit, if you wish to call it that, is a wicked heresy and devoid of all truth.

"After the passing away from the world of the Lord Buddha, the King of Kosala asked of the learned nun, Khema, the following questions:—

'Venerable Lady, the Perfect One is dead. Does he exist after death?'

'Great King, the Exalted One has not declared that he exists after death.'

'Then, venerable Lady, does the Perfect One not exist?'

'The Perfect One has not declared that he does not exist after death.'

'But, venerable Lady—does and does not? How is this possible?'

And, smiling a little, the learned nun replied:—

'Great King, have you an accountant or a mint-master who could count the sands of Ganges and lay the figure before you?'

'Venerable Lady, no.'

'Or who could measure the drops in the Ocean?'

'Again no, venerable Lady.'

'And why? Because the Ocean is deep, immeasurable, unfathomable. So also is it if the existence of the Perfect One be measured by any human category, for all statements of bodily form are abolished in the Perfect One; their root is severed; they are done with and can germinate no more. The Perfect One is released from the possibility that his being can be gauged in any human terms. He is now deep, immeasurable and unfathomable as the Ocean, and neither the terms of existence, or of non-existence as understood by the world, fit him any more."*

"There are," continued Neteru-Hem," three conditions of the mind. The first and lowest is the voice of the senses — or opinion. This is a terrible power, carrying with it an enormous responsibility, for it can be manifested in wrath and fury, ire and rage, bloodshed and carnage, hatred and estrangement. Or it can be displayed in love, mercy and goodness. And as this power is used, so it will draw — by attunement — the same conditions towards the performer of these attributes of the senses, or the higher or lower mind.

"The second state is that of the intellect. This is a condition of cold, hard and clear reasoning. All evidences of the imagination, of love, poetry or exaltation, find no place in the mind of the purely intellectual person when dealing with scientific investigations or rational pursuits. Only facts count, and proof must be piled on proof before these facts are accepted. This is excellent from a material point of view and a necessary stage in the development of the mind. Yet it leads nowhere in the end, for as intellectual science proceeds it discards every fact in turn for new facts, which are also disproved and discarded as time goes on, and eventually science returns to the first starting point, and the same cycle commences anew, but in a different manner.

"Only when Illumination is reached can the Mind — in its third round — become certain of having acquired WISDOM. Before it is thus perfected it endeavours to count the sands of the desert, or the drops in the Ocean, and it exists in a perpetual state of twilight; ever puzzled and perplexed by the multitudinous evidences of the variety of God's creations; and it is far removed from the Great Light of profound Omnipotence of the Infinite One Lord.

"Intellect constantly searches and rejects; Illumination finds and keeps.

---

* From "The Life of the Buddha," by L. Adams Beck.

"Until 'Illumination' has been reached, the 'Light' will be no more than a form of energy consisting of vibrations in the ether, which act upon the optic nerve and make vision possible. And how dark *that* light is when compared with the Uluminism of the Illuminati!"

PEARL

Limpid Streams of clearest Air,
Abundant, full of Forms Divine;
Realms of Peace, the Consummation
Of Knowledge of the Self as Heir
To final Great Initiation
Into the last Nirvanic Clime,
Where dwell the unseen Hosts Sublime.

* * *

Great Ashrum, Sacred, far Abode
Of Companies of Holy Men,
From which the Charioteers of God appear
As Harbingers of Dawn, and steer
Their mighty Steeds, that Wisdom veer
Its course to ev'ry silent Seeker.

* * *

Continuance of all the Logoi;
Of Will, Activity, Supremest Apprehension;
Where stay the Monads who deploy
In scintillating sparks that glow in that Dimension
Of all the Lights of Sacred Atma;
Auphanim of that vast extension,
Imperishable, of Holy Pitri-Deva.

* * *

Raise high the Golden Chalice,
So that the Gods may fill your Cup
With sparkling Dew of Revelation;
And give you Sight and Hearing,
So far beyond the ken of mortal man,
That ev'ry whisper of the Angels
Shall reach the Inner Soul of You,
And fill it full of rare Delight,
And deep Sagacity and Erudition;
So that a Shining Pearl you may
Become; A Rosy Light in Golden Dawn,
A Guiding Star! A Light unto your Brothers
On their weary Way.

VISION 11
THE DWELLERS IN THE CELESTIAL SPHERES

Upon the Great Light and within it, there seemed to gather an added Power, as if vast Hosts were preparing to invade that sublime state of awareness.

There blew an airy waft of inner warmth, encircling the Messenger and Ma-u and Ma-uti with silent movement of approaching vivid Life, as yet invisible.

There was a curious suggestion of ordered preparation, slowly accumulating in a vast concourse of happiness and bliss. There was the stirring of a million thread-like antennae, soft and downy and tender; unseen, but felt. The Soul of Light with lifting Wings astir on undulating pennons, but veiled in mystic curtains, spreading wide in shimmering lustrous vapours. Within that coloured Sea of Light there flashed a thousand Rays of puissant Radiations, emblazoned on the far-spread screens of rosy beauty in incandescent brilliance.

And in the Rays there whirled and danced a myriad tiny glowing motes in every hue imaginable.

There were the violet specks connected with the Astral Doubles of all Nature, the Paradigm of all Forms, and the combined hum of these small particles produced the musical note of B. And others were of the true indigo and rang the note A; they had to do with the Universal Mind, or Divine Ideation. Some were blue, and they represented the synthesis of Occult Nature; they gave the note G. Others were green, and were connected with the animal, or material Soul of Nature, and the source of animal and vegetable intelligence and instinct; F was their note. Then came the yellow specks, whose note was E, and on that note resounds the aggregate of Dhyân Chohanic Intelligences; fiery in its temper and beatitude. Also the note D was intoned by the orange particles, whose affinity is the Life-Principle in Nature. And finally the note C rang out in the red colour of the corpuscles connected with that principle which, on the spiritual plane, corresponds with the sexual affinity in the lower.

In the shining Light these atoms leapt with joy in perfect freedom; intermingling, or drifting in clouds resplendent, or rising up in sprays like bursting pyrotechnic bombs, ringing out their harmonies of ecstasy, keen with intellectual power and divine apprehension of super-spiritual penetration.

"These are the Monads which become Duads on the differentiated plane, to develop into Triads during the Cycles of Incarnation, knowing neither Space nor Time even when incarnated, but being diffused through the lower principles of the Quaternary. They are omnipotent and omniscient in their natures: An innate omniscience which can manifest its reflected light on the semi-terrestrial or material planes," said Neteru-Hem.

"But not all the Monads are so small as those you see here," he continued. "Remember the Angelic Monads from these spheres, who incarnated as men and gave mankind—which up to then had only the instincts of the other animals—understanding. Occult Wisdom teaches that the only difference between animate and inanimate objects on earth, and between an animal and a human frame, is that in some the various 'Fires' are latent, whilst in others they are active. Of course the *vital* Fires are in all things, and not an atom is devoid of them. But no animal has the three higher principles awakened in him; they are simply potential, latent. It was therefore only after the Progenitors had mingled with Man that the great miracle was wrought—the harmonious co-mingling of the Essence of the incarnating Angels, or Pitris, with Man—that Man became conscious of his divine descent, and was enabled to commence the long climb back to the regions from which he had first descended like a simple spark, or atom, to the lower realms of illusion in the objective World. In this manner the Angelic. Monads, the Ancestors of sentient Man, became, in reality, Man himself.

"Every atom becomes a visible complex unit, or molecule, and once attracted into the sphere of terrestrial activity, the monadic Essence, passing through the mineral, vegetable, and animal kingdoms, becomes man. God, Monad, and Atom are the correspondences of Spirit, Mind and Body in Man.

"The Monads are the minds of the Atoms; both are the fabric in which the Gods clothe themselves when a form is needed. So all these scintillating sparks you see here are Atomic Souls before they descend into pure terrestrial forms. They are the potential Creators, the Buddhi, the World-Saviours, the omnipotent Roots of Divine Intelligence, the Stars of the future. On Earth they are invisible, just as, according to an Occult Maxim, the real Sun and Moon are as invisible as the real man.

"The Earth itself was once one of them, as it is made up out of countless myriads of these atoms which have become ONE in Illusion.

"And Space, which has been wrongly proclaimed to be 'an abstract idea,' or a 'void,' is in reality the container and the BODY of the Universe in its seven Principles. Esoterically, it is the Unknown Container of All, the Unknown First Cause. It is a body of limitless extent, whose Principles, in Occult Terms, manifest in our phenomenal world only the grossest fabric of the sub-divisions of the septenary fountain of Being; and no-one has ever seen all the Elements in their fulness, as it is taught. These splendid atoms are re-created on Earth; but in an inverted sense, as in a *miner*. For these atoms to be evolved and developed into the complete septenary man, it is necessary to have two connecting principles, namely: the Soul, and the Mind in its higher and lower aspects. The latter some call personality and others individuality; and this is the outer, visible form of man and all his inner principles apart from the Soul; the higher Mind and the Body (or lower mind) being closely knit together during life on Earth—and the Soul accompanying them.

"The Higher Mind is the intellectual fruitage and the efflorescence of intellectual self-conscious Egotism in the higher spiritual sense. Thus he is neither God nor Pure Reason but a blending of these faculties *with* the Soul. Thence he may proceed to the higher states of bliss towards that fourth plane of consciousness wherein human evolution reaches the Divine.

"And so, from the highest Archangel, or Dhyan Chohân, down to the last conscious Builder of the inferior class of spiritual Entities, all such have been *men*, having lived æons ago in other cycles of time on earth in its earlier forms or incarnations, or in other spheres. In the same sense the inferior, semi-intelligent and non-intelligent Elementals are all future men; for all find their origin in these fiery, brilliantly coloured particles. The higher is on the upper rung of the Ladder of Being; he is the Watcher, the Divine Prototype, who observes his Shadows at the lower rung. Between them stretches a golden thread which becomes more radiant with every change in the consciousness of the Shadow as it evolves upward, until the Light of the Morning Sun has become the Noon-day Glory.

"The Monad, or luminous Atom, of every Shadow has full and distinct individuality and is entirely different from all the rest, although its primary, the spirit, is ONE with the One Universal Spirit. But the glowing spark that is enshrined in the shadowy Vehicle is part and parcel of that Dhyân-Chohanic Essence of the Watcher, and in this lies the mystery of the words: 'My Father, that is in Heaven, and I — are ONE.'

"The Sun is the medium whereby these Atoms are sent to Earth in a continuous stream which nothing can arrest or limit. Around the Sun are innumerable Choirs of Angelic Beings, like great Armies, continually watched over and directed by the Dhyân Chohans, who direct and observe all human things and actions. By it all creatures are preserved and nourished, and, even as the Heavenly Realms which environ the sensible world fill the latter with plenitude and universal variety of forms, so does the Sun also, enfolding all in His Light, accomplish everywhere the birth and development of all creatures. The Choir of Angels is under His direction. They are many and diverse, and their number corresponds to that of the stars. Every star has its Angels, good and evil by nature, or rather, by their operation; for operation is the Essence of these Angels. They preside over mundane affairs, just as the Gods, or Dhyânis do; they shake and overthrow the Constitutions of States and individuals; and they imprint their likeness on our Minds. They are present in our nerves, our marrow, our veins and arteries, and our very brain-substance. They permeate the mind so that it may receive the impress of their energy. But the Soul itself is not subject to them, for that is the part of God Himself, who enlightens it with His illuminating Ray. But all that which does *not* emanate from the Absolute is Illusion; for the Absolute, by reason of this qualification alone, stands as the One and Only Reality; hence, everything extraneous to it, the generative and causative Element, *must* be an illusion, most undeniably so from the purely metaphysical view-point.

"Mankind, psychically considered, is divided into various groups, each group being connected with one of the Dhyânic Groups, that first formed psychic man.

"There is one group whose inner Selves are primordially connected, by means of their descent, with that Group of Dhyân Chohans who are called the First-Born of Æther. This is the section of Mankind in which are born the Great Seers, Poets, Inventors, Artists, Musicians and Writers, for they are under direct control of the Mystic Watchers in the Higher Realms. They are the Leaders of humankind, whether humanity accepts them as such or not; for if at first they are rejected, the time must come when some of the rest of mankind will be able to obtain a glimpse of the Light they spread within the World. These leaders of thought, of whom there are said to be some 30,000, are under the control of the Lords who bestow Intelligence and

Inspiration; the All-knowing or Omniscient Lords. Each of these Lords has his own class of Adepts, knit together by its own bond of spiritual communion from this Heavenly Sphere. The only possible way to enter into communication with these Lords, of whom there are Seven, each operating on a special Ray, is by bringing oneself within the influence of the Spiritual Radiance which emanates from one of these Rays, which all radiate from this Central Spiritual Region here.

"The Dhyân Chohans are dual in their character, for they are composed of the irrational energy inherent in matter, and of the intelligent Soul, or Cosmic Consciousness, which directs and guides that energy, and which is reflecting the Ideation of the Universal Mind. They are known under various names, such as the Theoi (Gods), Genii and Daimones, by the Hermetic Philosophers; Kwan-Yin by the Buddhists; or Devas, Chitkala, Pitris, and many other names in different Philosophies. Although these Lords are so high in the Celestial Hierarchies, even *they* are Illusion, and therefore have no more permanence than Man. Nevertheless, all things are relatively real, for the cognizer is also a reflection, and the things cognized are therefore as real to him as he is to himself. On whatever plane our consciousness may be acting, both we and the things belonging to that plane are, for the time being, our only realities. But nothing is permanent except the one hidden absolute existence, which contains in itself the noumena of all realities. But as we rise in the scale of development we perceive that in the stages through which we have passed we mistook shadows for realities, and that the upward progress of the Ego is a series of progressive awakenings, each advance bringing with it the idea that *now*, at last, we have reached 'actuality'; but only when we shall have reached Absolute Consciousness and blended our own with it, shall we be free from the delusions produced by Illusion. Unchanged, the One Lord dwells in the profoundest depths of time, and during the intensest activities of the great Cycles.

Beyond Him is Divine Spirit, round whose Concealed Pavilion is the Darkness of eternal Illusion.

"The first seven Dhyân Chohans are those Entities who are born of the Mind of the Logos; they are the Pure Flames, or the Intellectual Breaths; those Angels who are said to have made themselves independent by passing from the passive and quiescent into the active state of Self-Consciousness. Some of them incarnated as men, others have made men the vehicles of their Reflections. One of those great Lords has said: 'I am the same to all Beings; those who worship me are in me, and I in them.' For this reason the Egyptian Candidate for Initiation always personified the God of the Temple he belonged to—each Temple having a special God, the equivalent of one of the Dhyan Chohans—just as the High Priest of that Temple always personified that God, and as the Pope personates Peter, and even Jesus Christ, upon entering the inner Sanctuary.

"The necessity for all these Hosts of Creators will be apprehended perhaps when it is understood that the One Lord of All is Infinite and Unconditioned. This One Lord, State of Consciousness, or Principle—call it what you will—cannot create, for It can have no direct relation to the finite and conditioned.

"If all the wonders we behold in Nature, from the great Suns and Planets to the tender blade of grass or a speck of dust, had been created by the Absolute Perfection and were the *direct* work of even the *First* Energy that proceeded from It, then all these things would have been perfect, eternal and unconditioned like their Author. The many imperfect works found in Nature testify that they are the products of finite and conditioned Beings, no matter how high they rank amongst the Dhyân Chohans, Gods, or Archangels. These imperfect works are the unfinished creations and the products of evolution, under the guidance of the finite Lords.

"The First-Born Logos is not an Emanation but an Energy inherent and co-eternal with the One Deity. It is an

Energy or Condition which proceeds through itself, not being due to the active or conscious will of the one that produces it. The Zohar speaks of emanations, but reserves the word for the seven Sephirod emanated from the first three, the triad of Kether, Chokmah, and Binah. As for these three, it explains the difference by calling them immanations, or something inherent to and coeval with the subject postulated, or, in other words, 'Energies.' These 'Auxiliaries,' the Auphanim, the half-human Prajâpatis, the Angels, the Architects under the leadership of the 'Angel of the Great Council,' with the rest of the Kosmos-Builders, explain the imperfection of the Universe. This imperfection is one of the arguments of the Secret Science in favour of the existence and activity of these Powers. Philo was very near the truth when he ascribed the origin of evil to the admixture of inferior potencies in the arrangement of matter—and even in the formation of Man—a task entrusted to the Divine Logos.

"Thus it is not the One and Unconditioned Lord, nor even Its reflection that creates, but the 'Seven Gods' and their Hosts, who fashion the Universe out of the Eternal Matter, vivified into objective life by the reflection into it of the One Reality, the One Life.

"In the ancient teachings it is said that: 'Descending on his region first as Lord of Glory, the Flame, having called into conscious, being the highest of the Emanations of that special Region (like our own Kosmos, for instance), ascends from it again to Its Primeval Seat, whence It watches over and guides its countless beams, or Monads. It chooses as Its Avatâras only those who had the seven virtues in them in their previous incarnation. As for the rest, It overshadows each with one of Its countless beams. Yet even the beam is a part of the Lord of Lords.'

"Therefore, as in the Egyptian Teachings, as in those of all others, Faiths founded on Philosophy, man was not merely a union of mind and body, but he became a trinity when Soul was added to it, the divine spiritual principle, which carries with it Wisdom and Understanding, with which the Mind eventually links up. They knew that Man was a septenary creation, consisting of:—

Kha—body.

Khaba—astral body or shadow.

Ba—Higher Mind.

Akh—terrestrial intelligence (or lower mind).

Sah—or mummy, whose functions commenced after the death of the body (actually, the Sah was the life-giving spark, but count mummy and life-giving spark as two separate principles); and

Osiris—the highest, uncreated spirit, or Soul.

"Each of these principles has its own ray or rays which are in direct communion with the Monads in the higher realms, each according to its nature.

"Once man has entirely merged his Self in the Universal Self he becomes a Dhyâni, and is identified with Supreme Intelligence, and thus he becomes a Dweller in the Celestial Spheres. 'They who shall be accounted worthy to obtain that World . . . neither marry . . . neither can they die any more,' as Jesus told the Sadducees.

"Then they are the prototypes which will again be reflected in future men, just as all the great characters like Jesus, Buddha, and other giants in the history of mankind were but the reflected images of human types which had existed for millions of years, rising, step by step in each incarnation to greater perfection. Thus, in their image, some men are born hypostatically animated by their divine prototypes, reproduced again and again by the mysterious Powers that control and guide the destinies of the world.

"The Higher Mind directs the Will: the lower turns it into selfish Desire. This explains the failures of some men, who, born to high destinies, pervert their powers to the illusions of Greed and Glory.

"The Dhyân Chohans are passionless and pure; they have long since discarded the lower mind and its fleshly snares. They have no more struggles, no more passions to crush. They have been through the School of earthly Life and graduated to higher realms. The highest state of consciousness is that which emanates directly from Absoluteness, and it is the First State of *Being* in the Universe. It corresponds with the Hierarchy of non-substantial primordial Presences in a place which is no place to us, and a state which is no state according to human comprehension. This non-substantial state or Hierarchy contains all that was, is, and will be from the beginning to the end of a Mahâmanvantara. It contains the highest Divinities in a condition where no progress is possible, for we can say that these Supreme Entities are crystallized in purity; in homogeneity.

"The next Heavenly Realm is that where dwell the Hierarchies of Celestial Teachers, Lords, Buddhas or Masters. It is related to the highest consciousness in man, and no Adept can be higher than this and live on Earth, for when he passes into that state he can return to Earth no more. These two states are purely hyper-metaphysical. The next five states have all to do with the higher and lower senses in man and his corresponding affinity, and make contact with each Ray on which these senses manifest.

"Man has thus within himself the seven pale reflections of the seven Divine Hierarchies; his Higher Self is in itself but the refracted beam of the direct Ray.

"The Seven Hierarchies are the seven Lights; intelligent, conscious and *living* Principles, manifested from the *un*manifested Light, which is Darkness to Man.

"When a World-Teacher appears, he contains within Himself all these Principles; nay, such a Teacher is in reality the Essence of all these Divine Attributes, created by the Lords of Wisdom especially in order to carry out the purpose of His incarnation, and give forth His Divine Message to Mankind.

"As to the Sovereignty of the Seven Great Lords, they wield enormous might but should not be termed 'All-Powerful,' for that is the Potency of the One Great Deity alone;

the Unknowable, the Unnameable, the *intra-cosioic* Deity; or Spirit and Matter inseparable from each other.

"The Seven Great Creator Gods, as represented in Esotericism, have a dual aspect; male or spiritual, and female or material, which is the same as Spirit and Matter, the two antagonistic principles.

"Synthetically, every creative Logos, or 'the Son who is one with the Father,' is the Host of the Rectores Mundi in Himself. Even Christian Theology makes of the seven 'Angels of the Presence' the Virtues, or the personified attributes of God, who, being created by Him, as the Manus were by Brahmâ, became Archangels. The Roman Catholic Theodice itself, recognizing in its creative Verbum Princeps the Head of these Angels and the Angel of the Great Council, thus recognizes the identity of Christ with them. If we limit the explanation to this Earth only, it was the duty of the first differentiated Egos—the Archangels or Gods—to imbue primordial Matter with evolutionary impulse and guide its formative Powers in the fashioning of its productions. Thus the Angels were commanded to create. After the Earth had been made ready by the *lower* and more material powers, the Gods were compelled by the evolutionary Law to descend on Earth, in order to construct the crown of its evolution—Mari. Thus the 'Self-created' and the 'Self-existing' projected their pale Shadows, except one Group who rebelled and refused to do so. Their piety was so great that it inspired them to refuse to 'create,' as they desired to remain 'Virgiri Youths' for ever, in order to anticipate, if possible, their fellows in the progress towards Nirvana-—the final *liberation*. They would not create will-less irresponsible men either, nor could they endow human beings with even the temporary reflections of their own attributes. Being of the class of Fire-Angels and belonging to another and a so much higher plane of consciousness, their reflections would leave man still irresponsible, hence interfere with any possibility of higher progress. They reasoned that no spiritual and psychic evolution is possible on Earth (which is the lowest and most material plane), for one who—on that plane at all events—is inherently perfect and cannot accumulate merit or demerit. Had Man remained the pale Shadow of the inert, immutable and motionless Perfection, he would have been doomed to pass through life on Earth as in a heavy dreamless sleep; hence he would have been a failure on this plane. But for the fact that the Gods communicated unto man a Ray of the Divine Light this would have happened-

"All this refers to man's spiritual awakening and not to his physical creation, since man existed in his animal form before the Gods descended and gave him evolving consciousness, cyclic and spiral; therefore progressive; an immutable Law of Nature, which is Eternal Motion in philosophical metaphysics.

"Thus we have a simultaneous evolution of seven human groups on seven different portions of the earth, created by the Seven Lords simultaneously. As the Divine Pymander teaches: 'This is the Mystery that to this day was hidden. Nature being mingled with the Heavenly Man [Elohim, Gods, Dhyân Chohans], brought forth a wonder . . . seven Men, all males and females [Hermaphrodites] . . . according to the nature of the seven Governors,' or the Seven Hosts, who projected or created him.

"These male-female men were destroyed as being imperfect, according to the Babylonian Legend of Creation, for the balance of the sexes was missing. They were destroyed by bringing into equilibrium those who did not yet exist, the Legend goes on.

"In other words, they were incarnated as the androgynes, men-women, who in later incarnations appeared as the sexual Race of Man. In this reference to the 'Governors' we find a confirmation of the 'Father-Mother' Gods of Spirit and Matter, eternally indissoluble.

"The Heavenly Man, or Tetragrammaton, who is the Protogonos, Tikkoun, the First-born from the Positive

Deity and the first manifestation of that Deity's Shadow, is the universal Form and Idea which engenders the Manifested Logos, Adam Kadmon, or the four-lettered symbol in the Kabalah of the Universe Itself, also called the second Logos. The Second springs from the First and develops the Third Triangle; from the last of which (the lower host of Angels) *Men* are generated. The Gods—the Regents and Instructors—are actual and existing Entities, which gave spiritual birth to, nursed, and instructed Mankind in its early youth. They are the Shining Ones, having efficacious eyes; they are great, helpful, imperishable and pure. All the Seven are of like Mind and Speech and they all act alike. They are the creators and destroyers of their human progeny, their protectors, overseers and rulers. Their shining efficacious eyes are the stars, and they are the Lords of the seven principal planets, and thus they are on the physical and sidereal planes. On the Spiritual plane they are the Divine Powers; the Watchers, Pitris or Fathers. Mortals need only to be sufficiently spiritualized to know this. There will then be no need to *force* them into a correct comprehension of this supreme Wisdom. They will *know* that there never yet was a great World-reformer or Teacher who was not a direct emanation of the Logos, under whatever name known to them. In other words, such a Being is an *essential* incarnation of one of the 'Seven,' of the 'Divine Spirit which is sevenfold,' and who has already appeared in many past cycles. Thus the Ideal Light comes from the Ideal Light, and the Luminous Intelligence, which was always, and its unity was the Spirit enveloping the Universe.

"The Dhyânis of the Seven Heavens—the seven planes of Being—are the Noumena of the actual and future Elements, just as the Angels of the Seven Powers of Nature are the still higher Noumena of still higher Hierarchies.

"The Elohim of the Bible, the word 'Elohim' being a *plural* noun and not a singular one, as translated by the Christian translators, were known to the Gnostics, the most philosophical teachers of all the early Christian

Churches, as the creators of mankind and as a *lower* order of Angels; and they are not even *exalted* powers in Nature. These Elohim correspond to the Prajâpati of the Hindus and were the fashioners of man's material and Astral frame *only*. They could not give him intelligence and reason, and therefore, in symbolical language, they failed to create man.

"The Chief of them is known as Osiris, or the chief Sephira, or the chief Amshaspend, or Ormazd. They form the second aspect of the higher order of Spiritual Beings and are in conformity with the dual aspect of all things in Nature. Thus the seven Cosmocratores of the World, the 'World-Pillars,' mentioned by St. Paul, are double. One set being commissioned to rule the superior worlds, and the other to guide and watch over the world of matter. They form two aspects of the same Deity in the formless Universe of Thought.

"So we see the union of blind matter, guided by the insinuations of the Spirit, by which is meant the *Astral* Spirit and not the Divine Breath, for the Astral Spirit is already tainted with matter on account of its double essence of Spirit and Matter. With regard to the inhabitants of the Celestial Worlds you may esoterically read in the Anugîtâ: 'Whatever Entities there are in this World, movable or immovable, they are the very first to be dissolved [at the end of a period when the life of a World, Chain, or Solar System is partially or wholly indrawn, activity or manifestation ceasing in part or in whole]; and next the developments produced from the Elements [from which the visible Universe is fashioned]; and (after) these developments [or evolved entities], all the Elements. Such is the upward gradation among Entities. Gods, Men, Gandharvas [or Devas, the celestial choristers, who are, Cosmically, the aggregate Powers of the Solar Fire, and constitute its forces: and psychically the Intelligence residing in the Solar Ray, the highest of the Seven Rays, or mystically the Occult Force in the Moon, and physically the phenomenal, and spiritually the noumenal causes of Sound and the voice of Nature;] the Pishachas [evil elementals, or the elementaries of deceased persons]; the Asuras [who are spiritual beings whose activity lies not only on the demoniac or discordant side of evolution, but also on the Cosmic or harmonious; or who in modern Theosophical literature are regarded as those Spiritual Beings belonging to the Fifth Creative Hierarchy, some of whom come from a past Universe, springing forth fully-grown from the Planetary Logos, and some the fruitage of the first Chain, the 'Rebels' of many Cosmic myths]; the Râkshasas [the semi-human Giants or Titans so named in the Hindu Sacred Books, belonging to the Fourth Sub-Race, or the Turanians]; all have been created by Nature [Svabhava, or Prakriti, plastic Nature], not by actions, nor by a cause [physically]. These Brâhmanas, the Creators of the Worlds, are born here [on earth] again and again. And whatever is produced from them is dissolved in due time in those very five great elements, like billows in the Ocean. These great elements are in every way [beyond] the elements that make up the world [or the gross elements]. And he who is released from these five Elements [the Logoi, or the seven emanations or Rays of the Logos], goes to the highest goal. The Lord Prajâpati created all this by the Mind only [by Dhyâna—the concentrated Mind engaged in abstract contemplation—also called the seventh stage of Yoga, the eighth stage being Samadhi, or ecstatic meditation].

"The Hosts of these Sons of Light are the very Root of Spiritual Man; omniscient and omnipotent divine Intelligence of the highest Logos, which descends 'like a Flame spreading from the Eternal Fire, immovable, without increase or decrease, ever the same to the end' of the cycle of existence, and becomes Universal Life on the Mundane Plane.

"Man derives his Spiritual Soul from the Essence of the Sons of Wisdom, and the Spiritual Man corresponds directly with the higher 'coloured circles,' the Divine Prism which emanates from the One Infinite White Circle, or the highest Logos. The Gnostics considered the Astral Gods to be the Sons of Ialdabaoth, who again was the 'Son' of Sophia, or Wisdom. Ialdabaoth produces from himself the six stellar Spirits who are Iao (or Jehovah), Sabaoth, Adoneus, Eloaeus, Oreus, and Astaphaeus, and they are to them the inferior Gods. And the Ancients never regarded the Sun as a planet but as a central and fixed star, whilst the seven planets are his Brothers, not his Sons.

"The seven planets, having a harmonious motion, also have 'intervals corresponding to musical diastemes, rendering various sounds, so perfectly consonant that they produce the sweetest melody, which is inaudible to us only by reason of the greatness of the sound, which our ears are incapable of receiving,' as Censorious says. The Monad is the principle of all things, as the pupils of Pythagoras taught. From the Monad and the indeterminate Duad (or Chaos), Numbers; from Numbers, Points; from Points, Lines; from Lines, Superficies'; from Superficies, Solids; from these, Solid Bodies, whose elements are four: Fire, Water, Air, Earth; of all which transmuted (correlated) and totally changed the World consists. The incipient Monads in the Celestial Spheres, who have never yet had terrestrial bodies, have no sense of separate personalities, or EGO-ism. None of them have individuality in the sense in Which a man says: 'I am myself and no-one else.' They are not conscious of distinct separateness, for individuality is the characteristic of their Groups, not their units; and these characteristics vary with the degree of the planes to which they belong. The nearer they are to the highest region the purer and the less accentuated is the individuality Of each Group. They are finite in every respect, with the exception of their higher principles, the immortal Essences reflecting the universal Divine Flame, individualized and separated only in the regions of Illusion by a differentiation as illusive as the rest. They *Live* because they are the streams projected on that Cosmic Screen of Illusion from the Absolute Life.

"The Pitris, who created physical man, shoot out from their ethereal bodies still more ethereal and shadowy similitudes of themselves which might be called doubles, or Astral forms, in their own likeness. Thus the Monad is furnished with its first dwelling, and blind matter with a model around and upon which to build henceforth.

"After the intelligent mind is added — although at first this intelligence is latent — then the Soul of Man, in its dual aspect, is added to that body and lower mind, together with all the body's other principles, and under the patient guidance of the Soul, the Higher Mind slowly awakens during its millions of years of; earthly incarnations, until at last it becomes one *with* the Soul. From Shadow to luminous Angel they evolve, each according to his own colour and kind. And when at last they have become the highest of the Dhyân Chohans they can but bow in ignorance before the awful mystery of Absolute Being. Nevertheless, the process of evolution does not stop there, and final liberation, or merging *with* Absolute Being is the end of the ascent from simplicity to complexity, ending in the simplicity of the One Life — when the *Actual* is reached and the *real* Work commences in the Body of Night which is the Body of the Great Day!

"That Day is surrounded with a Ring which none have ever passed, except the 'Recorders,' the Great Deities of the Kosmos who have the destinies of all within their hands; for this 'Ring-pass-not' is the Boundary that separates the Finite — however infinite in man's sight — from the truly Infinite. And this the ultimate Goal of ALL!!

"The human, conscious, lower minds are found in the Celestial Group called Rupas, or Atomic Forms. They are called the Imperishable Jîvas, and constitute, through the order below their, own, the first Group of the first septenary Host — the great mystery of human, conscious, and intellectual Being. From that Field descend the Mind-Germs that will fall into generation. These Germs will become the semi-spiritual potencies in the physical cells, and are the cause of hereditary transmission of faculties and inherent qualities in man. These inner souls of the physical cells—the semi-spiritual plasms that dominate the germinal plasms—are the keys that must one day open the gates of the *terra incognita* of the Biologist, now called the dark mystery of Embryology. The most powerful, occult, and mysterious region of the seven spheres, however, is that represented by the planet Venus—or Shukra, a *male* Deity, who is the Son of Bhrigu, one of the Vedic Sages. It is through Shukra that the double-sexed human Race descended from the first 'Sweat-Born.' Therefore, it is symbolized by the sign ⊖ of the circle and diameter during the Third Race of Man, the hermaphrodites, and by the sign ⊕ in which a vertical line runs up to the diameter during the Fourth Race, expressive of male and female, though not separated yet, after which it becomes a +, or male and female, separated and fallen into generation. The planet Venus is symbolized by the sign of a globe (the female sign) over a cross, which shows the former as presiding over the natural generation of Man. The Egyptian Ankh, ☥, life, is only another form of Venus, or Isis, and esoterically it means that mankind and all animal life had stepped out of the divine spiritual circle and had fallen into physical male and female generation. Pythagoras calls Shukra-Venus the *Sol alter*, the 'other Sun.' According to the Occult Doctrine, Venus is our Earth's primary and its spiritual prototype. It is taught that every sin committed on Earth is felt by Venus, and every change on Venus is felt on, and reflected by, the Earth. The Teacher of the Third Race is the Guardian Spirit of the Earth and Men, and Venus is represented as the Preceptor of the Giants of the Fourth Race of Men who at one time obtained the sovereignty of all the Earth, and defeated the minor Gods. It is with the Regent of Venus, the informing Dhyân Chohan, that Occult Mysticism has to deal. Venus, or Lucifer, also Shukra and Ushanas, the Planet, is the light-bearer of our Earth in both the physical and mystic sense. This was well known to the early Christians, and one of the earliest Popes of Rome is known by his Pontiff Name as Lucifer. Every World has its Parent Star and Sister Planet. Thus, Earth is the adopted child and younger brother of Venus, but the inhabitants of both differ, each according to their own kind. Each Sphere has its forms and organisms in full harmony with the nature and state of the Sphere they inhabit. There are numberless Spheres and on not a single one is there any Being that has a resemblance to the Beings on its companion Sphere, or to any other in its own special progeny. This is a flat contradiction of Swedenborg's statements as to what the various inhabitants of different Spheres looked like, and the famous Astrologer Huygens laboured under the same mistaken idea when he declared that the Beings on other planets are identical with those who live on Earth, possessing the same figures, senses, brain-power, arts, sciences, dwellings, even to the same fabrics for their wearing apparel!

"The informing Intelligences which animate these various Centres of Being are worshipped under all sorts of names and symbols, but the initiates honour in them only the manifestations of *THAT*—which neither our Creators nor their Creatures can ever discuss or know anything about. The *ABSOLUTE* is not to be defined, and no mortal or immortal has ever seen or comprehended it during the periods of Existence. The mutable cannot know the Immutable, nor can that which lives perceive Absolute Life. Therefore, man cannot know higher Beings than his own Progenitors in the Celestial Spheres, nor shall he worship them, but he should know how humankind was created.

"And so each Planet stands for a definite Sphere in both the Physical and Psychic Realms; and no two are alike. More than even this is taught; for it is known that not even the highest Creator God, such as the Dhyân Chohans, can realize completely the condition of the preceding

Cosmic Evolution. It is only the First Logos, the Self-manifested Son of the Unmanifested Father, the Creator of the Creators of the various Races of Man, who retains a knowledge of His experiences in all Cosmic Evolutions throughout Eternity.

"Man's destiny is to rise from the lowest Sphere—the Earth—to the Higher. Thus he can first attain the psychic state of Intelligent and good men; thence to the state in which he thinks more of his inner condition than of his personality; this is the Higher Psychic State: then comes the Holy State, (when he has lost all tastes and desires and has commenced on the path towards Reunion; then the Super-Holy State where his lower Self has lost all Affinity with the senses. These are the first four States of Evolution. When they have been mastered he reaches unity with the Highest Occult Hierarchies who help onwards the evolution of humanity, and he has Cosmic Self-Consciousness with the Buddhic World.

"Then comes the Innate Christos State, the Sphere of the Divine Flame, the dwelling place of the highest Angels in the Region of the Pitris and Devas. Arid, finally, the Realm where he reaches the highest possible ecstatic trance-like State of Supreme Consciousness, where he loses the ordinary Consciousness of every individuality, including his own. He is then at the threshold of the great Choice. The unreal has been transformed into conditionless Reality, and the realities of the Earth and all the Astral Worlds have vanished in their own nature into thin and non-existing air. Absolute Truth has conquered relative truth; he has reached the state of self-analyzing reflection, and the absolute consciousness of the personality is merged into the impersonal Ego, which is above illusion in every sense. Thence he can emerge, and, assuming an ordinary appearance, teach men. These incarnations, which take place but very occasionally, may be conscious as well as unconscious, so far as the realization by himself of his own high status is concerned when he dwells in a human body for a time. Or, he can go forward and reach a state of consciousness which is beyond all description and all human comprehension. He is free to choose, even as every human being is free to do so in a lesser way."

Neteru-Hem paused, and the multitudes of Divine Beings and Presences, unseen, because mortal eye cannot behold them and live, could yet be felt; and it seemed that the Celestial Spheres were filled with Angelic Voices, sweet and reverent and utterly blest. Spirits winged with activity they are and informed with power, everlastingly delightful, in exuberant glorious youth; pure and serene, with an intensity of flaming love, and luminous with ethereal life and joy. They are the Chariots of God's Will, ever blessing Him, and speeding through His vast Realms on His seraphic errands, enraptured and transcendent. Each one is an epitome of man's evolution—for all have once been men. Now, they are Lords of the Flame, Sons of Fire, the great Hierarchies of Spiritual Beings who guide the Solar System, and who later still will guide a Universe. Existing from Eternity to Eternity, they have descended down the Scale of being into the lowest form of Illusion, and risen again in mighty Arcs of Splendour, which will continue to extend in might and majesty and magnificence for ever and for ever; until they themselves become Lords of the Immortals, unmanifested but omnipresent; One in All, All in One.

This is the heritage of All Men.

DIAMOND

Out of the Highest, Unknown, Deity,
A Holy Essence forms in Hidden Logos.
A Secret Spring — from which come forth
The Seven Shining Sons
Who sparkle in the deep-blue sky,
And scintillate with gleaming Fire;
Beholding far below the waving Veils
That hide the Earth in shrouds fallacious,
In Fantasies, Deceptions of the Mind,
Concealing Radiant Truth.

* * *

O, may the Light now penetrate within the lowest worlds,
And cleanse away with Purifying Flame
All sin of ignorance and lack of comprehension.
And may the Blessings of Enlightenment
And Love and Wisdom bring the PEACE
To all the dwellers in the dark;
And lift them up towards the Glories
Of that Great Paraclete, the Ruler of the Universe,
Divine of Breath and full of Sacredness
Beyond all human apprehension

VISION 12
GOD
(IEUE)

It was an Apocalypse of Glory! An Empire of Absolute Being; affirming Itself eternally to its own immeasurable nobility of Divine Spirit; so far removed from the hydra-headed breed of Earth and the Spectres on the Threshold.

No more were seen the offspring of Unreason and the Hadean Night, nor the dwellers in the lower worlds — reflections cast upon the mist of the abyss, phantoms painted on the Veil of Illusion.

If only Ma-u and Ma-uti might stay here for ever they thought; and they looked upon the Messenger with pleading eyes. But this was not to be as yet, and they both realized that soon the moment must come when Netera-Hem would lead them back to the lower regions, so that they could spread the Message of what they had seen and heard.

An *old* Message, yet ever new; for Man forgets too soon the Holy Teachings, or tries to fit new explanations to the Golden Truths, which never alter!

Most men are blind, and there is, too, the ever-rising tide of younger souls, ascending like a mist from the morass of the material. All have to learn their lessons and climb the heights with painful effort and leaden feet; and with every upward step they take, there spread below them clouds of younger souls in never ending waves.

"Creation is as eternal as Eternity," said Neteru-Hem. " Although it proceeds in gigantic Cycles of activity and rest, it never really ceases; for as one Cycle slows down, another recommences in the Universe; every Kosmos being equivalent to an almost invisible atom in Space, when viewed from the Standpoint of Space-Dimensions, which in itself is a contradiction in terms, for Space — being both without beginning and end — can have no dimensions as understood in human terms of reasoning and is as eternal as what is understood by time.

"When people talk about the Central Sun of the Universe being the Abode of the Invisible Deity and have no idea of what the Occult meaning of this concept is, they are misled by their own limited conceptions of what a 'Universe' represents in Time and Space, Creation and Eternity. The NUMBER of Universes in Space is equally of such magnitude that here again we meet Eternity in a new form; that of a Number which — although it never had a beginning — has no end either; therefore, it becomes NO-number, and a Circle, as in the end it returns into itself: everything moving and evolving in circles, ovoids, and spirals in cyclic evolution of the Universes of Spirit and Matter — which are One!

"And Universes do not fall in Space at a terrific rate, nor contract, nor expand as science believes, formulating one theory after another, but they ever RISE spirally and during their ascent they awake and go to rest periodically — but ever on the UPWARD grade in cyclic Curves which narrow gradually until the unimaginable Apex is reached!

"And these untold myriads of Universes all follow the same Laws of motion, repulsion and attraction, and *they* again turn eternally around a still more gigantic Central Sun — the Abode of a still more mighty and Invisible Deity. And so on for ever and ever, without beginning or end.

"When we consider the Mystery of the One Concealed Deity, we are confronted with yet another Eternity — that of Mighty, Hidden Gods; each one more sublime, regal and majestic in his Grandeur than the one before, also without beginning or end. Yet all is in absolute unity, for as the Deity is Absolute, it must be omnipresent also; for as you have already learnt, there is not an atom but contains IT within itself.

"The Kabalah teaches that the Deity is One, because IT is infinite. It is triple, because IT is ever manifesting. It is triple in the manifestation of its aspects, for, as Aristotle says, it requires three principles for every natural body to become objective, namely, privation, form, and matter; privation, in the terms of Aristotle, meaning that which Occultism calls the prototypes impressed in the Astral Light—the lowest plane and world of the World-*Soul*.

"These principles can only be united by a fourth: that of Life; which radiates from the summits of the Unreachable, to become a universally diffused Essence on the manifested planes of Existence."

"Is there no end to the evolving Monads, dear Messenger?" asked Ma-uti.

"There *is* a limit, my child, although the Hosts of more or less progressed Monads are almost incalculable. But in spite of their numbers they are still finite in number and being, as all material things are finite. Through their assimilation of many successive Personalities they grow more and more perfect; and gradually they return to their Source—the Absolute Deity. But these limits apply only to each Universe as it evolves and becomes perfect. There is *no* limit to the number of newly evolving Universes, and they always were and will be.

"The seeming Eternity of these Monadic Pilgrims is but a moment in actual Eternity. Worlds, Solar Systems, and Universes are in appearance like a regular tidal ebb of flux and reflux.

"Just as these ebbs and flows have been observed by physical science and recorded in all departments of nature, so they appear and disappear in rhythms of the most colossal dimensions of Spirit and Matter in the Universe of Universes. No Divine Soul can have an independent conscious existence before the spark, which issued from the pure Essence of God, has passed through every elemental form of the phenomenal world of the great Life-Wave of a Logos, and has acquired individuality, first by natural impulse, and then by self-induced and self-devised efforts, thus ascending through all the degrees of intelligence, from the lowest to the highest. Until at last they bathe in the Light of God, and can nevermore be deceived by the Veil of Illusion.

"Matter is eternal also, becoming atomic only periodically. When talking about the Gods—the emanations from the One Logos—we must not confuse the purely meta-physical personifications of the *abstract* attributes of Deity with their reflections, the Sidereal Gods. These reflections are in reality the objective expressions of the abstractions; *living* Entities, and the models formed on the Divine Prototype. Deity is not God. It is Nothing, and Darkness to Man. The Highest God, the Unmanifested Logos, is Its Son.

"In the Revelations of Marcus, the chief of the Marcosians, who flourished in the middle of the second Century, he writes: 'When first its Father [that is: of the Tetrad]'. . . the Inconceivable, the Beingless, Sexless, desired that Its Ineffable [the First Logos] should be born, and Its Invisible should be clothed with form, Its mouth opened and uttered the Word like unto Itself. This Word [or Logos] standing near showed It what It was, manifesting itself in the form of the Invisible One. Now the uttering of the [Ineffable] Name [through the Word] came to pass in this manner. It [the Supreme Deity] uttered the first Word of its Name . . . which was a combination [or syllable] of *four* elements [letters]. Then the second combination was added, also of *four* elements. Then the third composed of *ten* elements; and after this the fourth was uttered, which contained *twelve* elements. The utterance of the whole Name consisted thus of *thirty* elements and of *four* combinations. Each element has its own letters and peculiar character, and pronunciation, and groupings and similitudes; but none of them perceives the form of that of which it is the element, nor understands the utterance of its neighbour, but, what each sounds forth itself, as sounding forth all [it can], *that* it thinks good to call the whole . .

. And these sounds are they which manifest in form the Beingless and Ingenerable *Æon* [First Logos], and these are the forms which are called Angels, perpetually beholding the Face of the Father' [the first Logos, or 'Second God,' who stands next Deity the Inconceivable].

"When the Occultists say that Deity is no Being, for It is Nothing—No-thing, they are more reverential than those who call God HE, and thus make of Him a Gigantic Male.

"The *Deity* Itself is ever concealed and called the Hidden One; It is connected only indirectly with Creation, and can act only through the Dual Force emanating from the Eternal Essence—which is the Supreme Hidden *Logos*.

"It is philosophically impossible to accept the idea of the absolute ALL creating or even evolving the Kosmos or the Universe, for absolute Unity cannot pass to Infinity, for Infinity presupposes the limitless extension of *something* and the duration of something; and the One ALL—like Space, which is its only mental and physical representation on the earth, or Our plane of existence—is neither an object of, nor a subject to, perception. If one could suppose 'the eternal infinite ALL, the omnipresent Unity, instead of being in Eternity, becoming through periodical manifestation a manifold Universe or a multiple Personality, that unity would cease to'be One. Therefore, it is never the Deity Itself which creates, but only Its Emanation, the Son, the Hidden First Logos, from whom all other Logoi are born, commencing with the first Seven Self-Generated Ones.

"It is not the One unknown ever present God in Nature we must reject, but the 'God' of human dogma, and his humanized 'Word.' Man, in his infinite conceit and inherent pride and vanity, shaped that conception himself with his sacrilegious hand out of the material he found in his own small brain-fabric, and forced it upon his fellows as a direct revelation from the unknown First Cause. The Occultist, on the other hand, accepts revelation as coming from divine yet still finite Beings, the manifested Lives, never from the unmanifestable *One Life*."

"How should one pray to the Spiritual Beings?" asked Ma-u. "For although they are finite they must have tremendous Powers, and if an unselfish prayer is directed towards them they can and will heagr and respond?"

"Yes," replied the Divine Messenger, "they can and do. But one should never address them with requests that have only to do with material advantages for the supplicant. The only things we may ask for are in regard to spiritual matters, such as will advance the World spiritually. With regard to material advantages, there are quite natural Laws one may put in action. But we are not concerned with those now.

"To address the Higher Beings you must never kneel down; for the act of kneeling down *lowers* the whole attitude of the petitioner, and brings him in attunement with the *lower* worlds of beings; with the material, or even lower. Therefore, the supplicant should stand upright, with arms crossed over the breast and one hand resting lightly on each shoulder. He should look UP. Furthermore, he should address his petition silently and mentally; for the spoken word issues from within outwards, and as soon as it is uttered it flows into the material realms of illusion and is lost there. It can then have material results only and, at the worst, they may be dire in the extreme, or be answered with Satanic laughter by the lower elementals if the prayer should be in connection with Spiritual conditions. The only powers that can be addressed with the spoken word are the dark beings, or the material. In order to petition the Divine Denizens of the Spiritual Realms, the prayer should be from without inwards; from the material to the Spiritual. That is the only way in which such prayers will reach the goal for which they are intended. At the same time, the supplicant should raise up his thoughts. They should go inwards and upwards, and always silently.

"Here is a Prayer which is absolutely Spiritual, and yet can have marvellous results for the good of *all* mankind if sincerely projected in the manner I have just described:—

'Light, Life and Love.
May the Spirit of Goodness reach out into all Space.
May the positive POWERS of these Principles overcome all negative conditions.
And may Peace Profound reign everywhere.
So mote it be.
Amén, Amén, Amén.'

"Face the East when doing this, and do it as many times each day and night as you can.

"This will help the World in general, for you will attune with the Great White Brotherhood of all the Divine and Spiritual Entities; and they will HEAR you and ACT.

"Once upon a time this Law was well known; but it has been lost to man on account of the selfishness or the ignorance—both of which are great sins—of the teachers and the priests, who should have kept it alive by reminding their disciples of it continually. Similarly, the Hierophants of the ancient times, in which these men gradually obscured more and more the sacred laws for selfish reasons, have combined so cleverly the dogmas and symbols of their scientific religious systems, that this ancient Wisdom can be grasped only if one has the combination and knowledge of *all* the keys.

"Although it was necessary to preserve the chief interpretations from the profane and wrap them in the greatest secrecy, yet the more simple laws should never have been hidden; for this has done incalculable harm to humanity. They grope in the dark and make the most appalling errors with the best intentions.

"A great thinker once said that: 'The possibility of rising to a comprehension of a system of coordination so far outreaching in time and space all range of human observations, is a circumstance which signalizes the power of man to transcend the limitations of changing and inconsistent matter, and assert his superiority over all insentient and perishable forms of being.' This is true and shows the godlike qualities inherent in man; who is a God in embryo.

"Occultism teaches that: 'Deity is an arcane, living or moving Fire, and the eternal witnesses to this unseen Presence are Light, Heat and Moisture; this trinity including, and being the cause of, every phenomenon in Nature.'

"All the great doctrines teach that the one infinite and unknown Essence exists from all eternity, and is either passive or active in regular and harmonious successions.

"In the Upanishads are contained the beginning and the end of all human knowledge; but the keys have been lost since the days of Buddha. The reason is that the Brâhmans abridged the texts by detaching from the MSS. the most important portions, containing the last word of the Mystery of Being. This was done because the Brâhmans were afraid that on account of the teachings of Buddha, who tried to save the world by popularizing these teachings, their Sacred Knowledge and Occult Wisdom was falling into the hands of the vulgar. The key to the Brâhmanical secret code remained henceforth with the Initiates alone, and the Brâhmans were thus in a position publicly to deny the correctness of Buddha's teachings by appealing to their Upanishads, which, in their condensed form, were silent for ever on all the chief questions.

"In a similar manner, throughout history, have the priests from time to time hidden the keys to the mysteries and obscured at least *some* of the Wisdom which is the heritage of ALL. This is done so that only a limited number of aspirants can have entrance to the mysteries, in order that the ranks of the priests shall not be swollen beyond control, for thus the power which is now in the hands of the comparatively few would be distributed among many, and thus lose potency.

"The various initiations are difficult enough in any case, for the pupil has to be in very strict training all the time if he wishes to qualify for Adeptship.

"The first stage is the 'entering of the stream,' when the neophyte has passed his first initiation and is on the first stage of the path. This is called Srotâpatti.

"After the second initiation he becomes a Sakadâgâmin, he who will now reincarnate once more; the second stage.

"Then comes the third initiation, Anâgâmin, or, not liable to return into incarnation.

"Then the fourth, when the aspirant becomes an Arhan.

"The aspirant, though he can see the Past, the Present and the Future, is not yet the highest initiate on the Four Paths to Nirvâna; for the Adept himself, the *initialed* candidate, becomes pupil to a higher Initiate. Three higher grades have still to be conquered by the Arhan who would reach the apex of the ladder of Adeptship. There are those who have reached it even in this present time of ours, but the faculties necessary for the attainment of these higher grades will be fully developed, in the *average* ascetic, only after many millions of years. Thus there will always be Initiates, as well as the profane, until the very end of this 'World-Cycle: until the Day when the Spark will re-become the Flame, when Man will merge into his Dhyân Chohan, or everything will be merged in God, or the Divine Unity.

"After that, the Great Gods and their Hosts 'awake' anew, and a new Universe springs into being.

"It is taught that the Deify, the ever invisible Presence, manifests like the sea from which outflows a stream called Wisdom, the waters of which fall into a lake named Intelligence.

" 'When the Elohim framed Adam Kadmon [the Heavenly Man], the Spirit of the Eternal shot out of His Body, like a sheet of lightning that radiates at once on the billows of the seven millions of Skies.'

" 'Life is drawn from below, and from above the source renews itself, the sea is always full and spreads its waters everywhere.'

"The Great Teachers of Mankind, the Illuminati, have within themselves the spirit of one of the Angels, apart from their own spiritual principles. Though often threatened by the lower elementals and the dark beings who dwell on earth and in the Astral Spheres, they cannot be destroyed, for no inferior being can withstand a single Ray from God. Thus the Messengers who spread God's Wisdom are always and ever protected, no matter how often appearances are to the contrary. They are the Gods come to Earth, to rekindle the Fire of Truth and light the Lamp of Spiritual Understanding, for in the intervals between the Blessings of their sojourns on the Planet that Fire gradually dies down, and the Lamp flickers and is extinguished by man's lack of spiritual intelligence and the deceptions of the Illusions of the senses.

" 'Motion is the Alchemical Solvent of Life; Spirit and Matter are the two States of the One Deity, which is neither Spirit nor Matter, both being the Absolute Life. Spirit is the first differentiation of and in Space; and Matter is the first differentiation of Spirit. THAT, which is neither Spirit nor Matter, that is IT — the causeless Cause of Spirit and Matter, which are the Cause of Kosmos. And THAT we call the One Life, or the Intra-Cosmic Breath, as it is taught in the Book of Dzyan.

"It is most necessary that the true Teachings shall again be spread among mankind. Is it not foretold in the Book called 'Vishnu Purina' that the whole world will be in a terrible 'turmoil? The writer of that book prophecies that there will be rulers upon the earth of churlish spirit, violent temper, and ever addicted to falsehood and wickedness. They will inflict death on women and children, seize the property of their subjects; they will be of limited power, their lives will be short, their desires insatiable. People of various countries will mingle with them and follow their example; the people will perish, wealth and piety will decrease day by day, until the world will be wholly depraved. Dishonesty will be the universal means of subsistence; weakness the cause of dependence; menace and presumption will be substituted for learning; a man, if rich, will be reputed pure. He who is strongest will reign; the people, unable to bear the heavy burdens will flee; thus decay will constantly proceed, until the human race approaches its annihilation. Then, a portion of that divine Being which exists of its own spiritual nature shall descend upon Earth, endowed with super-human faculties. He will reestablish, righteousness upon earth; and the minds of those who are still alive shall be awakened, and shall be as pellucid as crystal. The men who are thus changed shall be as the seeds of human beings, and shall give birth to a race which shall follow the laws of the Age of Purity. This prediction is already coming to pass, and as many men as will hear should be prepared *now* for the coming of that great enlightenment.

"The Secret Teachings establish three fundamental propositions: Firstly, an Omnipresent, Eternal, Boundless and Immutable Principle, on which all speculation is impossible, since it transcends the power of human conception and can only be dwarfed by any human expression or similitude. It is beyond the reach of thought; unthinkable and unspeakable. Secondly, the Eternity of the Universe in *toto* as a boundless Plane; periodically the playground of numberless Universes; incessantly manifesting and disappearing, called the manifesting Stars, and the Sparks of Eternity. Thirdly, the fundamental identity of all Souls with the Universal Over-Soul, the latter being Itself an *Aspect* of the Unknown Root. And further, the obligatory pilgrimage for every Soul—a spark of the former—through the Cycles of Incarnation during the whole term of each Universe or Kosmos.

"Remember again, that by Soul is meant the higher Mind, which is the negative aspect of the positive Soul—which never incarnates in the same manner as the higher Mind.

"Further, it is only 'with a Mind clear and undarkened by Personality, and an assimilation of the merit of manifold Existences devoted to Being in its collectivity [the whole living and sentient Universe], that one gets rid of personal existence, merging into, becoming one with the Absolute, and continuing in full possession of super-consciousness, which is the highest truth of Reality; hence the greater Consciousness, or *Self*, which scrutinises that lesser consciousness which is below, or outward; the reflection which analyses itself.

"The Worlds, to the profane, are built up of the known (?) elements. To the conception of the Spiritual Intelligence that has conquered, subdued, and trained inatter until his body is but the material expression of himself, it is divine Life.

"The Soul of Man is a God, and his Mind its counterpart, in spite of physiology, which admits Mind only as a temporary function of the material brain, and no more.

"It is equal to the various 'Creators' in the Sublime Regions, and it has been, and is, often in direct contact with these Gods through the Minds of the trained Occultists, who have both perceived and sensed them.

"These Creators have *Form*, represented by the pyramid of the triad, and therefore matter, the cube, making up the septenary Being.

"As the *Soul*, or Spirit — this being the *positive* Principle of both men and Gods — is without form, however, it must be the *Minds* of both [*their negative* principles] which are the material parts of both Gods and Men. And although the Soul-Minds of the Gods, Devas, Angels, or whatever else we call them, consist of both Spirit and Matter, and the *One Deity* is Pure Spirit, though transcended beyond human or Angelic conception, this proves that before Man or Angel can finally be liberated, and return to that Divine Essence of the Deity, he must either so sublimate that Mind-part of the Soul that it becomes pure Spirit, or lose it altogether.

"There is One Eternal Law, which always adjusts contraries and produces final Harmony. And it is by this Law of Spiritual development, superseding the physical and purely intellectual (matter and mind), that Gods and Men will become freed, and find themselves finally Self-redeemed.

"We must learn to distinguish between the various principles from the All-Cause downward.

"The All-Cause, the One Life, the Deity, is Supreme Spirit. It causes to come into being the Living Spirit of Nature. From this proceeds the Spiritual or Intellectual Soul. Thence the Living, or Life Soul. Then the embodied Soul, or Universe of Spirit and Ethereal Matter. And finally, the False Perception—or material Universe. This is the Esoteric Order of the effects of the All-Cause.

"Plato has said that: 'Beyond all *finite* existences and *secondary* causes, all laws, ideas and principles, there is an Intelligence or Mind (Nous), the first principle of all principles, the Supreme Idea on which all other Ideas are grounded, . . . the *ultimate* substance *from which all things derive their being and essence*, the First and efficient Cause of all the order, and harmony, and beauty and excellency, and goodness, which pervade the Universe.'

"From the transformation into energy of the supra-conscious Thought of the Deity, infused into the objectivation of the latter out of potential latency into the One Reality, spring the wondrous Laws of Matter out of unmanifested primordial Matter. These are the Noumena of which phenomena are the expression. Matter succeeds the Thought, but, *minus* Matter, the Thought is for all practical intents and purposes nonexistent. Thus closely knit together are Spirit and Matter; or Deity and the manifested Universe.

Space and Time are One; they are nameless, for they axe the incognizable THAT, which can be sensed *only* through its Seven Rays—which are the Seven Creations, Worlds, Laws, Gods. That the Ancients knew this is proved in the Papyrus of Ani, where it says: 'O God Ani, Thou residest in the agglomeration of Thy Divine Personages.'; the God Ani in this case being the Spiritual Sim.

"In the 'Secret Doctrine' it is justly said that: 'The true Ideal Deity, the One Living God in Nature, can never suffer in man's worship if that outward cloak, woven by man's fancy, mid thrown upon the Deity by the crafty hand of the priest greedy of power and domination, is drawn aside. The hour has struck . . . to dethrone the 'Highest God' of every nation in favour of One Universal Deity — the God of Immutable Law, not charity; the God of Just Retribution, not mercy, which is merely an incentive to evil-doing and to a repetition of it. The greatest crime that was ever perpetrated upon mankind was committed on the day when the first priest invented the first prayer with a selfish object in view. A God who may be propitiated by iniquitous prayers to 'bless the arms' of the worshipper, and send defeat and death to thousands of his enemies — his brethren; a Deity that can be supposed not to turn a deaf ear to chants of laudation mixed with entreaties for a 'fair propitious wind' for self, and as naturally disastrous to the selves of other navigators who come from an opposite direction — it is this idea of God that has fostered selfishness in man, and deprived him of his self-reliance. Prayer is an ennobling action when it is an intense feeling, an ardent desire rushing forth from our very heart for the good of other people, and when entirely detached from any selfish personal object; the craving for a beyond is natural and holy in man, but on the conditions of sharing that bliss with others.'

"For this reason the 'heathen' Socrates declared in his profound though untaught Wisdom that: 'Our prayers should be for blessings on all, in general, for the Gods know best what is good for us.' Official prayer — in favour of a public calamity, or for the benefit of one individual irrespective of losses to thousands — is the most ignoble of crimes, besides being an impertinent conceit and a superstition.

"The true God dwells *within* the heart of each human being, not without, and when St. Paul said: 'The first man is of the earth, earthy; the second man is the Lord from Heaven,' he meant to convey that each man is a Temple of his God, in which the Spirit of God dwells. That is the God — the 'God of our Hearts' — to which we should direct our petitions for the good of our brothers and the world in general.

" 'ONE is the Spirit of the Living God who (dwells in all and) liveth for ever. Voice, Spirit and Word: this is the Holy Spirit.' This is the God of every Philosopher, God infinite and impersonal, though personally present everywhere; God in Nature (the Universe) and Nature in God.

"Man's prayers and supplications are vain, unless to potential words, mentally spoken or softly uttered, he adds potent *acts*, which can make the Aura, which surrounds each, so pure and divine that the God within may act outwardly, or become as it were an extraneous Potency. Thus have Initiates, Saints, and very holy and pure men been enabled to help others as well as themselves in the hour of need, and produce what the foolish call ' miracles.' Iamblichus has shown how this union of our Higher Minds with the Universal Soul, or with the Gods, can be effected. He speaks of Manteia, which is Samâdhi, the highest trance. He speaks also of the dream, which he calls divine Vision, when man re-becomes again a God. By Theurgy a man arrives at Prophetic Discernment through our God (the respective Higher Ego of each of us) revealing to us the truths of the plane on which we happen to be acting; secondly, Ecstacy and Illumination; thirdly, action in Spirit, through the Will or in the Astral Body; fourthly, Domination over the minor, senseless elementals, by the very nature of our purified Egos. But this demands the complete purification of the latter. He calls this Magic, through Initiation into Theurgy. This has to be preceded by a training of man's senses and the knowledge of the human Self in relation to the *Divine Self*. This training is the *duty* of every Occultist and Mystic, who *dare* not leave off when once he has commenced, for the consequences are dire, since he has opened a portal to the disincarnate beings which must be constantly guarded, lest undesirable ones of the lower classes enter and take possession of his bodily Temple. There is no religion higher than Truth.

"It is only by intelligent and expert manipulation of Natural or Universal Principles that any spiritual or material results can be achieved. Such knowledge can only be attained under the wise guidance of masterly men who know the Laws underlying such Principles. Such Teachers are found mostly in the Great Mystic and Occult Schools, Orders, and Organizations, of which there are still a *few* in the present-day World.

"But let all beware of the little cliques, circles, and furtive 'meetings' of self-proclaimed 'masters,' who have neither authority, training or knowledge, except the cunning to fleece the aspirant who is misled by their bombastic claims.

"And now, my children, our pilgrimage is ended and I must lead you back to the realms of Illusion, for there is work awaiting you among your Brothers and Sisters on Earth."

Ma-u and Ma-uti heaved a deep sigh. To what depths of existence had they descended; risen to what Heights of Vision, Wisdom and Beauty!

There was no more a sense of separation in their consciousness. They were One with All, and All with One.

The Cosmic pulse throbbed within their minds and hearts, they were no longer pluralities nor separate entities, but One in Spirit with all Spiritual Souls which form the One Soul. Time and Space had taken on new meanings and robed themselves with Truth. The limitations of mere words could never reveal the greatness of their newly gathered Treasure.

Slowly they followed the Messenger as new surroundings of Splendour became visible on their way back to the Golden Path they had first ascended.

New Beings, dressed like butterflies in the Garden of Indra, floated about and roamed on the slopes of shining hills in all the beauty of Eternal Spring.

And a soft breeze, golden with the yellow pollen of the flowers, drifted in the verdant valleys, as if the scented blooms were a fragrant artillery of fairy cannons, whose spicy clouds of smoke perfumed the air.

It was like a Poetic Creator's Empire of all the nectar of loveliness. Happy are the Souls upon whom the Angels of these Regions look with smiling eyes; the refuge of virtue and comeliness of which the earthly ones can only dream.

And garlands of flowers draped the forms of these shining creatures, and they were anointed with magic unguents, drawn from the gracious trees that blossomed in red and orange, with pinnate leaves that glittered in the light.

There were sweet maids who gathered flowers at the entrance of gracious arbours and who with sidelong glances beheld the Messenger and his friends.

Like the flashing of the ruby amid green leaves they moved with gliding steps and nymph-like bearing, and Ma-u and Ma-uti expected every moment to see them rise up and fly in the lenitive, balsamic air like golden robins on rapid wings.

Auspicious sounds of silvery singing drifted upon the soft currents of aromatic atmosphere, like angels' voices heard in reveries beside cool rushing streams.

In golden palankeens, surrounded by swaying, dancing, slim-waisted shapes in festal array there rested delectable ladies with necklaces of priceless jewels and shimmering raiment in flowing folds.

And in the heavens floated gleaming swans with bodies of gold, like golden lotuses flowering in the waters of a holy lake; their eyes of pearl, their beaks and feet of coral, and wings be-tipp'd with emerald—glorious to behold.

A domain of unalloyed happiness and bliss.

And in the distance rose up palace after palace which seemed to swim among the rosy, feathery clouds in fadeless magnificence and lustre.

"This is the place where dreams come true for a while and all longings are satisfied," said Neteru-Hem.

"It is the habitation of beauty-starved mortals during their time of rest between two incarnations.

"Whatever man has wished for in vain whilst on earth is granted here; and there are millions of such climes within the Astral Realms. They are the Heavens and Paradises of all beliefs and creeds; and none intrudes upon another. Let us pass on."

And in passing they glimpsed once more the World of Astral Fire in its marvellous and timeless effulgence; and, too, the exaltation of some of the other splendid regions they had seen before.

At last they arrived at the noble cliffs and the pellucid Ocean first seen as a mirage in the sky at the end of the Golden Path that stretched from the earth upwards to the Sun. The descent began, and, passing down the Steps of Gold, there burst great rockets of magic fire up in the sky; and multicoloured sparks fell down. And great streamers of light in the seven colours of the rainbow and endless tints and shades rose up. All lines in the colours of the spectrum were represented, vibrating with life and trembling with radiant energy.

At the foot of the Golden Stairway there was a glory of vibrant hues. Soft shining rose dominated, with blue fading into ultra-violet, and gold and green and red and silver in tremendous agitation, quivering in fiery illumination. A blazing farewell and invitation to return again.

And as they walked down they beheld the *Souls* of the Unseeing, glowing with Tyrian Rays. But the Un-seeing wandered about in dull groups, in pairs, or alone, upon the earth; heads bent down and eyes to the ground, instead of lifted up to the glories in the heavens.

Bound to earth they are; enclosed and ensnared in the material. Their Souls watch and wait with endless patience and hope for the first look upwards and the opening of the blind eyes.

Once again the boundless beauties of earth and sky and all the wonders of Nature's dreaming Illusions unfolded themselves to Ma-u and Ma-uti. But how dull they seemed when compared with the Glory of the Realms of the Spirit!

Truly! they had forded the River of Death and returned again; laden with Knowledge and Wisdom.

"Dear Messenger," said Ma-uti, "how long has our journey lasted?"

"The answer, my child, was given you when you handed back the Cups at the Holy Well of Memory and Revelation," replied Neteru-Hem smilingly, "Remember — a thousand, years may pass in a flash, as though they had never been, and a flash in time may seem to last a thousand years; for Time and Space are both Illusions."

And now the Divine Messenger's kindly voice was heard for the last time, and he said: "Cleave to the Ideal, above and through all lesser mundane things. Do not be allured by worldly knowledge or the seductions of the 'senses, the lust for power or riches, and the blast of spiritual vanity: for they are all as nothing and must fade away like phantoms in the Light of God's everlasting inner Sun. So wilt thou canonise thy eternal Heritage, and to the pinnacle of thy Seership will be added the Sacredness of Divine Wisdom. Carry out thy task and fear not. There is no death in all the Universe; for every Soul is for ever *dis*-carnate, all bodily realization being illusion of the senses and unevolved Mind.

"Good-bye, my children, be not downcast, for we shall surely meet again."

Speechless with sorrow Ma-u and Ma-uti saw that Holy Shape dissolve slowly in the light of the evening Sun; and all seemed emptiness.

His Presence was no longer visible to mortal sight, yet deep within they knew that never again could they be isolated from His Holy Communion; and never would they forget His loving voice and wise Teachings.

And in the sky there shone the same marvellous spectacle still of Sea and Cliffs with the Path of Gold that stretched from Ra down to the place under the great oak where Ma-u and Ma-uti were standing — the same in every detail; for in a flash they had beheld some of the wonders of Eternity in all its Majesty and Splendour; and they had become conscious of a particle of the Divine Wisdom of the Gods — an Initiation and Illumination indeed!

* * *

O! God of Mercy, pour out Thy Sparkling Vials of Beauty upon the Mind of Man; so that he may bathe in Thy Effulgence, and his sight may be washed clean of all earthly matter. For with the realization of the beauty of all Thy Creations will come Love for Thee and Thy Creatures, so that evil shall be no more; nor Darkness or Shadow; but instead, Thy Eternal Light shall shine upon all. For once the scales have fallen from the eyes that behold Thy Glory there can be no more returning to Darkness and Ignorance; and those that are so Blessed will ever after look up to Thee and merge with Thy Holy Spirit.

So mote it be!

Amén. Amén. Amén.

OCCULT ENIGMAS
By J. MICHAUD, Ph.D.

1st EDITION MAY 15, 1939   2nd EDITION MAY 29, 1939
3rd EDITION JUNE, 30,1939   Dutch translation in preparation

CONTENTS

The Work of the Masters. Karma. Re-Incarnation. Evolution. Intellect, Instinct and Intuition. The Temple You Dwell In. The Astral World. Optimism *versus* Faith. Magic. Alchemy. The Soul.

PRICE 7/6 NETT

A FEW PRESS NOTICES
Occult Review
"Here is an important contribution to occult literature, vividly and vitally written . . . producing a depth of understanding rarely found in works of this nature . . . a sparkling, fascinating pattern . . . to read this book is an experience, and the student will undoubtedly obtain some solutions to his Occult Enigmas."

World Service and Psychic Review
"This book can be read by the many . . . when che presentation of facts is so cunningly presented as to keep alive curiosity from cover to cover. To the few, the initiates into occult lore. Dr. Michaud's book will be revealed as an elaborate portico to a temple of knowledge."

The Golden Dawn
"The author's answers to questions submitted to him . . .are illuminating. The book . . . is one you will not regret buying."

The Modem Mystic
"Author is well known . . . denial to Karma . . . reliable guides . . . a solid contribution . . . The Book has value."

One short extract out of hundreds of letters of praise:
"It is the class of matter that I have been seeking for a long time. It is very well written and expressed tersely and succinctly and I hope for all enquirers and yourself that the sales Will be prodigious. You have presented the facts in an unwavering manner nor cloaked the difficulties of the aspirant."

Now Published for the First Time by
THE UMA PRESS
Publishers of Unusual Books

40 Langham Street, London, W.l and from all Booksellers

THE WAY TO RADIANT HEALTH. By An Initiate.

Secret, ancient and mystical health exercises. Easy and delightful to perform. In sealed booklet. Price **6d.** post free.

THE POWER TO SUCCEED. By Oscar Brunler, D.Sc.

A complete treatise on Concentration leading to Power and Success. Written by a successful man. Dealing with Breathing, Concentration, Self-Control, Health and Energy, Control of the Body, the Mind, and of others, HypnQtic Power, Patience and Determination, Resistance, Mirror Paxctice, the Use of Odic Rays, and other fascinating subjects. Price **1/6** post free.

ASTRO-PHYSICS. By Oscar Brunler, D.Sc.

A series of lectures on the Influence of the Planets on our Life; on Friendship, Meditation, Concentration, Wisdom, Education, Personality and Philosophy. Written in the clear scientific and concise manner the readers of Dr. Brunler's books expect, these lectures will appeal to all. They contain many important lessons on life, the mind, health, the emotions, and will give you a key to the philosophy of this highly gifted and popular author.

Paper covers **4/-**. Cloth volumes **5/6**.

GOD'S GIFT TO MAN. By Dr. Flora Ames.

Presents to you the Legends and Uses of Herbs as natural remedies for most ills. Written in the form of a beautiful and highly dramatic story. The many patients and friends of this well-known Woman Doctor and Lecturer will welcome this book for many reasons. Price 4/6.

THE INFLUENCE OF COLOURS ON OUR MIND AND HEALTH. By Oscar Brunler, D.Sc.

A series of lectures on Colours, Hope, Faith, Loneliness, The Mind, Rays, Experiences. Paper covers **4/-** each; cloth with dust wrapper **5/6** each. **Only a few copies left.**

Full morocco, antique paper, top edge gilt, other edges uncut, numbered 1 to 75 and signed by author. **One guinea each, SOLD OUT.** These morocco-bound copies will not be reprinted.

N.B.—We have one morocco bound copy as good as new, which we can offer as a collector's item at Two guineas net. As this is the first book printed by us it should appeal to the collector of rare and precious volumes.

REJUVENATION — The Way to Health and Long Life.

By Dr. Henry Chellew, D.Sc., Ph.D., etc.

(Sometime Lecturer of the University of London)

A Most Unusual Book. — Our claim to be publishers of unusual books is justified in all our publications, but in this book especially we are establishing our rlainn to the unusual in literature. It took over 30 years of intense sttfdy by thjg brilliant mind to give to the world the results of his extensive researches in every department of science in order to benefit humanity. You cannot do without this book, which deals with Dietetics, Biotherapy, Psychology, etc., in a popular manner. This book is "The Philosopher's Stone" for which the ancient alchemysts sought for centuries — The Secret of Youth and Long Life. Before publication is was submitted to several most eminent Harley Street Specialists, whose letters of approval are unqualified; approving most highly, of both matter and the method outlined in this remarkable book. Price **3/6**.

Publishers of Unusual Books

UMA PRESS

40 Langham Street, London, W.1

www.ingramcontent.com/pod-product-compliance
Lightning Source LLC
Chambersburg PA
CBHW021848230426
43671CB00006B/305